D1413262

LETHAL LOGIC

Other Titles in Current Affairs from Potomac Books

Getting Immigration Right: What Every American Needs to Know
edited by David Coates and Peter Siavelis

Counting Every Vote: The Most Contentious Elections in American History
Robert Dudley and Eric Shiraev

*The Cure for Our Broken Political Process: How We Can Get Our
Politicians to Resolve the Issues Tearing Our Country Apart*
Sol Erdman and Lawrence Susskind

*The Four Freedoms Under Siege: The Clear and Present Danger from
Our National Security State*
Marcus Raskin and Robert Spero

*Transforming America's Israel Lobby: The Limits of Its Power
and the Potential for Change*
Dan Fleshler

New Common Ground: A New America, a New World
Amitai Etzioni

LETHAL LOGIC

EXPLODING THE MYTHS THAT PARALYZE AMERICAN GUN POLICY

DENNIS A. HENIGAN

POTOMAC BOOKS, INC.
WASHINGTON, D.C.

Published in the United States by Potomac Books, Inc. All rights reserved. No part of this book may be reproduced in any manner whatsoever without written permission from the publisher, except in the case of brief quotations embodied in critical articles and reviews.

Library of Congress Cataloging-in-Publication Data
Henigan, Dennis A.
  Lethal logic : exploding the myths that paralyze American gun policy / Dennis A. Henigan. — 1st ed.
    p. cm.
  Includes bibliographical references and index.
  ISBN 978-1-59797-356-4 (alk. paper)
  1. Gun control—United States. I. Title.
  HV7436.H46 2009
  363.330973—dc22
                                    2008055634

Printed in the United States of America on acid-free paper that meets the American National Standards Institute Z39-48 Standard.

Potomac Books, Inc.
22841 Quicksilver Drive
Dulles, Virginia 20166

First Edition

10 9 8 7 6 5 4 3 2 1

For Tara, Matt, and Kylie Quinn

CONTENTS

ILLUSTRATIONS

ACKNOWLEDGMENTS

THIS BOOK WAS born of countless conversations, phone calls, e-mail exchanges, meetings, and bull sessions I have had with my colleagues at the Brady Center over the course of twenty years. Most of those discussions, in one way or another, addressed how best to convince policymakers, legislators, judges, and the American people that the NRA's arguments against gun control are pure bunk and that overcoming the gun lobby's opposition to sensible gun laws will save countless lives. There is little in the book that has not been inspired, in some way, by the insights of my Brady colleagues, a remarkably talented and dedicated group of advocates.

I also could never have written this book without having daily access to the immense collection of material about gun violence and gun control available to me through my work at the Brady Center, including books, research studies, news articles, congressional hearings, court decisions, law review articles, and publications of other groups on both sides of the gun issue. This collection is updated continuously to provide the latest and most relevant additions to the available literature. I have done my best to bring this material to bear on the issues addressed in the book.

Through my involvement in litigation against the gun industry, I also have gained access to many thousands of internal gun industry documents and to the sworn testimony of gun industry officials elicited by the determined work of Brady Center lawyers and other attorneys working to achieve justice for gun violence victims. Through the skill and hard work of these lawyers, the industry's efforts to hide these materials from public view were overcome in courtrooms throughout the nation. As a result, the public, through this book and otherwise, will better understand how the industry's decisions about how to conduct its business threaten our safety every day.

I am thankful to the Brady organization and its leadership, present and past, for giving me the opportunity to use my talents in one of the most personally rewarding jobs imaginable. From the moment I first stepped through the door of the Brady Center, I have been acutely aware of my good fortune in being able to devote my work life to the lifesaving, and life-affirming, cause of preventing death and suffering from gun violence. I'm very lucky, and I know it.

I am especially indebted to the late Pete Shields, one of the founders of the modern gun control movement and former chair of the Brady Center, who gave me my chance to be part of this noble effort. His memory inspires me to this day, and his wife, Jeanne, continues to be part of the Brady family. I once told Pete that he reminded me of my father, George Henigan, who was a beloved professor of argumentation and debate at George Washington University. Not only was there a physical resemblance (both had thick, white hair), but Pete also exemplified the standards of principled advocacy that my father taught me, and his students, many years ago. I have tried to measure up to those standards in this book.

I also have been privileged to know, and learn from, many others in the gun violence prevention movement, as well as many independent scholars. I have tried to be vigilant about giving credit where credit is due for the information and analysis that originated with others, both from within Brady and from other sources.

My greatest source of inspiration has been the victims of gun violence and their families, including many I have been honored to represent in court and with whom I have shared every emotion, from grief to anger to frustration to the quiet satisfaction of turning profound feelings of loss into accomplishments that will spare others from similar heartache in the future. Starting with my heroes Jim and Sarah Brady, I salute them all and thank them for all they have done to save lives.

Although this book has its roots in my work with the Brady Center, it is not a book produced by the Brady Center nor does it necessarily reflect the views of the Brady Center. I'm confident that my colleagues at the Brady group will like much of what I have written here and will find it helpful in advancing our goals. But the book was not officially authorized by the Brady organization, and there may be portions of the discussion that some at Brady would treat differently or may take issue with. In short, the book reflects my views and no one else's.

I need to make the same point about the individuals who reviewed various portions of the manuscript and endeavored to improve it. The book was immeasurably enhanced by their ideas and suggestions. At the same time, they are in no way accountable for its content and should feel entirely free to disavow (or embrace) it in whole or in part.

Among those who generously gave of their time and talent to help me with this project are Luis Tolley, Bob Walker, Doug Mitchell, Chris Ritter, David Hemenway, Jens Ludwig, Becca Knox, Robyn Steinlauf, Heather Schatz, Doug Weil, Doug Pennington, Bruce Nicholson, Ken Lerer, and my dear wife, Tara. Because of their contributions, the book is far better than what I could have written without them. I can never adequately repay my debt to them, but perhaps this expression of thanks will be a start.

I also owe much to Peter Hamm of the Brady Center for connecting me with Hilary Claggett of Potomac Books. Hilary believed in the book from the outset and has been an invaluable guide to me as a novice author. I also am grateful to Chris Ritter, Guy Grogan, and Dennis Duong of The Focal Point LLC for devoting their creative skills to preparing and presenting the tables and graphs that appear in the book. Thanks also to Jon Vernick of Johns Hopkins University and Scott Vogel of www.gunguys.com for providing me additional material for inclusion.

Finally, and above all else, I am grateful to my loving wife, Tara, and to my children, Matt and Kylie, for their understanding as I worked my way through this project, while trying to do justice to them and to my day job at the Brady Center.

PROLOGUE

THE GUN CONTROL debate in America causes people in other parts of the developed world to look at this country and shake their heads. They just don't get it. They don't understand why so many Americans have such passion for their guns. They don't understand why gun control is such a contentious issue. Most of all, they don't understand how Americans tolerate the chronic carnage of deaths and injuries from gunfire, particularly when children are involved. As of the late 1990s, the rate of firearm deaths among children fourteen years and younger was nearly twelve times higher in the United States than in twenty-five other industrialized countries combined.[1] President George W. Bush, of all people, noted that an American teenager is more likely to die from a gunshot than from all natural causes of death combined.[2] God bless America.[3]

This uniquely American tragedy is often viewed from a political perspective. At every level of government, a powerful lobby, the National Rifle Association (NRA), disproportionately influences gun policy. If it is true, as some have argued, that gun control proponents are overly focused on the NRA as their opponent, their obsession is understandable. In 2001 *Fortune* magazine named the NRA the most powerful lobby in Washington, eclipsing such notable competitors as the American Association of Retired Persons.[4] A 2005 poll of "congressional insiders" by the *National Journal* found that Democrats rated the NRA the "most effective" interest group on Capitol Hill; Republicans ranked it number two. One insider hastened to add, "Effective does not necessarily mean ethical."[5] In fact, a 2006 Harris Poll found the NRA one of the most recognizable, and least trusted, public policy organizations in the nation.[6] The NRA's reputation as "least trusted" was reinforced when it was revealed in 2008 that the gun lobby had sponsored a paid spy who had infiltrated various gun control organizations, posed as a committed gun control activist, befriended grieving gun violence victims

1

under false pretenses, and no doubt passed along inside information to the NRA for more than a decade.[7]

What is truly astounding is that the NRA is able to block the enactment of legislation that is spectacularly popular among the American people. Seventy-eight percent of the American people support reinstating the ten-year ban on AK-47s, UZIs, and other military-style assault weapons, while only 16 percent oppose it.[8] Yet Congress, under NRA pressure, allowed this ban to lapse. Despite surveys showing upward of 80 percent public support for requiring background checks for gun sales between private persons,[9] legislation to extend the Brady Act background checks to private sales at gun shows continues to languish in Congress. Even mandatory registration of handguns has the support of 75 percent of Americans,[10] yet has no serious support in Congress. Gun owners and nonowners alike favor stricter gun control. Of gun owners, 61 percent favor mandatory registration of handguns, while 62 percent favor requiring a police permit for the purchase of a handgun.[11] Even most self-identified NRA members support handgun registration and mandatory safety training before purchasing a firearm.[12] The NRA is successful in resisting legislation that even its own members support.

The NRA's power, of course, can be overcome. The Brady Bill was enacted into law in 1993 and is still stopping criminals from buying guns from gun dealers. From a different perspective, though, even the Brady Bill experience can be seen as an illustration of the NRA's clout. Even though the Brady Bill had public support consistently in the 85 to 90 percent range,[13] it took *seven years* to become law.

THE CURRENT STALEMATE

After the 2000 election the NRA did a masterful job of deceiving the political punditry, and many in the Democratic Party, into believing that Al Gore's support for gun control cost him the election. (The gun lobby successfully distracted commentators from the highly material fact that Gore won more popular votes than his NRA-supported opponent.) No doubt in an effort to demonstrate the Democratic Party's capacity for political courage, President Bill Clinton asserted that the party's support for the Brady Bill and the assault weapon ban cost it a decisive number of congressional seats in the 1994 elections. "The NRA could rightly claim to have made [Newt] Gingrich the House Speaker," the former president wrote in his autobiography.[14] The president's words, of course, played right into the NRA's hands.

The conventional wisdom formed around the idea that the gun issue is too politically risky for Democrats, particularly in swing rural and outer suburban areas. When in 2005 the party chose Howard Dean, who had received the NRA's support in Vermont, as chair of the Democratic National Committee (more on Dean later), an insider Capitol Hill publication pronounced the appointment as "the last nail in gun control" and called it "a crippling blow to the gun-control movement."[15]

The conventional wisdom does not account for President Clinton's success in campaigning on the gun issue in 1996 (two years after the issue supposedly cost the Democrats control of Congress) or for the stunning defeats of NRA-supported candidates in key 2000 Senate races (John Ashcroft of Missouri, Spencer Abraham of Michigan, Bill McCollum of Florida, and Slade Gorton of Washington State come to mind). Nor have the "run from gun control" Democrats even attempted to explain why both John Kerry and George W. Bush endorsed renewal of the assault weapon ban during the 2004 presidential campaign. If gun control has become such political poison, how could this be?

The case of President Bush is particularly striking. When asked about the assault weapon ban in the third presidential debate against John Kerry, Bush not only endorsed its renewal, he went further to support closing the "gun show loophole" through extending Brady background checks to all gun show sales, *even though he was not even asked about gun shows*. Although the Republican Party, since the Reagan years, has become strongly identified with pro-gun interests (with some exceptions), Karl Rove obviously thought there was a political price to be paid for Bush to be associated with the NRA's opposition to sensible gun laws. Rove seemed to understand what some Democrats have forgotten: that it also can be politically risky to appear extreme on the issue by opposing sensible gun laws.

Of course, Bush wasn't sincere about his support for gun control. The NRA knew this and also knew that it would be politically damaging for Bush to publicly support the NRA's agenda. With a wink and a nod, the gun lobby worked to elect a candidate who claimed to support two of the major priorities of the gun control movement.

The conventional wisdom should have an even more difficult time explaining the 2008 elections, particularly the Barack Obama landslide victory. After solidly pro-gun candidates like Fred Thompson, Mike Huckabee, Ron Paul, and Bill Richardson failed in the primaries, the NRA had little choice but to endorse a candidate—John McCain—who the gun lobby had long vilified for his support of legislation to mandate background checks at gun shows. In 2001 the NRA had called McCain "one of the premier flag carriers for the enemies of the Second Amendment."[16] To the gun lobby, however, he was by far a "lesser evil" than Barack Obama.

To put it mildly, the NRA went "all in" to defeat Obama. It said Obama and Biden constituted "the most anti-gun ticket ever to run for the White House" and "a clear and present danger" to Second Amendment rights.[17] It launched a website, www.gunbanobama.com, dedicated solely to defeating Obama and claimed to spend at least $10 million on the presidential race (and millions more in the election generally). Top NRA officials personally campaigned for McCain in such states as Pennsylvania, Colorado, Nevada, and Minnesota—all won by Obama. It ran TV and radio ads against Obama in Colorado, New Mexico, Ohio, Virginia, Florida, Michigan, Minnesota, Wisconsin, North Carolina, and Pennsylvania—all won by Obama. It advertised nationally in *USA Today*.

Although the NRA consistently lied about Obama's gun control record—outrageously accusing him of favoring a ban on the "use of firearms for home self-defense,"[18] for example—it is certainly true that no presidential ticket in history had a stronger record supporting gun control than Obama/Biden. Nor did candidate Obama run away from the gun issue during the campaign or retreat from any of the pro-control policy positions he had taken in the past. Indeed, in his convention acceptance speech—the single most important speech of his campaign—Obama directly addressed the issue with the words "don't tell me we can't uphold the Second Amendment while keeping AK-47s out of the hands of criminals." The NRA did everything in its power to defeat Obama, and he won in a landslide.

Nevertheless, fear of the gun issue persists within the Democratic Party. Some argue that Obama succeeded in red states because he downplayed the gun issue and emphasized his belief in the Second Amendment. In politics, perception is power. And, despite the weight of the evidence from recent presidential and congressional election cycles, the perception continues to persist that crossing the NRA is risky business.

At the state level, the NRA's top priority in recent years has been to make it easier to carry concealed handguns in public places, and it has been impressively successful in doing so. By 2006 thirty-four states had passed "shall issue" concealed weapons laws. Generally speaking, these laws require police to issue permits allowing the carrying of concealed weapons in public places to anyone who does not have a criminal record. In the few states that still have "may issue" concealed weapons laws, the police have discretion to deny a permit to someone they believe presents a risk of violence, even though he or she may not have a criminal record.

Still, gun control forces also have an impressive list of victories in the states. Since 1989 they have succeeded in passing child access prevention (CAP) laws in eighteen states. These laws hold gun owners criminally responsible for leaving guns accessible to children. In recent years the NRA also has suffered key legislative defeats in New Jersey (legislation requiring that guns be child-proofed), Maryland (legislation requiring internal locks on guns and limiting handgun sales to one per month), and Illinois (legislation requiring background checks for private sales at gun shows).

The gun control movement has found its most fertile ground in California, where the NRA and its allies have suffered repeated setbacks in recent years. Indeed, the state has become a recurring nightmare for the gun lobby. Since 1989, in addition to enacting a CAP law, California passed legislation to ban semiautomatic assault weapons, require background checks for all gun sales from all sources, restrict handgun sales to one per month to curb gun trafficking, require gun dealers to sell child safety locks with guns, require handgun buyers to pass a safety test and be fingerprinted, mandate certain safety features on handguns, ban .50-caliber sniper rifles, and require gun makers to use new technology to allow guns to be traced from spent cartridges at crime scenes. After most states had acceded to NRA demands to immunize gun sellers from lawsuits brought by municipalities, in 2002 California went in the other direction and repealed a twenty-year-old law protecting the industry from certain lawsuits. Considering that one of every eight Americans resides in California and that it is the largest gun market in the United States, this record is deeply embarrassing for the NRA. Nevertheless, with the exception of the assault weapon ban, which passed the California legislature in 1989 and led directly to a federal ban in 1994, California's pioneering gun control laws have done little to generate momentum for similar laws at the national level.

Although it is absurd to pronounce the political death of gun control, it is certainly true that the nation is at a stalemate on the gun issue. To explain our inability to move decisively toward sensible gun regulation entirely in terms of raw political power begs the question, why is the NRA able to exercise that power? Surely the NRA could not command such strength if there weren't something in its message that resonates with large numbers of people. Is there something about the gun control debate itself that contributes to the policy paralysis on the gun violence issue? Speaking as a longtime participant in that debate, I believe the answer is yes.

THE TRIUMPH OF BUMPER STICKER LOGIC

Shortly after I began my career as a lawyer and advocate for the nation's leading gun control group, I started to notice a peculiar repetitiveness in my opponents' arguments. Whether it was on radio or TV talk shows or panel discussions or speeches with audience Q&A, there was a striking similarity in the substance of the arguments, and even the language, used by my opponents. Over and over again, I would hear that "Guns don't kill people. People kill people." I would hear "When guns are outlawed, only outlaws will have guns." I would hear "An armed society is a polite society." I had seen these sayings on bumper stickers for years, but I discovered that my opponents actually argued in these terms. Even when these exact phrases weren't used, the thoughts they express were conveyed in other words. In more scholarly settings, critics of gun regulation would dress up their arguments in the arcane language of academia and in mountains of statistics, but their basic claims could, to a remarkable degree, be boiled down to the same themes I had heard on countless talk shows.

For gun control advocates, the sad fact is that the bumper sticker arguments of the National Rifle Association and its allies have a persuasive power that cannot be denied. Their impact on the gun debate needs to be acknowledged. I am not suggesting that these arguments cause most people to oppose specific gun control proposals; as already noted, a wide range of proposed restrictions on guns have broad public support. However, because the arguments sound like they have more than a kernel of truth, they have had an important long-term effect on the intensity with which the public favors gun control. Years of public opinion polls on guns suggest that support for gun control is a mile wide and an inch deep. People will tell a pollster that they favor a host of gun restrictions, but surveys show few gun control supporters feel strongly enough about it to make it a major factor in determining their support or opposition to a particular candidate for office. Even fewer are motivated to take any action to influence legislators to pass new laws. (The exceptions tend to be those who have lost loved ones to gunfire or who have been wounded themselves.)

This phenomenon may well be related to the resonance of at least some of the NRA's oft-used bumper sticker arguments. Let's take, for example, the assertion "Guns don't kill people. People kill people." The suggestion that the violence that has long plagued our society is rooted in the evil that lurks in the hearts of men or women is effectively used to marginalize, as relatively insignificant, issues related to the specific instrumentalities of violence. As discussed in chapter 1, the slogan has been remarkably effective in diverting attention from the issue of gun regulation to the endless and difficult search for more "fundamental" causes of criminal violence.

To take another example, discussed at greater length in chapter 2, a great paradox of opinion polling on gun issues is that the public consistently supports enactment of gun legislation, even though it does not think it will be effective. In 1994, the year following the enactment of the broadly popular Brady Bill and the year the assault weapon ban passed with overwhelming public support, one poll showed that only 34 percent of the American people believed that gun control laws would reduce violent crime, while 62 percent said they would not.[19] Thirteen years later, an ABC News poll revealed similar attitudes; although 61 percent of those surveyed supported stricter gun laws, only 27 percent thought they would do "a lot" to reduce violence.[20] In other words, at some basic level, the public is convinced that "When guns are outlawed, only outlaws will have guns." This belief cannot help but diminish the intensity of public support for further gun restrictions.

This book is an effort to tackle the pro-gun slogans head on. Each chapter focuses on a specific slogan, asking two questions: First, what arguments against gun control does the slogan convey? Second, do the arguments make sense? Throughout this discussion I will endeavor to apply to the gun issue the same reasoning typically applied to other public policy issues. As to the arguments made against regulation of guns, it is always legitimate to ask whether we would be persuaded by those same arguments if applied to other issues. If we would not be persuaded, then either there is something wrong with the argument, or there is something different about the gun issue that makes the argument valid as to guns, but invalid as to other issues. By identifying those differences, our understanding of the gun issue is enhanced.

The discussion in this book, then, is largely concerned with the *logic* of the arguments against gun control and, secondarily, about the evidence marshaled in support of those arguments. As will be seen, in the last twenty years there has been an explosion of new learning about gun violence, much of it from the public health community, laying to waste the empirical claims often made by gun control opponents and attacking the work of pro-gun researchers. Apart from any flaws in the scientific methodology of pro-gun researchers, there is the separate and even more fundamental problem that the pro-gun arguments represent flawed thinking, whether by NRA officials or by the academics whom the NRA offers in support of its positions. Under close examination, they turn out to be arguments that we would reject out of hand if used in contexts other than the gun control debate.

There may well be a good deal of bad science marshaled in opposition to gun control. There is also a good deal of bad thinking.

WHAT'S LOGIC GOT TO DO WITH IT?

Some will think this discussion reflects an embarrassing level of naiveté about the politics of gun control. If the barrier to progress is the raw political power of the NRA, they will say that it will never be enough to show that the NRA's arguments make no sense. As one columnist said about the gun control debate, "This dispute isn't about logic any more than the stem-cell dispute is about science. It's about the power of an interest group to impede what looks to most of us like genuine public progress."[21] Let me be clear. I am not arguing that destroying the NRA's mythology will be sufficient to overcome its political influence. I believe, however, that the gun lobby's political power will never be overcome until these myths are destroyed. Political power is not unconnected to ideas. The source of the NRA's disproportionate political power is not simply its money and the intensity of its supporters' beliefs; it also is its effective communication of several simple themes that resonate with ordinary Americans and function to convince many that gun control has little to do with improving the quality of their lives.

Democratic Party strategists James Carville and Paul Begala nicely demonstrate the connection between politics and ideas on the gun issue in their 2006 book, *Take It Back*. Carville and Begala are solidly in the camp of Democrats who believe their party has been damaged by its identification with the gun control issue. They, like their former boss President Clinton, are convinced that "gun control played a major role in the defeat of congressional Democrats in 1994" and blame the gun issue for costing Al Gore states he'd carried when he was on the ticket with Bill Clinton, including Arkansas, Tennessee, Louisiana, Missouri, Kentucky, and West Virginia.[22] Their political analysis leaves something to be desired. They do not account for the 1996 victories of the Clinton/Gore ticket in those states, after having campaigned on a gun control platform that year and even having Jim and Sarah Brady speak in prime time at the 1996 Democratic Convention.

Although President Clinton's margin of victory decreased in some of those states from 1992 to 1996, the president's own analysis of the returns did not attribute the decline to the gun issue alone.[23] And his winning percentage actually went up in some states, such as Louisiana and New Hampshire, not usually thought of as friendly to gun control. Nevertheless, Carville and Begala argue that Democrats should "defuse" the gun issue, essentially by agreeing with the NRA that we should simply enforce existing gun laws, but not pass any new ones.[24] (This particular NRA canard is discussed in chapter 5.)

Those who believe that destroying the gun lobby's bumper sticker fallacies would have no effect on the politics of gun control should consider this passage from *Take It Back* on the issue of whether the Democrats should push to require background checks on gun sales at gun shows:

Sponsored by Senators Joe Lieberman (D-CT) and John McCain (R-AZ), the bill would require that people who buy guns at gun shows pass the same background check required for purchases made in stores. Okay. Sounds reasonable. But what is the political cost-benefit analysis? A study by the Clinton Justice Department showed that just 1.7 percent of criminals who used guns in the commission of a crime obtained their gun from a gun show. By extending the Brady Bill to catch such a small percentage of transactions, Democrats risk inflaming and alienating millions of voters who might otherwise be open to voting Democratic. But once guns are in the mix, once someone believes his gun rights are threatened, he shuts down.[25]

Notice the question: "What is the political cost-benefit analysis?" What Carville and Begala are saying is that gun control simply doesn't do enough good, as a policy matter, to be worth the political cost of advocating it. Presumably, the "political cost-benefit analysis" would be different if they were convinced that stricter gun laws would really save thousands of innocent lives and prevent untold suffering.

Dig beneath the surface of this passage and it is easy to uncover two of the NRA's favorite fallacies. The cavalier dismissal of the need for gun show background checks is a variation on the theme of "When guns are outlawed, only outlaws will have guns." It turns out that, on the issue of gun shows, Carville and Begala don't know what they are talking about. They cite a Justice Department survey of federal firearms offenders showing that only 1.7 percent of the offenders said they got their guns at gun shows.[26] This ignores the well-established fact that many gun criminals buy their guns from gun traffickers who, in turn, bought their inventory at gun shows. Many criminals simply don't know that their guns originated at gun shows. Carville and Begala overlook the Bureau of Alcohol, Tobacco and Firearms (ATF) study identifying gun shows as the second leading source of guns trafficked into the illegal market[27] and the joint Justice-ATF study of federal trafficking investigations showing "a disturbing picture of gun shows as a venue for criminal activity and a source of firearms used in crimes."[28] Perhaps their "political cost-benefit analysis" should consider Ali Boumelhem and his brother Mohamed, who purchased an arsenal of shotguns and assault weapons at Michigan gun shows to supply Hezbollah in Lebanon.[29] Or perhaps they should talk to Peter Langan, former head of the Aryan Republican Army and an accomplished bank robber, who told the *Kansas City Star* that gun shows in Missouri and Kansas were a quick way to buy and dump weapons. "It was incredibly easy," Langan explained.

"Gun shows, just for the sheer volume and selection, you just couldn't beat 'em."[30]

The reference by Carville and Begala to gun owners feeling that their "gun rights are threatened" by background checks implicitly invokes, and validates, the classic "slippery slope" argument, treated in chapter 3, that moderate measures such as gun show background checks eventually will lead to destruction of the right to bear arms. Chapter 3 will address the slippery slope argument from several angles, including the impact of the Supreme Court's recent ruling in *District of Columbia v. Heller* striking down the District's handgun ban as a violation of the Second Amendment.

This is not to say that these two leading Democrats would see the light and change their minds if presented with the arguments in this book. But the persuasive power of their political argument to fellow Democrats likely is enhanced because the NRA's lethal logic has managed to sink in to our collective consciousness about the relationship between guns and violence. Conversely, exposing that logic as transparently empty and dangerous would make it more difficult for Democrats to defuse the gun issue by embracing the NRA's view.

It should be self-evident that any position on a controversial public issue carries with it some political cost; that is, after all, part of what it means for an issue to be controversial. If the issue is seen as a matter of principle, though, political leaders should be prepared to pay the political price because so much is at stake. As president, Lyndon Johnson led the historic battle for civil rights legislation, culminating in the enactment of the Civil Rights Act of 1964 and the Voting Rights Act of 1965. He confided in longtime Democratic Party insider Ben Barnes, "Ben, I'm proud of these Civil Rights bills, but they're going to hurt the party in the long run."[31] As a historical matter, the Democratic Party paid a high political price in the South for its aggressive support for civil rights laws. Because equal justice was seen as a core Democratic principle, the party did not waver in spite of the political price.

Democrats continue to pay that price in the South to the present day, but it would never occur to Carville and Begala, both southerners, that Democrats should turn the clock back on civil rights to regain the South. They are willing to jettison the gun issue precisely because they don't see gun control as a core principle. I am not here suggesting that gun control should be as fundamental to Democrats as civil rights, only that if Democrats were convinced that strong gun laws could save thousands of lives, the political price to be paid in some parts of the country would perhaps be seen as something that must be endured because the stakes are so high.

It is revealing to compare Carville and Begala's view of gun control politics with that of President Clinton. I noted that the president agrees with his former advisers that the gun issue cost the Democrats dearly in the 1994 congressional elections. However, unlike his advisers, Clinton understands the political benefit of standing up to a special interest lobby, *as long as the case can be made that the public's health and safety are at stake.* In his autobiography, President Clinton's reflections on gun control bring to mind President Johnson's on civil rights. When Clinton refers to the political cost of gun control, he nevertheless concludes that the benefits in lives saved were worth the electoral damage. About the Brady Bill, he says "it had saved countless lives," but "exposed many of those brave enough to vote for it to harsh attacks, which were effective enough to drive several of them from office."[32] About the assault weapons ban, he said if he had listened to Democratic leaders like Tom Foley, Dick Gephardt, and Jack Brooks and stripped the ban from the crime bill, "I would have left more police officers and children at the mercy of assault weapons. *I remain convinced that those hard decisions were good for America* [emphasis added]."[33]

This is exactly how President Clinton framed the issue during his second term. His message was that his administration's support for sensible gun laws was a profile in courage in which he put the interest of the nation above the political risk of facing down a powerful special interest lobby. He did not run from gun control in his second term. Instead, his administration expanded the existing ban on imported assault weapons, pushed for background checks at gun shows, proposed handgun licensing, and even threatened to support a massive lawsuit by public housing authorities against the gun industry. Unlike Begala and Carville, Clinton believed that gun control's political cost was worth it. He further knew that if he could make a convincing case to the American people that a powerful special interest lobby was blocking legislation that would make Americans safer, the gun issue could be a positive factor politically, particularly at the national level. In this way, Clinton actually used the NRA's perceived power to derive political benefit for himself and his gun control policies.

Yes, the NRA is the classic schoolyard bully and is capable of inflicting great damage in a fight. But standing up to the schoolyard bully to protect the safety of the innocent is an appealing image that communicates a powerful message in the political context. Its political potency, however, depends on whether those who the politician is trying to protect really believe that the bully threatens their safety. On the gun control issue, as with other issues, politics and policy *are* connected.

In December 2003, President Clinton spoke at the celebration of the Brady Act's ten-year anniversary in Washington, D.C. Obviously delighted to relive one of his administration's greatest triumphs, he spoke expansively about the way the gun debate is conducted in this country. He said he was always struck by the disconnect between the gun lobby's arguments and what is happening in real life. "This is all about getting people to stop thinking," he said. "Ignoring the human consequences of a practical problem." He went on: "But the consequences here are quite severe, because the landscape of our recent history is littered with the bodies of people [who] couldn't be protected, under sensible gun laws that wouldn't have had a lick of impact on the hunters and sportsmen of this country."

I was in the audience that day, and I was struck with his observation that "this is all about getting people to stop thinking." This is, in fact, the impact of the pro-gun slogans. They do not stimulate thoughtful, rational discussion of the "human consequences of a practical problem." They end thoughtful, rational discussion and replace it with clever catchphrases in service to an immovable ideology. I think President Clinton was getting at the disturbing truth about the gun debate in America. Our nation does a bad job of thinking about guns. Until we get the reasoning right, we will do little to address the "human consequences" of gun violence. It is no exaggeration to say that our nation's gun policy is paralyzed by a series of fallacies—arguments that appear sound on first hearing but crumble in the face of careful thought and analysis.

Although exposing these fallacies is necessarily an exercise in reason, it should not be coldly intellectual. It is my hope that the task will awaken the same emotion in the reader that it did in me. It should, in fact, make us angry. It should lead us to realize that too many of our fellow citizens have perished, or been severely injured, because the pro-gun fallacies have held sway for far too long. They have excused inaction and justified misguided policies. Because gun violence is, literally, a life-or-death issue, the NRA's tortured logic has cost too many innocent lives for us to tolerate it any longer.

1.

"GUNS DON'T KILL PEOPLE.
PEOPLE KILL PEOPLE."

THIS IS, NO DOUBT, one of the greatest advocacy slogans ever conceived. Its first sentence seems plainly false on its face—that is, until one reads the second sentence, which is both plainly true and, at the same time, appears to confer truth on the first sentence. The first sentence captures our attention; the second persuades us with a proposition we cannot deny.

The slogan is, of course, intended to convey the idea that guns are simply inanimate objects, which are not dangerous unless and until they come into contact with human beings. As pro-gun partisans have been known to say, "I've never seen a gun get up off a table and fire itself." The slogan makes the point that guns are morally neutral. They are not dangerous in and of themselves. They become dangerous only in the hands of evil or disturbed or careless people. As one Idaho gun dealer put it, "Firearms are not guilty of crime; the individuals who possess the firearm are guilty of doing something with it."[1] Countless gun owners have observed that they have owned guns for years and none of their guns has ever been involved in a crime or other violent act. No less an authority than best-selling author Tom Clancy has pointed out that "no firearm has ever killed anyone unless directed by a person who acted either from malice, madness or idiocy."[2] There is no gun problem. There is only a people problem. For the gun control opponent, this means that the only laws that make sense are those directed at how people use guns, not at guns themselves. When Charlton Heston was the NRA's president, he was asked by then-senator John Ashcroft during a congressional hearing, "What can be done, and

13

specifically what can Congress do, to stem the tide of violent crime?" His answer: "Punish criminals, Senator."[3]

How does this thinking fit with how we treat other "inanimate objects" that tend to become dangerous only when they come into contact with human beings? Are we content simply to punish the person who misuses the product? Or are we interested also in placing barriers between the product and those most likely to misuse it?

CARS DON'T KILL PEOPLE. PEOPLE KILL PEOPLE.

Automobiles do not often exceed the speed limit without a driver behind the wheel. Sitting in a driveway, a car seems pretty innocuous indeed. Does this mean that the sum total of our public policy response to reckless driving should be severe punishment of drivers who violate the law? Few would think so.

For example, most of us are quite comfortable with the idea that before anyone is permitted to operate an automobile he must be licensed by the government to do so. Although the requirements vary from state to state, this generally means prospective drivers must be of a legal age to drive, have undergone driver training, have passed a written test, and have shown they can safely operate a car. When I was a teenager in the Commonwealth of Virginia, I had to endure a "behind the wheel" test (which included the dreaded parallel parking requirement) with a very large and intimidating state trooper in the passenger seat. No one seriously argues that since cars are not dangerous unless driven by dangerous people, we don't need to license drivers, only to punish dangerous driving. It makes sense to have a system in place to prevent potentially high-risk people from driving in the first place.

If you find this logic compelling, you will be mystified that, for decades in this country, convicted felons were legally prohibited from buying guns from gun dealers, yet there was no uniform system of background checks to ensure against such sales. Before President Clinton signed the Brady Bill into law in 1993, in thirty-two states it was possible for a convicted felon to walk into a gun store, fill out a federal form falsely claiming to have no criminal record, and walk out with a gun.

The NRA vehemently opposed the Brady Bill, arguing that background checks at gun stores make no sense because criminals don't buy guns at gun stores; they either steal them or get them "on the street." An NRA lawyer wrote that the Brady Bill was "simply not workable" because "criminals do not, to any appreciable degree, buy handguns from federally licensed firearms dealers."[4] This, of course, was always an example of muddled thinking; even if some criminals acquire guns through theft or "on the street," it is hard to believe that other criminals don't simply go into gun stores and lie on the federal form. After all, as we will explore in more detail later, gun stores *are where the guns are.* There is a nice selection, there is a store clerk to offer help, and the store will provide a warranty against defects. A Justice Department survey of adult prison inmates, taken before the Brady Bill was enacted, asked those who had used a handgun in a crime where he or she had acquired the gun. The guns were as likely to have come from a gun store as from the black market and three times more likely to come from a gun store as from theft.[5]

One additional reason we know the NRA was wrong in saying criminals don't buy from gun stores is that they are still trying to buy from stores *after* the enactment of the Brady Bill. According to the Department of Justice, since the Brady Bill became law, over 1.5 million legally prohibited gun buyers have been blocked from completing their purchases at licensed gun dealers, and most of those were convicted felons.[6] The Brady background checks not only block these prohibited gun purchases, they also expose the prospective buyer to a risk of prosecution for lying on the federal form. If thousands of criminals still try to buy guns from stores in the face of a background check system that provides evidence of their criminal culpability, can you imagine how many bought them from stores before such a system existed?

That guns are inanimate objects that require the intervention of people to inflict injury is, therefore, not a sound argument against public policies designed to screen those who seek to own and use guns. Thanks to the Brady Act, we at least have a system to screen gun buyers at gun stores. In all but a handful of states, however, gun buyers do not face the equivalent of a parallel parking test; that is, there is no licensing requirement for gun ownership that would require training and testing to establish that the people who want to handle guns know what they are doing. If we are to treat guns like cars, such licensing, with its training and testing mandates, should be part of a sound gun policy. Nothing in the notion that "Guns don't kill people. People kill people," should counsel otherwise.

The NRA has a creative response to the guns/cars licensing analogy. "A license and registration," it points out, "is not required to merely own a vehicle or operate it on private property, only to do so on public roads."[7] If all you do with your car is drive it on your own property, as opposed to a public thoroughfare, you need no license. (I presume they have in mind a rancher driving his pickup around the north forty, not a suburbanite driving the family SUV up and down the driveway.) Therefore, the argument goes, you should not need a license merely to own a gun, but rather to carry it, concealed, in a public place. (As explained above, the NRA position is, however, that the police should be required to give concealed carry licenses to anyone who does not have a criminal record and can legally buy a gun.)[8]

The problem with this argument is that the risk posed by the gun owner's use of a gun on her property is far greater than the risk posed by the car owner's use of a car on her property. How many auto accidents occur on the property of the owner of the automobile? It is unlikely that such a bizarre statistic has ever been determined, since it is surely true that a virtually undetectable percentage of driver miles occurs within the confines of the owner's real estate. Conversely, a substantial part of the risk posed by guns is created by the use of guns in or around the home of the gun owner. Large numbers of unintentional shootings occur in the home. Indeed, one study, examining only shootings in which the gun involved was known to be kept in the home, showed that guns in the home were four times more likely to be involved in accidents than to be used to injure or kill in self-defense.[9]

Gun suicide, a significant but often underemphasized part of the gun violence problem, also occurs largely in the home. A landmark study by Dr. Arthur Kellerman and his colleagues published in the *New England Journal of Medicine* showed that a gun in the home increases the risk of suicide by nearly five times.[10] Depressed adolescents commit many of those suicides with guns left accessible by adults. Indeed, firearms are the most common method of suicide by adolescents, accounting for 60 percent of suicide deaths among youth under the age of nineteen.[11]

The risk of unintentional shootings and adolescent suicide could be substantially reduced by safety training emphasizing the increased risk posed by guns in the home and the elements of safe handling and storage practices. Thus, the analogy between cars and guns strongly supports licensing gun owners. With respect to both products, persons should be licensed before they engage in the risk-producing activity with the product. With cars, that activity is driving on public streets. With guns, the activity is possession of the gun, whether in the home or on the person in a public place.

Not only is there a broad consensus favoring government intervention to screen drivers of cars, that consensus extends to regulation directed to the cars themselves. The fact that an automobile is innocuous sitting in the owner's driveway does not persuade us against government regulation to make the car safer when a driver is at the wheel. The National Highway Traffic and Safety Administration (NHTSA) has long had the power to issue minimum safety standards for cars, to test cars for their crashworthiness and to recall defective cars. Only the most extreme libertarians would argue that government has no proper role in the design of cars, even though some form of driver negligence, recklessness, or illegal behavior often causes traffic injuries and fatalities. Does any reasonable person argue that the government should not mandate seat belts, air bags, shatterproof windshields, and crash-resistant bumpers because "cars don't kill people, people kill people"? No, because it is more likely that people will kill people, including themselves, with unsafe cars than with safe ones.

REGULATE TOY GUNS, NOT REAL ONES

The authority of NHTSA regarding cars is loosely replicated by the Consumer Product Safety Commission (CPSC) regarding consumer products generally. For lawn mowers, playpens, cigarette lighters, and a myriad of other consumer products, there are federal regulations designed to reduce the risk of harm to consumers and others.

Most Americans are quite surprised to learn that no federal agency has the power to set safety standards for guns, test guns for safety, or recall defective guns. As will be seen throughout this text, our laws regulating guns repeatedly illustrate the triumph of irrationality, backed by a powerful lobby, over common sense. The absence of federal consumer product standards on firearms is a compelling example. As is typical of statutory provisions that bestow inexplicable benefits to a special interest, the consumer safety exemption for guns is buried in the morass of parts and subparts in the law that gave birth to the CPSC. The pertinent language is the exemption for "any article which, if sold by the manufacturer, producer or importer, would be subject to the tax imposed by section 4181 of the Internal Revenue Code of 1954." Those "articles" are guns. Of course, Congress could simply have written that the law "does not apply to guns," but then the irrationality of the exemption would leap screaming from the face of the statute.

The father of this clever indirection is Representative John Dingell (D-Michigan), the famously combative congressman who has been a proponent of strong consumer protection laws as long as he has been an opponent of strong gun control laws. He quietly inserted the exempting language in the bill. Later, Representative Dingell led the effort to use the power of the CPSC against lawn darts, which were banned in 1988 because their use in outdoor games had killed three children.[12] Nevertheless, he opposes legislation to extend safety standards to guns, even though, in the years 1996–2000, an average of 270 children and teens lost their lives in unintentional shootings alone[13] and four times as many were injured.[14] For

Representative Dingell, three dead children are enough to ban lawn darts, but hundreds of dead children every year and thousands injured is not enough to justify imposing minimum safety standards on guns. Lawn darts kill kids, but guns don't?

Thanks to the handiwork of Representative Dingell and the power of the gun lobby, we have a federal consumer protection agency with authority to regulate toy guns but not real guns. The CPSC's regulatory authority over toy guns has resulted, for example, in a recall of a toy cork-shooting shotgun because of a single incident involving an eye injury to a small boy,[15] as well as a recall of caps for toy cap guns that resulted in burns to at least five children.[16]

The cruel irony of it all was obvious to Ann Brown, when she was chair of the CPSC in 1994. In October of that year, Ms. Brown issued a statement challenging the toy industry to stop producing toy guns that look like real guns. "Fatal accidents with guns involving kids are tragic," she said. "Real-looking toy guns may be a small part of the problem of violence in our society, *but it is the part of the problem we can solve* [emphasis added]."[17] There is something truly plaintive in those words. Ms. Brown was faced with the absurd reality that she could address the risk that a child might be shot because he was holding a toy gun that *looked* real but was powerless to address the far greater risk that he would be shot because he was holding a gun that *was* real.

It ought to be clear, at the very least, that the "morally neutral" status of guns is hardly a good reason to resist regulation of guns directed both at screening those who would use them and ensuring that they meet minimum safety standards. However, "Guns don't kill people. People kill people" also conveys the idea that if dangerous people are denied access to guns, they will simply use some other dangerous product to inflict harm. The homicidal have many alternatives: knives, baseball bats, and fists, for example. The suicidal have alternatives as well. Therefore, the argument goes, policies directed at guns themselves, rather than their users, are destined to fail.

The "Guns don't kill people. People kill people" argument requires us to more seriously consider what it is about guns that may distinguish them from other products that can inflict serious injury or death. Automobiles are subject to far more regulation than knives and baseball bats. Are guns more like cars or more like knives and baseball bats? For purposes of deciding appropriate public policy toward guns, what characteristics of guns are relevant? How are they relevant?

Let's start by stepping back and asking the question: What, exactly, is a gun, anyway?

GUNS AS WEAPONS

Listen to any of the endless series of talk radio shows on gun control and you will eventually hear the following point made, in virtually the same words: "Guns are merely devices to expel a projectile at a high rate of speed. A gun is simply a tool. It can be a tool for good, or for evil, depending on the user."

Well, yes, but the question is: Why does the user want a device to expel a projectile at a high rate of speed? The answer should be obvious. Such a device is an effective and efficient weapon. Unlike other dangerous products we allow to be widely available, guns are desired by their users primarily because they can be used to inflict serious injury or death on living beings, whether human or animal. This proposition is implicit in the survey results asking gun owners why they own guns. Although pro-gun interests like to emphasize the use of guns to shoot holes in paper targets or blast clay pigeons out of the sky, relatively few gun owners report target or sport shooting as their primary reason for owning guns. According to a Police Foundation survey, three-quarters of handgun owners cited "self-defense" as their primary reason for gun ownership, while only 11 percent cited "target and sport shooting" and less than 1 percent said "gun collection." For long gun (rifle and shotgun) owners, 70 percent named hunting and 15 percent named self-defense, while only 6 percent named target and sport shooting and less than 1 percent named gun collecting.[18] (I am not suggesting here that owning guns for use as weapons for self-defense or other lawful purposes is somehow improper, although, as explained later, it is often unwise.)

There is, of course, another major reason for owning a gun that will never be measured by a survey of gun owners: for use as a weapon in crime. No gun owner will admit in a survey that he owns a gun to engage in illegal activity. Yet we know that from 1993 to 2001, an average of 846,000 violent crimes were committed each year with firearms.[19] More crimes were committed with firearms than with knives, baseball bats, or any other products.[20]

Whether owned for lawful or criminal purposes, therefore, it is undeniable that guns are owned primarily as weapons. This distinguishes guns from other potentially dangerous products. Autos, of course, can be used as weapons, as is proved from time to time by disgruntled spouses who have been known to run down their mates in the family Buick. They are, however, not generally purchased for their killing capacity. Baseball bats are another example. They can, of course, be used as weapons. Some years ago, this became painfully apparent to Los Angeles Dodger catcher John Roseboro, when he was attacked by a bat-wielding Juan Marichal of the San Francisco Giants in perhaps the most famous baseball brawl in major league history.[21] Despite Roseboro's painful injuries, it is nevertheless true that baseball bats are not designed as weapons nor desired by consumers primarily as weapons.

The gun industry is fond of claiming that it is the "most regulated" industry in America because the sale of guns is regulated in ways that transactions in other products are not. A car dealer can sell one a car without contacting the authorities for a criminal background check. There is no minimum legal age to buy a baseball bat, as there is for the purchase of guns. (Under federal law, you must be twenty-one to buy a handgun; eighteen to buy a rifle or shotgun.)[22] That's true, but so what? Of course guns are, and should be, subject to such regulations *because guns are designed and sold as weapons.* Because few purchasers of cars and baseball bats buy these products to use as weapons, there is little reason to subject their purchasers to the same screening for past criminal conduct that is justified for gun purchasers.

The point is that the kind and extent of regulation should follow from the nature of the risk from the transaction. The purchase of a product sold as a weapon presents a different kind of risk than the purchase of a product sold for another purpose. As compared to other potentially dangerous products, the weapon will, by its nature, attract a far higher percentage of consumers who desire it to inflict injury on others (or themselves). The issue is not whether the gun industry is "more regulated" than other industries. The issue is whether the regulations we have are appropriate to the nature and extent of the risk.

It would be overstating matters to say that guns are the only widely available products desired primarily as weapons. For example, certain kinds of knives are designed, and marketed, as weapons to be used against human beings and animals. As weapons, however, even the most lethal knives are inferior substitutes for guns. It brings to mind the expression, "never bring a knife to a gunfight." It turns out that being able to "expel a projectile at a high rate of speed" is a most valuable attribute for a weapon.

For one thing, such a feature makes it unnecessary for the user to be in close physical proximity to the victim, thus reducing the attacker's risk of detection and making successful resistance by the victim more difficult. As Florida State University professor Gary Kleck, one of the NRA's favorite researchers, has recognized, "guns provide a more impersonal, emotionally remote, and even antiseptic way of attacking others, and could allow some attackers to bypass their inhibitions against close contact with their victims."[23]

In October 2002 this advantage was on horrifying display in the Washington, D.C., area, as snipers used a Bushmaster XM-15 E2S .223-caliber military-style assault rifle in a series of long-range shootings that killed ten innocent people and wounded four more, while paralyzing an entire metropolitan area in fear for weeks. Sniper Lee Boyd Malvo told authorities he could "hit you with metal sights from 300 yards away."[24] Although not all the shootings were from that range (Malvo accurately estimated that his shooting of a Home Depot shopper was from about 160 yards away),[25] they were far enough away that witnesses could not locate where the shots had come from. No knife has yet been invented that could afford such anonymous killing power.

The sniper example is only an extreme illustration of the obvious advantage of a gun over other potential weapons in most scenarios. Although handguns (pistols and revolvers) lack the range of rifles, they can do far more damage at longer distances than knives or other weapons. A cheap handgun in the hands of a dangerous racist terrorized two Midwestern states on Independence Day weekend in 1999. Benjamin Nathaniel Smith—a white supremacist with a shaved head and the words "Sabbath Breaker" tattooed on his chest—rampaged through Illinois and Indiana, targeting ethnic and religious minorities by firing his Bryco .380 pistol from his car and driving away. He drove to a predominately Jewish neighborhood in Chicago and shot six people in front of a synagogue. In a quiet residential neighborhood in Skokie, Smith killed Ricky Byrdsong, an African American and the former Northwestern University basketball coach, as he walked along the street with his children. The next day he shot and wounded an African-American minister outside his home in Decatur, Illinois, and an Asian-American student at the University of Illinois in Urbana. On July 4 he fired into a crowd of people entering a Korean Methodist Church in Indiana and mortally wounded Won-Joon Yoon, a Korean doctoral student in economics at Indiana University.

Smith's choice of a gun, over other weapons, was no accident. To put the general point another way: When is the last time you heard of a drive-by knifing?

A second advantage of the gun as a weapon is that it affords the opportunity to inflict multiple wounds, quickly and efficiently, on the same target. Even a six-shot revolver can inflict horrendous damage on the human body in a matter of seconds; fully automatic or semiautomatic guns with high-capacity ammunition magazines can inflict scores of wounds, again in seconds, with little physical effort by the attacker. As high-capacity semiautomatics replaced revolvers as street guns in the 1980s, urban trauma centers reported a substantial increase in the average number of gunshot wounds suffered by victims.[26] Multiple gunshot wounds are associated with higher mortality, more days in intensive care, and longer hospital stays.[27]

A third advantage of the gun is that it can inflict wounds, quickly and efficiently, on multiple targets. This capacity has been tragically demonstrated time and again in recent American history, from Charles Whitman's sniper attacks from the University of Texas tower in 1966 (fourteen dead and thirty-two wounded), to Patrick Purdy on a schoolyard in Stockton, California, in 1989 (five killed, all children, thirty wounded, all but one a child), to Eric Harris and Dylan Klebold at Columbine High School in Littleton, Colorado, in 1999 (twelve students and one teacher dead, twenty-three students wounded), to Seung Hui Cho at Virginia Tech in 2007 (thirty-two students and teachers dead, seventeen wounded). If only these killers had been armed with knives or baseball bats—so many lives would have been saved.

It is remarkable how often the opponents of gun regulation forget the obvious advantages of guns over other weapons. For example, after the September 11 attacks, the NRA repeatedly pointed out that the terrorists' weapon of choice was not the gun, but the box cutter. According to NRA lawyer Stephen Halbrook, "The hijackers of September 11, armed with box cutters and then with airliners, proved terrorists don't need firearms."[28] Is this trenchant observation meant to suggest that the hijackers would not have preferred to carry semiautomatic pistols on those planes rather than box cutters? For all the failings of our airport security system, at least it deterred the terrorists from using guns. Indeed, the terrorists were forced to use a product not even designed to be a weapon at all. If they had been able to use guns, perhaps the heroic passengers of United Flight 93 would not have been able to bring their plane down in a field in western Pennsylvania, thus preventing the destruction of the Capitol building or the White House.

The NRA's box cutter argument illustrates a recurring fallacy in the gun debate. Simply because other weapons (or products used as weapons) can be used to do great harm, does not mean that guns should be subject to no greater regulation than other weapons or dangerous products. To put the point another way, the case for stringently regulating guns does not require a showing that guns are the only product that can be used to cause harm. Yes, Juan Marichal did great damage to John Roseboro with a baseball bat. What would have happened if the Giants' right-hander had a Glock strapped to his waist?

THE INSTRUMENTALITY EFFECT

Every fan of rock music knows that two members of the Beatles were victims of criminal attacks during their lifetimes. John Lennon was shot. George Harrison was stabbed. John died. George survived. Of course, we can't necessarily say that if John had been stabbed and George shot, their fates would have been different. We can say that, as a statistical matter, John's death and George's survival were the most likely outcomes. Simply put, *guns are more lethal than other weapons.*

Professor Franklin Zimring has done the pioneering work on this "instrumentality effect" of guns. Zimring's landmark 1968 study compared fatal and nonfatal gun and knife assaults over a three-year period in Chicago and found that gun attacks were about five times more likely to kill than knife attacks.[29] Almost a quarter century later, Zimring's instrumentality effect was confirmed by a study in the *Journal of the American Medical Association* of fatal and nonfatal assaults involving family members or intimates. Domestic assaults with firearms were three times more likely to result in death than assaults with knives or other cutting instruments; firearm assaults were more than twenty-three times as likely to be deadly than assaults with other weapons or bodily force.[30]

Further support for the greater lethality of guns is found in the effect on the murder rate from the use of guns in robberies. Professor Philip Cook of Duke University looked at the incidence of robbery and robbery murder in forty-three cities for the period 1976–1983. He found that, on average, an additional thousand robberies committed with guns "produced" more than three times as many murders as an additional thousand robberies not involving guns.[31] Thus, gun involvement in robberies more than tripled their lethality. Undeniably, when criminals use guns, as opposed to other weapons, crime becomes more lethal. Although Professor Kleck takes issue with some of these studies, ultimately even he is forced to concede that "part of this positive association between aggressor gun use and victim death is probably due to the greater lethality of guns."[32]

It is hardly coincidental that, although guns are not used in most crimes, they are the weapons of choice for homicide. Guns are used in only 4 percent of all felonies, which, of course, include many nonviolent offenses. As to felonies involving threatened or actual bodily injury—homicide, rape, robbery, and aggravated assault—the involvement of guns increases fivefold, to 20 percent. For homicides alone, gun involvement jumps to 70 percent.[33] It may be that guns do not kill without people to use them. It is also true that people kill people more often with guns. Guns don't kill people. They *enable* people to kill people.

The data suggesting that firearms are more lethal than other weapons used in criminal assault is consistent with the data on the use of firearms versus other methods of suicide. Suicide attempts with firearms are more likely to be completed than attempts by other means. One study of over a thousand suicides and over sixteen hundred attempted suicides in Allegheny County, Pennsylvania, found that attempted suicides by gun were successful 92 percent of the time.[34] The next most lethal means were carbon monoxide (78 percent), hanging (77 percent), and drowning (66 percent). The differences in lethality, however, were far greater when gun suicide attempts are compared to attempts with other instruments that can be considered weapons. The 92 percent lethality of guns far exceeded the lethality of poison (23 percent), drugs (11 percent), or, most relevantly, cutting with a knife or other sharp object (4 percent). Thus, for persons trying to kill themselves, guns were over twenty-three times more deadly than knives.[35] Again, as weapons go, whether used against others or against oneself, guns are more deadly.

Pro-gun critics respond to these lethality figures by suggesting that those who use guns in crimes against others, or to hurt themselves, may simply be more determined to kill than those who choose other weapons. According to this argument, if guns weren't available, these highly motivated killers would simply try harder with other weapons and would succeed just as often.

Note the premise of this argument: that persons more serious about killing will choose guns over other weapons. This implies, of course, that the truly motivated killers at least *believe* that guns are more lethal. They could, of course, be wrong. Zimring's research suggests that they are not. Zimring analyzed the location and number of wounds inflicted in assaults for a one-month period in Chicago in 1967 as a basis for judging the seriousness and intent of the assailants.[36] He found that whereas 77 percent of the knife attacks reflected an intent to cause serious injury or death, only 60 percent of the gun attacks reflected such intent.[37] According to Zimring, "nothing about the data suggests that the average knife attack is any less seriously intended than the average gun attack."[38] Thus, the greater lethality of gun assaults reflects the greater lethality of guns, not a more deadly intent of those who attack with guns.[39] Zimring concluded that "if knives were substituted for guns, the homicide rate would drop significantly."[40]

For suicides, it turns out that the choice of a gun as the instrument of self-destruction does not necessarily indicate a greater determination to complete the task. The Allegheny County suicide study found that those who unsuccessfully attempt suicide with guns are actually less likely to later commit suicide (by any means) than those who unsuccessfully employ other means. Although gunshot was the most lethal suicide method, it ranked only sixth as a predictor of future suicide, behind smothering oneself with a plastic bag, carbon monoxide, drowning, gas, and poison. Unsuccessful suicide attempters using guns were only slightly more likely to eventually kill themselves as unsuccessful attempters who cut themselves. Whereas 6.25 percent of the gun attempters eventually committed suicide by some means, 4.83 percent of the cutting attempters did so. Even if this reflects a somewhat greater determination among the gun users, it does not come close to accounting for the overwhelming difference in lethal results described earlier (92 percent versus 4 percent).

Of course, any suicide is a devastating tragedy. But suicides of young people, who have everything to live for but often don't realize it, are particularly tragic. The *Omaha World-Herald* did a series on guns and teen suicide, finding that the unique deadliness of guns, and their ready availability to teens in Nebraska, was taking far too many innocent young lives. In 2003 Nebraska hospitals treated 553 children for self-inflicted injuries or suicide attempts. The hospitals discharged 386 children who swallowed pills or poisons, but only three who used guns.[41] The gun users went from the hospital to the morgue. Seattle pediatrician and researcher Dr. David Grossman makes the point this way: "If we can get them to take pills instead of a gun, it is more likely to turn a suicide into a suicide attempt."[42]

But the "guns don't kill people" fallacy has a powerful hold on people, even parents whose children have become victims. The *World-Herald* interviewed Darrell Schramm, whose fifteen-year-old son Ryan had killed himself with his father's hunting rifle after his mother had discovered he was abusing amphetamines. Four years after the tragedy, Mr. Schramm was still ambivalent about guns. "I suppose if I wouldn't have ever owned a gun, he might be alive today. But the gun didn't kill the boy. The boy killed the boy."[43] No, Mr. Schramm, the gun enabled your son to kill himself, as difficult as it is to face that awful truth.

The question, therefore, is not whether people can kill other people (or themselves) with weapons other than guns. Of course they can. The question, rather, is whether guns are more effective and efficient in achieving lethal results than other weapons. Of course they are.

THE INSTRUMENTALITY EFFECT ACROSS NATIONS

If guns are more lethal than other weapons, we would expect that nations with a greater use of guns in crime would have more lethal crime. Conversely, if the lethality of a nation's criminal activity were relatively low despite its relatively high involvement of guns in crime, we might begin to doubt the instrumentality effect. Professor Zimring's more recent work, with collaborator Gordon Hawkins, has focused on comparative analyses of U.S. crime with that of other Western industrialized nations. The Zimring/ Hawkins findings will be surprising to most Americans, although they are entirely consistent with the instrumentality effect.

We generally think of our country as comparatively lawless when stacked up against other Western democracies. Indeed, there has been endless speculation about the causes of peculiarly high American crime rates, and possible answers have been found in everything from the unique individualism of American social thought, to the violent conquests that made possible our western expansion, to various demographic explanations. Zimring and Hawkins find, however, that the basic premise is wrong. America actually does not have dramatically more crime than other Western democracies. America's crime is simply more deadly.

Their analysis of crime victimization rates for eighteen industrialized nations shows, for example, that high rates of property crime (that is, crimes not involving force against a person) are not unique to the United States. The United States has a rate of property crime slightly lower than that of Poland and only slightly higher than those of New Zealand, the Netherlands, Australia, and Czechoslovakia. Even as to violent offenses, the rate in Australia actually exceeds that in the United States, and three other countries—New Zealand, Poland, and Canada—have rates within 10 percent of those prevailing in the United States.

Perhaps most surprising, rates for assault in the United States are actually lower than those in Canada, New Zealand, and Australia and are nearly identical to those in Finland, the Netherlands, and Poland. However, the rate of assaults leading to death is several times higher in the United States than in Canada, New Zealand, and Australia. Homicide rates in Finland, the Netherlands, and Poland are a fraction of the American homicide rate.[44] Other Western countries have our crime problem. None has our lethal crime problem.

No country, moreover, has our gun crime problem. The United States is the only large industrial democracy that reports firearms as involved in a majority of its homicides.[45] To take one dramatic example, Zimring and Hawkins report a comparison of the United States with England and Wales. Killings by all means other than guns occur in the United States at a rate per million population that is 3.7 times the nongun killings in England and Wales. However, the gun homicide rate in the United States is *sixty-three times* that in England and Wales, yielding an overall homicide rate that is 8.5 times greater in the United States.[46] The United States has greater involvement of guns in crime, and its crime is more lethal.

These kinds of international comparisons are not offered here to establish that countries with more guns, or less gun control, necessarily have more crime or violent crime. They are offered because, insofar as they show that greater gun involvement in crime yields more deadly crime, they are entirely consistent with the basic proposition that guns are more lethal than other widely available weapons. As might be expected, it turns out that, across twenty-six developed nations of the world, there is a significant correlation between gun ownership levels, gun homicides, and total homicides.[47]

THE LETHALITY OF GUN ACCIDENTS

The instrumentality effect, as discussed above, has to do with the deadliness of guns when used intentionally, either in crimes or suicide attempts. However, unintentional uses are also instructive on the relative lethality of guns. Unlike other weapons, guns often kill or inflict serious injury even when the user does not intend to inflict injury at all.

My earliest recollection of really thinking about guns concerned an incident in my neighborhood when I was about twelve years old. I was a child of the 1950s' American suburbs; my family lived in the solidly middle-class community of Springfield, Virginia. One day our neighbor, Mrs. A., was rushed to the hospital with a bullet wound. She had been accidentally shot by her husband while he was cleaning his handgun at the kitchen table. The bullet shattered Mrs. A.'s leg, and she walked with a pronounced limp from that day on. Even the idea that a family three doors away would own a gun was jarring to learn. That the family's own gun would end up changing Mrs. A.'s life forever was absolutely chilling to me. That the bullet might have taken a different, and deadly, path was unthinkable. I really liked Mrs. A. A couple of summers later, she and I rode the bus together to meet up with my family at our hotel on the beach at Ocean City, Maryland. I remember thinking how she was still so much fun, even after all she had been through.

I also remember being very angry at Mr. A. How could he be so careless with such a dangerous weapon? He also had two small children in the home. But my thoughts also were directed at the gun itself. When guns are concerned, is it possible for human beings, with all their limitations and frailties, to be careful enough? I remember my father asking about Mr. A., "Why in the world did he have a gun in the first place?" I thought it was a good question.

The Mrs. A. incident also provides a different kind of response to the "Guns don't kill. People kill people" argument. If Mr. A. owned a knife for self-defense, or a baseball bat, he likely would not have seriously injured his wife unless he intended to do so. He could not have come close to killing her accidentally. As the late columnist and humorist Molly Ivins once observed, "People are seldom killed while cleaning their knives."[48]

Because guns are meant to shoot projectiles, they have a certain complexity that other weapons, like knives, do not have. For example, many gun accidents occur because the user does not know the gun is loaded. Others occur when the gun is dropped. Hunting accidents often occur because the long range of hunting rifles and shotguns makes it sometimes difficult to know whether one is shooting at an animal, or human, target. (Just ask Dick Cheney.) Of course, there is much that can be done to train gun users to avoid accidents, through myriad gun safety and safe hunting courses. But there is no denying that the relative complexity of guns makes their users more susceptible to accidents than users of knives.

There is also no denying that mistakes in gun handling and use are more likely to be fatal than mistakes with knives. The National Safety Council calculates the odds of dying from various kinds of injuries. In the year 2004 accidental firearm discharges caused 649 deaths; the lifetime odds of dying from such firearm discharges come to 1 in 5,808. For the category "contact with sharp objects," which likely includes many more sharp objects than knives purchased as weapons, there were one-sixth as many deaths in 2004 and the lifetime odds of dying from such contact is 1 in 35,563.[49] The odds of death from firearm accidents, therefore, are six times greater than the odds of death from "sharp object" accidents. This is true despite the undeniable fact that knives and other sharp objects are far more prevalent in American households than guns. If we were to compare guns with only those "sharp objects" actually owned and used as weapons, the relative propensity of guns to accidentally kill would be astronomically higher.

Instead of comparing accidents with guns to accidents with other weapons, defenders of firearms would rather compare guns to other potential causes of accidental deaths. For example, Gary Kleck points out that the accidental death rate for motor vehicles is thirty-three times that for guns, when based on the total number of cars and guns in existence.[50] Kleck offers this comparison as "a meaningful point of reference,"[51] but it is meaningful only until one thinks about it.

As pointed out earlier, guns are owned primarily as weapons; cars are not. This means, of course, that the uses of guns and cars will be dramatically different. The average American car owner uses his or her car virtually every day, sometimes for lengthy periods of time. Moreover, auto owners use their cars in a way that involves constant interaction with other car owners using their cars (i.e., on crowded roadways). Gun owners, in contrast, do not typically use their guns every day, nor for long periods of time during the day, nor in a manner involving interaction with other gun owners using their guns. This is true even if we define the "use" of guns to mean contact with them that does not involve shooting (e.g., carrying them). Indeed, many gun owners go for months, if not years, without ever touching their guns. It is difficult to even imagine a general usage of guns that could be meaningfully comparable to our usage of cars. (Such a comparison would be only fanciful; for example, suppose virtually all gun owners went hunting virtually every day of the year.)

The point is a simple one that seems to have escaped Dr. Kleck and other gun enthusiasts: if gun owners actually used their guns as frequently as car owners use their cars, there is every reason to expect that the accidental death rate from guns would be far *greater* than the accidental death rate from cars. Since there is no way to actually control for differences in usage between guns and cars, Dr. Kleck's comparison is the classic "apples and oranges" fallacy. It makes no sense to conclude from such a comparison of accidental death rates that guns are somehow less dangerous than cars or should be less regulated than cars.

Dr. Kleck also cannot resist another common comparison of accidental death rates that is common in gun debates: that between drownings of young children in swimming pools and shootings of young children. Of all categories of gun deaths, shootings of young children are the most shocking and senseless. For this reason, gun advocates are particularly determined to minimize their significance. Kleck points out that each year about five hundred children under the age of five accidentally drown in residential swimming pools, compared to about forty killed in gun accidents. Considering that far more households have guns than swimming pools, Kleck estimates the risk of a fatal accident among young children is over one hundred times higher for swimming pools than for guns.[52]

Again, if this comparison is meant to suggest that swimming pools are one hundred times more dangerous for young children than guns, it borders on the silly. The comparison is illegitimate because it fails to control for exposure to the risk. To make the accidental death rate comparison meaningful, we would have to imagine a world in which young children are as exposed to the risks posed by guns as they are exposed to the risks posed by residential swimming pools. Of course, we can't imagine such a world because most adults are not crazy enough to expose young children to guns in any way similar to their exposure to swimming pools. Parents typically allow five-year-olds to use residential swimming pools, with active adult supervision. Indeed, the benefits of teaching young kids to swim are widely acknowledged. What would be the accidental death rate for gunshots among five-year-olds if gun owners frequently allowed five-year-olds to use loaded guns under active adult supervision? Of course, it would be astronomical, to say nothing of the fatal casualties inflicted on the adults supervising their young shooters. No sane gun owner would think of allowing a five-year-old to handle a loaded gun under any circumstances.[53]

Guns are weapons. They are purchased as weapons. They are used as weapons. When one assesses relative risks, guns should be compared with other weapons. When such a comparison is made, it is striking that guns are far more likely to kill, even when their users have no intention to kill. This is a measure of the lethality of guns that should not be obscured by phony comparisons of guns with other dangerous products.

THE LESSONS OF COLUMBINE

What, then, is the core fallacy of the argument, "Guns don't kill people. People kill people"?

If the argument is meant to convey the idea that guns cannot inflict injury without human involvement, it is both true and irrelevant. As to public policy issues involving regulation of cars and other dangerous products, it is hardly sufficient to oppose regulation simply because injuries from those products occur only when they are used by human beings. Why should such reasoning have any more validity when the issue is regulation of guns?

If the argument is meant to convey the idea that gun regulation cannot be effective because criminals will simply substitute other weapons for guns, it ignores the central reality that guns are more lethal than other weapons. Thus, reducing gun involvement in violent crimes (as well as in suicide attempts) can be expected to save lives.

In other words, "Guns don't kill people. People kill people" is a fallacy because, although guns *alone* do not kill people, they *enable* people to kill people more effectively than other weapons. They more effectively enable those with criminal intent to inflict mortal injury on others; they more effectively enable the suicidal to inflict mortal injury on themselves. They enable mortal injury even when no one intends such injury. This lethal enabling potential is a key justification for regulation designed to reduce access to guns by persons likely to use them in violent acts and to make guns themselves less susceptible to unintentional discharge. Perhaps the point was made best by renowned social scientist Ozzy Osbourne when he was asked about "the recent epidemic of violent youth." He responded, "I keep hearing this [expletive] thing that guns don't kill people, but people kill people. If that's the case, why do we give people guns when they go to war? Why not just send the people?"[54] Ozzy's insight shows more common sense about the gun issue than the NRA has demonstrated in decades.

"Guns don't kill people. People kill people" is, however, a fallacy with a powerful hold on how the problem of gun violence is addressed in America. Consider, for example, the public response to one of the most traumatic American gun tragedies since the John F. and Robert Kennedy and Martin Luther King Jr. assassinations: the Columbine school shooting of 1999.

On April 20, 1999, two seniors at Columbine High School in Littleton, Colorado, Eric Harris and Dylan Klebold, entered the school with two sawed-off shotguns, a Hi-Point semiautomatic rifle, and an Intratec TEC-DC9 assault pistol. In sixteen minutes they killed twelve fellow students and one teacher, and wounded twenty-one others, before taking their own lives.[55] It was the most deadly of a horrifying series of school shootings in suburban and small town America during the late 1990s. These were the places where kids were not supposed to kill kids. These were the places where schools were supposed to be safe. Springfield, Oregon. Jonesboro, Arkansas. Paducah, Kentucky. Pearl, Mississippi. For many Americans, deadly youth violence was no longer just a "city problem." It was in their neighborhoods and, worse yet, in their schools. It could happen anywhere.

A stunned nation struggled to answer the question, Why? Because Klebold and Harris had planned their assault for months without detection from their parents, many said lack of parental involvement was to blame. Since the killers were fans of *Doom*, others said violent video games were responsible. The Family Research Council cited the "alleged bisexuality" of the shooters.[56] In his first speech after leaving Congress, Newt Gingrich blamed the shootings on the elimination of school prayer, violent movies and video games, high taxes that force parents to spend more time working and away from their children, and the decline in "core values" among youth, "so that young people may not know who George Washington is . . . but they know what MTV is."[57] The NRA's Charlton Heston blamed the absence of an armed security guard in the school, even though there actually *was* an armed security guard in the school.[58] He also said the school should not have allowed Klebold and Harris to wear black trench coats to school.[59]

A national discussion of how teenagers like Klebold and Harris could be so alienated and infected by hatred as to massacre their classmates was well worth having. With hindsight, however, it is now clear that the Why? debate served to obfuscate the most obvious and simple lesson of the Columbine tragedy. Columbine was a national tragedy not because two teenagers were morally bankrupt and filled with hatred, but because two morally bankrupt and hate-filled teenagers *were able to kill thirteen innocent people and seriously injure twenty-one others.* They were *enabled* to be mass killers because of guns. Knives or baseball bats would have been woefully inadequate to the task. Yes, the killers also were armed with homemade bombs, but most of them did not detonate.[60] If explosives were regulated as loosely as guns are, Klebold and Harris would not have had to resort to the less dependable homemade variety.

The killing and wounding was done with guns, with even many of the surviving victims suffering multiple wounds. Seventeen-year-old Richard Castaldo was shot five times in the chest, back, and abdomen. Valeen Schnurr, eighteen, had four bullet wounds in her chest, abdomen, and arm. Sean Graves, fifteen, was shot four times in the back and stomach. Seventeen-year-old Anne Marie Hochhalte was shot three times in the chest and liver.[61] Harris fired 121 rounds, 96 from his semiautomatic rifle and 25 from a sawed-off shotgun. Klebold fired 67 rounds, 55 with his TEC-DC9 assault pistol and another 12 from his sawed-off shotgun.[62] Without the guns, the problem was two deeply troubled kids. With the guns, the problem was fourteen dead kids, including Klebold and Harris. A bumper sticker emerged after Columbine, but the message was not the NRA's. It read, "It's the guns, stupid."

Nevertheless, the political aftermath of Columbine was a triumph for the "Guns don't kill people. People kill people" fallacy. No new federal laws to curb access to guns by dangerous kids were enacted, even though Klebold and Harris obtained their guns by exploiting the weaknesses in America's gun laws. At the federal level, and in most states, gun sales by licensed dealers are regulated, but sales by private citizens are not. The Brady Act's background check system, for instance, applies only to sales of guns by licensed gun dealers, not to sales by private citizens who claim they are merely selling guns from their personal collections. This leaves a huge, unregulated secondary market of gun sales between private citizens at gun shows, through classified ads, and by other means. About 40 percent of gun sales occur in these private transactions.[63]

Klebold and Harris turned to this secondary market to acquire their arsenal. Indeed, Eric Harris was chillingly well informed about the loophole allowing purchases from private sellers at gun shows. In his personal journal, amid the nauseating profanity, racism, and promises to "burn the world" and "kill everyone," he wrote, "If we can save up about $200 real quick and find someone who is 21+ we can go the next gun show and find a private dealer and buy ourselves some bad-ass AB-10 machine pistols."[64]

Because, at age seventeen, the boys were under the minimum age of eighteen to buy guns from a dealer, they recruited Klebold's eighteen-year-old prom date, Robyn Anderson, to act as a "straw purchaser" for them. (She was not old enough to be an effective straw purchaser for the "machine pistol" referred to by Harris, for which the minimum age was twenty-one, but she was old enough to buy rifles and shotguns.) Anderson first went to a licensed dealer but did not complete the purchase because she would have had to fill out a federal form to trigger the Brady background check. Even though she presumably would have passed the check, she later said, "The dealer asked me if I would fill out some paperwork and I said, 'No, I didn't feel comfortable with that.' I didn't want to put my name on something that I wasn't going to have control of." She and the two boys instead went to the Tanner Gun Show in Adams County, Colorado, where she paid cash to a private seller for the two shotguns and the Hi-Point semiautomatic. She said it was clear to the seller that the guns were for the boys. "They were the only ones asking all the questions and handling the guns." There were no questions asked and no paperwork to fill out. She said, "I would not have bought a gun for Eric and Dylan if I had had to give any personal information or submit to any kind of check at all."[65] The fourth gun—a machine pistol—was purchased directly by Klebold and Harris from a private seller who, in turn, had purchased it from an unlicensed vendor at the Tanner Gun Show.[66]

Paradoxically, however, this tragic illustration of the weakness of America's gun laws failed to result in a new surge of public support for stronger laws. An analysis of public opinion before and after the Columbine shootings by the National Opinion Research Center (NORC) concluded, "There is little indication that Littleton generally increased support for gun control in the short term and no sign that it did so after about six months."[67] The NORC survey did cite other polls finding that, in the immediate aftermath of the shootings, mentions of gun violence as one of the most important problems facing the country increased several-fold,[68] but apparently that view did not translate into greater support for specific gun control measures.

Public support for background checks on private sales of guns, the specific legislative reform most relevant to how the Columbine shooters obtained their guns, actually declined slightly after the shootings.[69] Both before and after Columbine, public support for private-sale background checks was extraordinarily high—79.5 percent in 1998 and 78.6 percent in 1999. It may be that, given such a stratospheric starting point, any event is unlikely to spark public support to a new, higher level. The small minority of opponents is likely so committed that no new information will change their minds. Nevertheless, it is surprising that such a cataclysmic episode of gun violence registered on the public opinion Richter scale as a spike in concern about gun violence but not in support for gun control.

The results suggest that although the American public overwhelmingly and consistently believes gun control makes sense, it did not take from the Columbine shootings the lesson that stronger gun laws are an urgent national priority. It seems quite plausible to believe that an uptick in gun control support was absent because the public interpreted the shootings as a "people problem," not a "gun problem."

In July 2003, more than four years after Columbine, a survey conducted by the Marttila Communications Group for the Brady Campaign to Prevent Gun Violence showed the school shootings had hardly shaken the power of the "people, not guns" fallacy. The survey asked the following question:

Recently, there have been a series of school shootings in the news, perpetrated by high school and elementary school students. Which of the following statements is closest to your own view?

A. Weak gun laws deserve a large part of the blame for these tragedies. It is much too easy for children to get access to guns.

B. People kill people, not guns. Stronger gun laws would make little difference in stopping school shootings. It is not fair to blame guns or gun owners when children take guns to school.

Fifty-one percent of those responding said that "People kill people, not guns" was closest to their view, while only 43 percent attributed blame to weak gun laws.[70]

In May 1999, a month after the Columbine shootings, legislation to extend the Brady background checks to private sales at gun shows passed the U.S. Senate, but only by Vice President Gore's tie-breaking vote. A month later, however, the House of Representatives defeated a similar proposal by a comfortable margin of 235–193.[71]

The echo of "Guns don't kill people. People kill people" could be heard throughout the floor debate in the House. Listen to Representative Lamar Smith of Texas: "The violence and crimes committed with guns are not the root problem, just the manifestation of it. The root problem is the destruction of American values. Our efforts should be directed towards strengthening those values, and not passing restrictive amendments which are going to be considered later tonight and which do not solve the problem."[72] Or Representative Terry Everett of Alabama: "The erosion of America's morality has desensitized our children's ability to discern right from wrong, and even to value human life. This debate should not be about more laws on guns, or adding even more laws at any point. It should be about our culture and values that have gone really, really wrong."[73] Or Representative John Peterson of Pennsylvania: "Something has changed in this country. The people do not value life. That is what we need to deal with. It is not guns."[74]

Of course, if it is true that Dylan Klebold and Eric Harris were typical of large numbers of young people who truly do not know the value of human life, that would seem to be a rather compelling reason to limit their access to the instruments of killing. Shouldn't Columbine have made keeping guns out of the hands of violent kids our most urgent national priority, while we also figure out how to deal with the far tougher challenge of the hardness of so many young hearts? No one can deny the importance of addressing the root causes of youth violence, but the need to do so is simply not a good reason to oppose laws to make it more difficult for kids to get guns. Representative Steven Rothman of New Jersey responded to the root causes argument during the House debate: "There were many factors that contributed to the recent school killings: lack of parental involvement, the prevalence of violent, cruel and sadistic video games, television shows, and movies. But when all is said and done, the main culprit was the easy accessibility of guns to the children."[75]

Congress, however, was not persuaded. As the House debate drew to a close in the wee hours of the morning on June 18, Representative Carolyn McCarthy of New York, the primary sponsor of the gun show legislation, took the podium knowing that defeat was inevitable. She had been elected to Congress three years before as a strong gun control advocate, after her husband was killed and her adult son was badly wounded in a shooting on the Long Island Railroad. The futility of the debate had brought her to tears. "I am sorry that this is very hard for me. I am Irish, and I am not supposed to cry in front of anyone. But I made a promise a long time ago. I made a promise to my son and to my husband. If there was anything that I could do to prevent one family from going through what I have gone through . . . then I have done my job." Carolyn McCarthy thought what she was trying to do seemed so simple and sensible. "I am trying to stop the criminals from being able to get guns. That is all I am trying to do." She concluded, "If we do not do it, shame on us."[76]

Today, it is still possible, in all but a few states, for another Dylan Klebold or Eric Harris to buy high-firepower guns at gun shows. The search for the root causes of youth violence continues.

2.

"WHEN GUNS ARE OUTLAWED,
ONLY OUTLAWS WILL HAVE GUNS."

IN HER FIRST NETWORK interview as a candidate for vice president, Alaska Governor Sarah Palin was asked by ABC's Charlie Gibson whether she supported a ban on semiautomatic assault weapons, as did 70 percent of the American people. She responded by proudly proclaiming her lifetime membership in the NRA and then explaining that she opposes an assault weapon ban because if "you start banning guns . . . you start taking away guns from people who will use them responsibly" and then it's "the bad guys who have the guns, not those who are law-abiding citizens."[1] In other words, "If guns are outlawed, only outlaws will have guns."

This clever slogan embodies two ideas, each of which has some surface plausibility. First, it invokes the "futility argument," that is, the belief that criminals are so determined to arm themselves, no gun control laws can possibly disarm them. Second, it implies the corollary argument that, because only law-abiding citizens will obey gun control laws, the law-abiding will be defenseless against the well-armed criminal.

Although those two propositions are embodied in the slogan, they are not directly expressed by it. Instead, the slogan, by its literal terms, addresses the imagined consequences of the most extreme of gun control proposals (i.e., the legal prohibition of gun ownership). It is worth noting that the proposal to "outlaw" all guns, or even just handguns, has little to do with the contemporary gun policy debate. A legal ban on the manufacture, sale, and possession of handguns has virtually no support in the U.S. Congress. Although bills barring the future manufacture and sale of handguns occasionally are introduced in Congress, they have attracted only a handful of supporters. Some localities have enacted broad handgun bans, but no state has done so. Public opinion surveys show large majorities supporting virtually every conceivable proposal for stricter gun laws, with the conspicuous exception of a handgun ban, which polls in the 30–40 percent range.[2]

This is not to say that the proposal to ban handguns, or even all guns, is not worthy of public debate. It is merely to note that the argument "When guns are outlawed, only outlaws will have guns" seems unresponsive to most proposals for strengthening our gun laws that have dominated the gun debate for at least the last two decades. Instead, the argument often functions as a classic "red herring."[3]

For example, the proposal to require background checks for private gun sales at gun shows and through the classifieds obviously is not equivalent to a proposal to "outlaw guns." Indeed, the evidence indicates that requiring background checks at gun shows does not even have an adverse effect on the number of gun shows, as shown by the experience of various states that have closed the "gun show loophole." One study found that of the five states that hosted the most gun shows in 1998, three states—Pennsylvania, Illinois, and California—already require background checks or licenses for private purchases.[4] Nor would the extension of background checks to gun shows have the effect of depriving gun buyers with no criminal background or other disqualifying record of their access to arms. Dr. Garen Wintemute of the University of California–Davis studied gun shows, both in states that have closed the "gun show loophole" and states that have not. He concluded that "gun shows can be regulated so as to diminish their importance as sources of crime guns without greatly diminishing attendance or commercial activity."[5] Whatever the arguments against outlawing guns, they appear quite irrelevant to gun show background checks and other policy ideas that have been animating the gun debate in recent years.

This does not, however, stop opponents of gun control from invoking the specter of banning guns in response to far more modest policy proposals. Indeed, this is one reason gun control debates often have a "ships passing in the night" quality. The gun control advocate will argue for additional regulation on some aspect of gun manufacture, sale, or possession (e.g., required safety devices on guns, limits on the numbers of guns sold to specific buyers, requirements that guns be stored safely). The gun control opponent will respond, at least in part, by talking about how important gun possession is for self-defense and to preserve our basic liberties, as if the issue is whether the government should allow people to own guns at all. This is an understandable, if objectionable, effort to change the subject (i.e., to shift the debate from proposals that enjoy broad popular support to a more radical idea that does not). "What the opposition *really* wants," said one NRA official, "is a total ban on the private ownership of all firearms. I have no doubt whatsoever."[6] This change-the-subject tactic also enables the NRA to make the gun control issue salient to gun owners, convincing them that even modest controls are merely a first step to the eventual elimination of guns for self-defense and hunting.[7]

One of the challenges for gun control advocates is that their opponents have had great success in causing many people to equate the words "gun control" with the concept of banning gun possession. More than once I have attended a social gathering and made the mistake of revealing what I do for a living to persons whose views on the gun issue are unknown to me. If they are hostile to my work, they usually are not shy about denouncing "gun control" as an attack on their rights as Americans. However, more often than not, it will turn out that even the strongest opponents of "gun control" will have views on specific gun laws that do not differ from my own. If I ask them whether they support the Brady Act, they will almost always say yes. If I ask them whether people should be allowed to buy assault weapons, they will say, "Of course not." They will, however, not retreat from their opposition to "gun control."

To many Americans, the words "gun control" equate with opposition to guns per se. This was not always the case. When I was a teenager, the U.S. Congress enacted a law called the Gun Control Act of 1968, which did not ban a single gun. A poll taken thirty-five years later, in July 2003, by the Marttila Communications Group showed a large minority of likely voters—45 percent—agreed with the statement, "The hidden agenda of most gun control advocates is to ban all guns."[8] This sentiment gives force to the so-called slippery slope argument, discussed at length in chapter 3. Any proposal to tighten gun restrictions is treated as if it were equivalent to a proposal to outlaw gun ownership because it is a slippery slope from one to the other.

The equation of "gun control" with "banning guns" also is aided and abetted by the media, which frequently uses the shorthand label "anti-gun" in reference to any person advocating stronger gun laws. The use of this label assumes that the advocate is motivated by an animus toward guns in general and that his agenda really is to ban gun ownership. I have been involved in countless television debates and interviews in which I am identified on the screen as "anti-gun" or a "gun opponent," even before I have uttered a word. In most cases (Fox News excepted), the media likely is not intentionally being misleading. The use of the anti-gun label more likely reflects the tendency of the media (particularly television) to oversimplify issues and to portray every issue (whether it be guns, abortion, immigration, or others) in the starkest possible terms as a clash between polar opposite positions. The intention, obviously, is to make the coverage as dramatic and interesting as possible, but in the case of guns, it plays directly into the NRA's hands.

To the extent that the NRA and others have been able to frame the debate as about "outlawing guns," their success, surprisingly, may be threatened by the greatest "gun rights" victory in American legal history, the landmark Second Amendment ruling issued by the Supreme Court in *District of Columbia v. Heller.*[9] In a 5–4 decision issued in June 2008, the Court found the Second Amendment's "right of the people to keep and bear Arms" violated by D.C.'s handgun ban, as well as its highly restrictive requirements for storage of guns, which the Court read to make impossible the use of those guns for self-defense. *Heller* marked a radical departure from the longstanding view, endorsed by the Supreme Court almost seventy years before,[10] that the right to be armed relates exclusively to service in a "well regulated Militia." Justice Antonin Scalia's majority opinion in *Heller* found that the amendment "elevates above all other interests the right of law-abiding, responsible citizens to use arms in defense of hearth and home."[11] Because handguns are commonly used for self-defense in the home, they cannot be banned. As Justice Scalia put it, "the enshrinement of constitutional rights necessarily takes certain policy choices off the table," including, in this case, "the absolute prohibition of handguns held and used for self-defense in the home."[12]

If a handgun ban is "off the table," this may make it more difficult for the pro-gun advocate to change the subject when the issue is reasonable gun laws, like background checks at gun shows, that fall far short of a handgun ban. How can the gun lobby argue as if the issue is whether to allow guns for self-defense, if the issue now *cannot* be whether to allow guns for self-defense? If the argument is, "When guns are outlawed, only outlaws will have guns," now a new response is possible: "Not only are we not talking about outlawing guns, but guns *cannot* be outlawed. So let's talk about ways of strengthening our laws to keep guns out of the wrong hands, while abiding by the new Constitutional right created in *Heller.*"

In succeeding chapters, I will explore the implications of *Heller* for the gun lobby's slippery slope argument, as well as the decision's legal significance. For now, it is sufficient to at least recognize the possibility that, in achieving a great legal victory, gun rights advocates may well have made it easier for their opponents to focus the debate on a set of policy proposals that have broad public support, free from the distracting charge that the debate is really about whether law-abiding citizens should be allowed to have guns.

WHAT CRIMINAL WOULD OBEY GUN LAWS?

It should be recognized, though, that the "When guns are outlawed . . ." slogan, although literally about "outlawing guns," makes a broader argument about gun laws in general. The core of the argument is that because gun control laws, by their very nature, are obeyed only by the law abiding, they cannot possibly be effective in curbing violent behavior by criminals. "Criminals will always break the law and obtain firearms illegally," says NRA President Sandra Froman.[13] Here is how two academic critics of gun control laws put it:

> Attempts to reduce drive-by shootings by restricting access to firearms are doomed to failure. It must be borne in mind that in all cases of drive-by shooting, the weapons themselves and the use to which they are put are already illegal and carry heavy penalties. . . . The prospect of all these penalties appears not to deter drive-by shooters, and why should it? They are, after all, on their way to commit first-degree murder, punishable by no less than a death penalty. Further gun control laws could hardly be expected to offer more deterrence than that.[14]

If, in fact, the effectiveness of gun control laws depended on the willingness of determined killers to obey them, their success would be unlikely indeed. In fact, however, the premise of the argument is wrong. The success of gun control laws in curbing access to guns by dangerous people is not at all dependent on the willingness of hardened criminals to obey them.

Let's take the drive-by shooter himself. If he is a minor, already has a felony record, or is a batterer with a domestic violence record, his mere possession of a gun is illegal. This creates the possibility that he may be arrested and charged with a gun crime before he is able to shoot anyone. Were it not for gun control laws barring gun possession by certain categories of high-risk people, the police would not have this enforcement tool at their disposal.

Gun possession offenses also can be valuable even if the offender is successful in committing a crime with the illegal gun. They can be useful to prosecutors in obtaining longer sentences in plea bargains, particularly since they may be easier to prove than the more serious, violent offense.

Even the NRA says it supports laws barring possession of guns by convicted felons,[15] although it goes without saying that many convicted felons will not obey those laws.

The problem is that, under federal law, the categories of prohibited possessors are insufficiently broad. For example, although a misdemeanor involving domestic violence, i.e., violence committed by the victim's current or former spouse, parent, or guardian, bars the offender from gun possession,[16] other violent misdemeanors do not. One study showed that violent misdemeanors are predictors of future, more serious violent behavior.[17] Persons with at least two violent misdemeanors are fifteen times more likely to be charged with murder, rape, robbery, or aggravated assault. The "prohibited person" gun control laws would be an even greater law enforcement tool if they were broadened to include more high-risk people. Their value, even in dealing with hardened criminals, in no way depends on whether such criminals will obey them.

Moreover, there is an obvious circularity in arguing that gun laws must be futile because criminals disobey them. Of course, as to the criminals who are willing to disobey them, the laws are futile by definition. But what about the possibility that there are potentially violent individuals who are deterred from carrying guns by the illegality of doing so? Although this notion escapes some opponents of gun control, it should be clear that compliance with a law cannot be determined merely by looking at the instances of when the law is violated. If it could, we would regard all our criminal laws as ultimately futile because all of them are frequently violated. I have never heard anyone argue that laws against murder are futile because murderers don't obey them.

It turns out that there is substantial evidence that many criminals may refrain from gun carrying because of gun control laws. In one survey, incarcerated felons who had not carried weapons during the commission of their crimes were asked why they decided against being armed. Seventy-nine percent chose the response, "Get a stiffer sentence," and 59 percent chose "Against the law."[18] It seems clear that, although some criminals will ignore gun laws, they will deter others.

Returning again to the drive-by shooter (who obviously is not worried about a possible illegal gun possession charge), what about laws designed to prevent him from getting his hands on guns in the first place? Does the effectiveness of these laws depend on the willingness of hardened criminals to obey the law? To answer this question, we must think about the sources of guns for the criminal market.

THE SOURCES OF CRIME GUNS

Guns do not fall from the sky into the hands of criminals. Few black market guns started their lives as black market guns. Virtually every gun illegally possessed or used in a criminal act was first made by a government-licensed gun manufacturer and sold by a government-licensed gun dealer. This establishes a critical connection between the legal and the illegal market in firearms. As the director of the Bureau of Alcohol, Tobacco and Firearms (ATF) put it several years ago, "Virtually every crime gun in the United States starts off as a legal firearm. Unlike narcotics or other contraband, the criminals' supply of guns does not begin in clandestine factories or with illegal smuggling. Crime guns, at least initially, start out in the legal market, identified by a serial number and required documentation."[19]

This does not mean that every crime gun was sold directly by a licensed dealer to a criminal, although this was a more frequent kind of transaction before the Brady Act was passed. It does mean that the gun used by our drive-by shooter is unlikely to have been smuggled across the border or manufactured in a garage gun factory. It also means that regulation directed at the legal sources of guns—those who are in the business of legally making and selling them—may well have an impact on their availability to illegal users.

Take the Brady Act, for example. The effectiveness of the Brady Act does not depend on criminals' willingness to obey the law. The statute's requirements are not directed at the gun user but at the licensed dealer who is selling the gun. It requires gun dealers to submit the purchaser's name for a background check and to refuse the sale if the check reveals a disqualifying record. If the dealer is willing to obey the law, the criminal's preferred source of guns will be denied him. Of course, there are scofflaw dealers who will sell guns "under the table" without doing the necessary background checks. Increasing enforcement resources and criminal penalties directed at those dealers may well reduce the incidence of illegal dealer sales. The point, however, is that the effectiveness of the Brady Act in curbing retail sales to criminals does not depend on the willingness of prospective murderers to obey gun laws.

Of course it may be argued that those who are blocked from buying guns from retailers will simply get them elsewhere. Some, of course, will succeed in doing so. It is perfectly plausible to believe, however, that some prohibited gun buyers will either lack the determination or the knowledge or the money (as we will see, there is a considerable markup for illegal guns) to find guns from other sources. We have already seen that over 1.5

million prohibited gun buyers have tried to buy guns from gun stores even after the Brady Act. If alternative sources are so readily available, why aren't they using them instead of running the risk of criminal prosecution by lying on a federal form about their criminal history and being nabbed by a Brady background check? As gun salesman Ed Riddle told the *Pittsburgh Tribune-Review*, "So-called 'bad guys' often are so eager to get their hands on a weapon that they'll submit to a background check—only to be arrested on the spot for outstanding warrants."[20]

To look at it another way, if criminals are so dumb as to continue to subject themselves to Brady background checks, why are we so sure they are smart enough to find alternative sources of guns?[21] One study showed that individuals who were denied purchases of handguns because of prior felony convictions were less likely to commit subsequent crimes than those who had been arrested but not convicted and thus were able to legally obtain handguns.[22] The study found that denial of a handgun purchase is associated with a reduction in risk for later criminal activity of approximately 20 to 30 percent.

Of course some criminals will obtain guns despite being closed off from retail gun dealers. This does not mean that there is no benefit to preventing criminal access to guns from that source. As prominent gun control critic Gary Kleck has acknowledged, even though some highly motivated criminals may evade the Brady background checks by resorting to unlicensed sellers or other alternatives, "there are some persons who will commit serious acts of violence in the future but who would not be sufficiently motivated and able to make use of these evasion strategies."[23]

Kleck's conclusion is supported by the statistics. Although, as the NRA often points out, violent crime rates began declining shortly before the Brady Act went into effect, the use of firearms in violent crime did not begin its sharp decline until Brady's inaugural year of 1994. In the five years preceding Brady, the percentage of violent crimes committed with firearms increased every year.[24] Beginning in 1994, a stunning reversal occurred. The proportion of nonlethal violent crimes committed with firearms declined by 45 percent from its high point in 1993 to 2004. Even more remarkable is the decline in the absolute number of nonlethal violent gun crimes, from 1,054,820 in 1993 to 280,890 in 2004, *a drop of 73 percent.*[25] During the same period, gun homicides dropped 37 percent,[26] driving a 34 percent decline in all homicides.[27] During those same years, an estimated 1,228,000 criminals and other prohibited purchasers were blocked by Brady background checks from buying guns from licensed gun dealers.[28]

FIGURE 2.1

FIREARMS CRIMES (MURDERS, ROBBERIES, AND AGGRAVATED ASSAULTS), 1973–2003

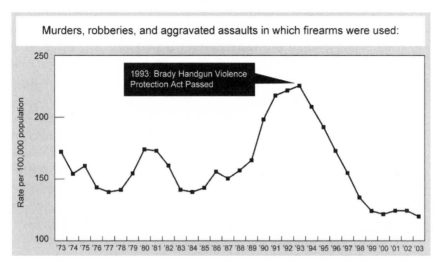

Source: Adapted from *CQ Researcher*, November 12, 2004, based on data from U.S.
Department of Justice, Bureau of Justice Statistics.

Is it plausible to believe that the Brady Act was not one of the causes of our nation's historic decline in gun crime? The impact of the Brady Act in no way depends on criminals being willing to obey gun laws. And, as we will see later, the existence of alternative sources of guns for criminals is a reason to shut off those sources, not to despair of the futility of gun laws.

A particularly strong indication of the close relationship of the legal to the illegal gun market is the impact of so-called one-gun-a-month laws. Here the surprising pioneer was my home state of Virginia, also now home to the National Rifle Association, whose impressive headquarters building sits along Route 66 in Fairfax. Although the NRA's move some years ago from the District of Columbia to Virginia took it to a far more gun-friendly environment, in July 1993 the Old Dominion had a moment of gun control sanity that made the NRA cringe. It enacted a statute limiting handgun purchases by individuals to one gun a month, with an exception for gun collectors.

To many observers, the Virginia law was an odd gun control law indeed because it seemed unlikely that a law allowing individuals to purchase twelve guns a year would have much of a beneficial impact on the availability of guns. The law, however, was a direct response to Virginia's burgeoning reputation as a primary source state for crime guns in the cities of the Northeast.

Since 1989 the ATF has used the unique serial numbers on guns to trace many thousands of crime guns—guns confiscated in connection with criminal investigations—to their last retail seller. When ATF traces a gun, it begins with the manufacturer, who reveals its distributor, who then reveals its retailer. Based on its database of these crime gun traces, ATF had determined that 41 percent of a sample of guns seized in New York City in 1991 had originated with Virginia gun dealers. Virginia similarly was a primary source state for crime guns traced in Washington, D.C., and Boston, Massachusetts.[29] Indeed, Interstate 95 from the Southeast to the Northeast became known to ATF as the "Iron Pipeline." Interstate gun trafficking investigations revealed that traffickers could make impressive profits by recruiting Virginia residents as "straw buyers" to purchase guns in bulk in Virginia gun stores, for shipment in the trunks of cars up Route 95 to the illegal gun markets of the large cities of the Northeast.[30] Virginia wasn't the only source state—Florida and Georgia also accounted for large shares of northeastern crime guns.

The Iron Pipeline, however, ran in only one direction: from the states of the Southeast, with their weak gun control laws, to the states of the Northeast, with their strong laws. Because New York, Massachusetts, and the District of Columbia had strong gun laws that made it difficult for criminals to get guns at gun stores, the street value of Virginia guns in those areas greatly exceeded their legal retail price. As one ATF agent observed, "On the streets of New York, an illegal handgun often can be sold for more than $1,000 in cash or drugs—a markup of five times or more over the price in Virginia."[31] The trafficker could maximize profits and keep costs down by buying large numbers of guns from Virginia dealers during each gun store visit.

In fact, law enforcement authorities have long regarded the purchase of multiple handguns by a single buyer as an indicator that the buyer intends to traffic the guns to the illegal market. If someone buys two or more handguns in a five-day period, the purchases are regarded as so suspicious that the seller is required by federal law to file a special "multiple sale" report with ATF.[32] Federal law does not, however, prohibit multiple sales. By restricting handgun purchases to one per month, Virginia sought to disrupt these trafficking operations by undermining their profitability.

A landmark study by my colleagues Douglas Weil and Rebecca Knox in the *Journal of the American Medical Association* showed a dramatic decline in Virginia's relative contribution to the Northeast crime gun problem following the statute's enactment. Prior to the law, 35 percent of all guns originating in the Southeast and traced in the Northeast came from Virginia gun shops. Shortly after the law took effect, Virginia accounted for only 16 percent of the southeastern guns traced to crime in the Northeast.[33] For southeastern-sold guns traced in New York State alone, Virginia's share dropped from 38 to 15 percent.[34] The law's statistical impact was confirmed by the experience of federal law enforcers. An ATF spokesperson told the *Washington Post,* "We do not see the trafficking the way we used to."[35]

The success of Virginia's law is best illustrated by a trafficking operation that began after the law took effect. Since the new statute prevented one straw buyer from purchasing a large number of guns at one time, trafficking revenue could be maintained only by recruiting many Virginia straw buyers to buy one gun every month. In 1995 federal authorities busted a trafficking ring that had recruited fifteen members of a college marching band in the Norfolk area to act as straw buyers for guns that were sold on the streets of Washington, D.C.[36] The ring made their gun purchases between June 1995 and October 1995. By the fall of 1996, twenty-five of the guns already had been recovered from criminals, many in the hands of drug dealers. Some of the guns already had victims—a wounded police officer, a young man whose spine was severed by a bullet, another murdered on the street, and the owner of a vending machine company, shot in the face during a robbery at his office.[37]

As musically talented as its members were, this was a marching band destined to entertain only their fellow prison inmates. There were just too many people who could implicate too many other people. "The larger the animal, the easier it is to catch," said Mike Brooks, the ATF agent who cracked the case.[38] Virginia's law was making gunrunning too complicated, too costly, and too risky.

Of course, gun traffickers can simply avoid Virginia and use gun shops in other states. This may well be happening. In one particularly high-profile case, in July 2000 a West Virginia pawnshop, Will Jewelry and Loan, sold twelve handguns in a single all-cash transaction to a New Jersey cocaine dealer named James Gray and his recently recruited West Virginia straw buyer and drug user, Tammi Lea Songer. Despite her history with drugs, Songer had a clean record. She would buy Gray his guns. She would receive drugs and cash in return. Songer stood next to the cash register while Gray told the clerk which guns Songer would buy. Songer filled out the ATF purchase forms and paid the clerk thousands of dollars in cash. Gray carried the guns out of the store, destined for the streets of northern New Jersey. Songer said she "kind of" suspected she was getting involved in a criminal enterprise, but "I was so strung out I didn't care."[39]

On a frigid night six months later, one of those guns, a Ruger 9 mm semiautomatic, serial No. 313-07198, was in the hands of three-time felon Shuntez Everett as he approached a gas station in Orange, New Jersey, that repeatedly had been victimized by armed robbers. Everett matched the description of someone who was suspected in several gas station robberies in the area. When approached by Detective David Lemongello, who was staking out the gas station, Everett drew the Ruger out of his pocket and started firing. Lemongello was hit in the chest, stomach, and left arm. Unable to return fire, he radioed for help. Officer Ken McGuire responded and chased Everett into the backyard of a nearby house. Everett again started firing, hitting McGuire in the stomach and leg. Knocked to the ground, McGuire returned fire and killed Everett at the scene. Both officers survived, but their police careers were over.[40] Incredibly, some months before the shooting, McGuire had taken from a suspect a handgun that was traced back to the same batch of twelve guns. What happened in that West Virginia pawnshop turned out to be a clear and present danger to a community, and two of its bravest police officers, several states and hundreds of miles away.

Virginia's experience with curbing multiple handgun sales supports two propositions. First, the Virginia law is working to curb trafficking from Virginia gun shops. Its effectiveness, moreover, does not depend on traffickers like James Gray obeying Virginia law. If the licensed gun dealers obey the law, the traffickers find it far more difficult to conduct their deadly business in Virginia. Second, if the Iron Pipeline is being detoured to West Virginia or other states, it means we should adopt a strong *federal* law to curb bulk handgun sales. To the extent that the weak laws of other states are undercutting the effectiveness of Virginia's law, the solution is a federal law that bans multiple sales in *all* states. Like the Virginia law, a federal statute would reduce gun trafficking because the new legal mandates would be directed at legal gun dealers as a means of reducing the supply of guns to the criminal element. The law's success would depend not on the willingness of criminals to obey the law, but on the willingness of gun dealers to adhere to new legal requirements that curb a primary avenue by which criminals get their guns.

Remember the gun lobby's assertion that the Brady Act was doomed to failure because criminals don't buy guns from gun stores but rather get them "on the street"? To support this argument, opponents of gun regulation often cited surveys of prison inmates about where they obtained their last handgun. The surveys showed that, prior to the Brady Act, somewhere between 16–27 percent of imprisoned felons had acquired their last handgun from a retail dealer.[41] The gun trafficking transaction that occurred in Will Jewelry and Loan shows why such figures drastically understate the connection between licensed gun dealers and criminal acquisition of guns. Take the New Jersey criminals who bought their guns from James Gray. If you asked them where they got their guns, they would not answer, "from a gun dealer." They would say they got them "on the street" or, if they knew Gray, they might say, "from a friend." Yet we know that the guns were available to them "on the street" or "from a friend" because it is possible, and highly profitable, for gun traffickers or their straw buyers to buy large numbers of guns from gun dealers.

Another indication that the illegal market is largely the result of guns trafficked from gun stores is how quickly the guns are traced to crime after they leave the store. According to ATF, experienced trafficking investigators have found that recovery of crime guns within three years of their last retail sale is a "significant indicator" that the gun was trafficked out of a gun shop.[42] This "time to crime" is merely a rough measure of how long it took a gun to move from retail shelf to the illegal market; of course, a gun could have been possessed by a criminal, or used in a crime, long before it was recovered and traced by police. In twenty-seven communities in which all guns recovered in crimes were traced, ATF found that between 32 and 49 percent of the guns recovered from persons aged eighteen to twenty-four had been sold by a retail dealer or pawnshop less than three years before. The range for adult purchasers was 27 to 40 percent.[43] This suggests a flood of guns moving quickly from retail gun outlets into the illegal market.

Opponents of gun regulation are anxious for the public to think about the black market in guns as mysterious in its origins and somehow self-generating. If the public believes that criminals buy their guns "on the street," without asking how those guns got to the street in the first place, it is more likely to support the NRA's idea that the only productive response to gun crime is to punish the criminal. If the black market is generated by the criminal element itself, with no relationship to the legal market, then it is easier to make gun control seem ultimately futile. The fast-flowing stream of guns from gun dealers to the illegal market tells a different story. So does the successful operation of the Brady Act and the Virginia one-gun-a-month law.

WAR BETWEEN THE STATES

Virginia's longtime position as the prime supplier of guns to crime markets in northeastern states is but one example of a broader pattern of the movement of guns across state lines. For many cities, crime guns are largely homegrown, that is, they originate with gun dealers in their home states. For example, over 80 percent of the crime guns in Houston, Atlanta, and New Orleans originate from gun dealers in Texas, Georgia, and Louisiana, respectively.[44] For other cities, the vast majority of crime guns originate in other states. For New York City and Newark, New Jersey, for instance, about 85 percent of the crime guns originate with gun shops outside New York State and New Jersey.[45] For Boston, about 60 percent originate outside Massachusetts. What explains the difference between these groups of cities? It is almost universally true that cities in states with relatively strong gun laws import their crime guns from other states. Cities in states with relatively weak gun laws get their crime guns right at home.

What does this pattern tell us? There obviously is no reason for a criminal in New Jersey to prefer out-of-state sources for his weaponry. If it were easy to buy guns from New Jersey gun dealers, he would do so. If the opponents of gun regulation were right that gun laws can have no effect on the arming of criminals, Newark's crime guns would come from New Jersey gun shops just as often as Houston crime guns come from Texas gun shops. The fact is that the strict gun laws in states like New Jersey, New York, and Massachusetts have the effect of forcing gun traffickers in those states to use sources in other states for their guns. Strict gun laws have a direct impact on the arming of criminals in those states, not because criminals obey gun laws in those states, but because it is more difficult for criminals to buy guns in the "strict law" states from sellers who do obey the gun laws. The well-established pattern of gun movement from weak gun law states to strong ones demonstrates that regulating the legal market in guns affects the illegal market.

Looking at it from another perspective, the pattern of interstate movement also shows that the weak laws of some states undercut the effectiveness of the strong laws of other states. Criminals in New Jersey, New York, and Massachusetts would have a tougher time getting guns if the supply of trafficked guns from other states were reduced. Because guns cross state lines so easily, ultimately a federal solution is required.

During the Democratic presidential primaries in 2003, Howard Dean, in trying to establish his bona fides as a candidate for people who "display confederate flags on their pickup trucks," explained that gun control was an issue better suited for resolution by the states, because although "states like California and New Jersey want more gun control . . . , it is unreasonable to apply laws that may be necessary in California to rural states like Montana or Vermont."[46] Dean failed to acknowledge the obvious problem that, because guns so easily cross state lines, the effectiveness of gun laws in states like California and New Jersey is consistently undercut by the flow of guns from the states that don't want strong laws. This, of course, is the reason gun control cannot be left solely to the states.[47] I wonder if Dean thinks pollution control should be left to the states as well?

A favorite argument of gun control opponents is that gun laws clearly don't work because places like Washington, D.C., and Chicago, with their strong laws, have much higher homicide rates than places like Georgia and Montana, with their weak laws. This comparison is silly on so many levels it is difficult to know where to begin in responding to it.

For one thing, it compares *cities* with *states*. Obviously, urban areas are plagued with particularly high concentrations of poverty, unemployment, family disintegration, poor housing, illegal drugs, substandard schools, and a myriad of other contributors to violent crime.[48] Indeed, no comparison of the effect of state gun laws could possibly be valid without controlling for the degree of urbanization in the states being studied.

If *city* homicide rates are compared, it is manifestly *not* true that cities in states with strong gun laws generally have higher homicide rates than cities in states with weak gun laws. In 2004, for example, the homicide rate in New Orleans (in a state with notoriously weak gun laws) was eight times the homicide rate in New York City (in a state with strong gun laws). The homicide rates in Atlanta and Dallas (in weak gun law states) were more than twice as high as in Boston (in a state with strong laws).

However, it is also true that Baltimore (in a strong gun law state) has a higher homicide rate than Las Vegas (in a weak gun law state). In any given year, the cities with the ten highest murder rates will include cities in states with both strong and weak gun laws. The point is that the strength of a jurisdiction's gun laws is only one of many factors bearing on its homicide rate, and snapshot comparisons of cities prove little. Comparisons between cities and states are even less helpful.

Apart from the obvious invalidity of comparing cities with states in this context, the comparison never considers the origins of the guns that are plaguing cities such as Washington, D.C. Licensed gun dealers within its borders originally sell only 3 percent of the guns used in crime in that city.[49] The high murder rate in the District is not evidence of the ineffectiveness of its gun laws; indeed, as discussed above, if D.C.'s gun laws had no effect on the criminal market, far more of its crime guns would be homegrown, not imported. D.C.'s high murder rate reflects a complex of socioeconomic and other factors, including the movement of guns across state lines ensuring that its crime will remain highly lethal.

FIGURE 2.2

TOP-TEN LARGE CITIES RANKED BY MURDER RATES: OFFENSES KNOWN TO THE POLICE PER 100,000 POPULATION

2004		2003		2002	
1. New Orleans	56.0	New Orleans	57.7	New Orleans	53.1
2. Baltimore	43.5	Washington, DC	44.0	Washington, DC	45.9
3. Detroit	42.1	Baltimore	41.9	Detroit	41.8
4. Washington, DC	35.8	Detroit	39.4	Baltimore	37.7
5. Atlanta	25.8	Atlanta	34.3	Atlanta	34.9
6. Philadelphia	22.2	Oakland	26.8	St. Louis	31.4
7. Dallas	20.2	Philadelphia	23.3	Oakland	26.1
8. Kansas City	19.9	Chicago	20.6	Newark	23.3
9. Miami	17.9	Miami	19.4	Memphis	22.5
10. Cleveland	17.1	Memphis	19.3	Chicago	22.1

Source: U.S. Census Bureau, Statistical Abstract of the United States, 2004–7.

THE "CRIMINALS WON'T REGISTER" ARGUMENT

What about gun laws that are directed at individual gun owners, not licensed dealers? Eleven states regulate transactions between individuals by requiring the buyer to present to the seller a license or permit to purchase issued by a government agency only after presentation of a valid identification and completion of a background check. In some of these states, the licensing system is supplemented by a requirement that the seller register the sale with the government. At first glance, these seem to be gun laws destined to fail because criminals would be the last people who would ever obtain licenses or register their guns. As longtime pro-gun activist Joseph Tartaro put it, "There is little, if any, evidence that such registries would accomplish much" because "most criminals acquire their arms outside the legal, federally regulated commerce in firearms."[50] The "registration record" of a gun would, at most, be a record of transactions between law-abiding citizens, at least those sufficiently law abiding that they bothered to register. Our drive-by shooter would not be among them.

This analysis, however, misses the point of licensing and registration laws. Like the Brady Act and state one-gun-a-month laws, laws requiring that gun owners be licensed and gun sales be registered do not depend for their success on compliance by criminals. Rather, they seek to reduce access to guns by criminals by regulating gun sales by lawful gun owners.

Let's assume that a licensed dealer initially sold the gun used by our drive-by shooter to a law-abiding homeowner. Call him Good Guy. He keeps the gun for two years, then sells it to another law-abiding citizen and license holder (Good Guy #2). Good Guy registers the sale, providing the government the name of Good Guy #2. So far, so good. Sometime thereafter, Good Guy #2 decides to sell the gun. He is contacted by a prospective buyer who appears to be a solid citizen but has no license to buy a gun. The buyer is in fact a convicted felon and a member of a violent gang. We'll call him Bad Guy. Good Guy #2 has two choices. He can obey the law and refuse the sale, in which case Bad Guy is denied the gun. Or he can sell the gun to Bad Guy, thinking no one will ever know. Let's assume he chooses to roll the dice and sells the gun to Bad Guy. Bad Guy uses the gun in a drive-by shooting and then sells the gun to Bad Guy #2, a black market sale that goes unregistered. In a drug raid, the police arrest Bad Guy #2 on illegal gun possession charges and confiscate the gun. Without registration, the police can trace the gun to Good Guy, the buyer from the retail dealer, but no further. With registration, the gun can be traced to Good Guy #2, who now can't account for what he did with the gun and is, therefore, exposed to criminal liability. He also is a potential source of valuable information about his buyer, our drive-by shooter, Bad Guy. Therefore, under a properly constructed licensing and registration system, either Bad Guy is denied his gun, or he is at far greater risk of apprehension for using it in the drive-by shooting.

Any pro-gun partisan worth his ammo will ask, Why wouldn't Good Guy #2 simply say the gun was lost or stolen? This loophole could be closed by adding to the licensing and registration system a further requirement that gun owners must report lost or stolen guns promptly to the authorities. Such a requirement exists for guns stolen from, or lost by, gun dealers.[51] Why shouldn't gun owners have the same obligation?

The point is that gun owners should be accountable for what happens to their guns. If they sell them, the sale must be to a properly licensed individual and must be reported to the government. If the guns are stolen or lost, that must be reported to the government as well. As former ATF Special Agent William Vizzard has observed, "Registration records would allow investigators to track every gun to its last legal owner. This alone would deter most gun owners from making an illegal transfer. Even persons who routinely violate other laws would have reason to avoid illegal gun transfers.

They do not welcome police attention and thus would have reason to avoid transferring guns registered to them."[52]

The objection that registration is doomed to fail because only law-abiding citizens will register presumes that people are easily and forever divided into the categories of "criminal" and "law-abiding" citizen. Real-world experience shows that sometimes people who are convicted of violating the law actually registered their guns *before* they were convicted. (The NRA has a difficult time accounting for this because its worldview assumes that every criminal has always been a criminal, whether they have been convicted yet or not, and criminals, by definition, don't obey the law and register their guns.) If gun sales have been registered, authorities can identify gun owners who became legally prohibited from owning guns after they registered.

In 2002 the California legislature enacted a statute directing state authorities to use the existing gun sale registration records to identify persons who own guns despite being prohibited by law from doing so. In the first three years the law was in effect, over four thousand firearms, including over a thousand assault weapons, were seized from felons and other prohibited persons.[53] Oddly enough, the NRA actually supported the legislation that allowed the registration system to be used in this way. As we will see in the next chapter, the NRA decries registration of guns because, by allowing the government to know who owns the guns, it makes confiscation of guns much easier. Nevertheless, it supported legislation in California that disarmed convicted felons and other high-risk persons, precisely because registration enabled the government to know that such people owned guns.

Licensing and registration systems also make it more difficult to use straw buyers without detection. Criminals who would fail a Brady background check frequently recruit people with clean records to serve as straw buyers. According to one Wisconsin gun dealer, straw buying sometimes happens "two, three times a day" at his store.[54] A straw buyer violates federal law because he must lie on the federal firearms transaction form when it asks whether he is, in fact, the actual buyer of the gun. However, it is difficult to prove the violation, unless the straw buyer and the prohibited real buyer made it obvious to the dealer that they were working as a team *and* the dealer is willing to testify against them. With licensing, registration, and theft reporting in force, a case can be made against the straw buyer simply because he no longer has the gun (having given it to the real buyer), yet has neither reported the sale of the gun nor its theft or loss. There is no need to prove that he was merely acting as the intermediary or agent for the real buyer. Of course, the straw buyer's obvious violation of his legal obligations under the licensing and registration laws also gives the authorities leverage to obtain information about the real buyer.

The efficacy of a properly constructed licensing and registration system does not, therefore, depend on compliance with the system by criminals. Rather, licensing and registration, by regulating the last *legal* sale of a gun, constructs barriers to the flow of guns from the legal into the illegal market. Whereas the Brady Act and state one-gun-a-month laws regulate the last legal sale of a gun by a lawful dealer, licensing and registration laws regulate the last legal sale by a lawful owner.

An important study by researchers at Johns Hopkins University supports the idea that strong licensing and registration systems make it more difficult for criminals to acquire guns.[55] Using the crime gun trace data from twenty-five of the cities that did comprehensive tracing through ATF, the study found that states with strong licensing and registration systems tend to import their crime guns from other states. The researchers divided the twenty-five cities into three groups: (1) those in states with gun licensing *and* registration, (2) those in states with *either* gun licensing *or* registration, and (3) those with *neither* gun licensing *nor* registration. In the five cities located in states with both licensing and registration, a mean of 33.7 percent of crime guns were first sold by in-state gun dealers, compared with 72.7 percent in cities that had either licensing or registration (seven cities) and 84.2 percent in cities without licensing or registration (thirteen cities). The cities with the lowest proportion of homegrown crime guns—Boston, Jersey City, and New York—were in the states with the toughest licensing and registration laws, requiring fingerprinting of purchase applicants and longer waiting periods, as well as giving police greater discretion to deny licenses to buy guns. According to the Johns Hopkins team, "Our findings suggest that comprehensive gun sales regulations that include permit-to-purchase licensing and registration can affect the availability of guns to criminals."[56]

The interstate movement of guns from weak gun law states to strong ones is replicated, to a great extent, by the international movement of guns. It is well established, for instance, that many of the guns used in crime in Mexico, with laws far more stringent than in the United States, originate in American gun shops. In November 2005, for instance, ATF arrested two Arizona men, Antonio Moran and Francisco Coronado, for purchasing at least eighty-four guns at Arizona gun shops, including AK-47 assault rifles, which then were smuggled into Mexico and sold for twice their retail value.[57] Obviously, if such guns were as readily available in Mexico, the smuggled guns would not command such a premium from Mexican buyers.

The Brownsville, Texas, *Herald* reported in August 2005 that "Federal gun seizures show that a majority of weapons used in violent crimes in Mexico were smuggled into the country from the United States or bought through other sources in a lucrative black market."[58] In a display of twisted logic, the *Herald,* citing unnamed U.S. law enforcement officials, blamed the Mexican illegal gun market on Mexico's strong gun laws. It explained that the use of American guns in Mexican crime means that "Mexico's strict gun control laws are contributing to an illegal gun market and easier access to weapons." Really? Doesn't it rather show the effectiveness of Mexico's gun laws? Mexico's laws, of course, cannot be expected to affect American guns. Their effectiveness must be judged by their effect on Mexican guns. If Mexico's laws had no effect on the availability of Mexican guns to Mexican criminals, then why would those criminals be dependent on American guns and willing to pay a premium for them? The blame for Mexico's gun violence should be placed on America's weak gun laws, not Mexico's strong ones.

GUN CONTROL CATCH-22

Some have commented that the reason it is difficult to show the positive impact of gun control laws is that they have never been tried. There is much truth in this. Our gun laws are a hodgepodge, full of unexplainable gaps and bizarre distinctions. As we have seen, other states' gun laws inherently undermine a state's gun control efforts. Occasionally Congress has been persuaded to pass national gun laws, but they invariably involve painful legislative compromises that result in gaping loopholes and irrational limitations. In this way, the gun lobby does its best to maneuver the country into a gun control catch-22. The NRA and its allies claim gun control laws don't work. When comprehensive controls are proposed, the NRA then works to ensure that they will be as weak as possible. Then the NRA argues, once again, that gun control laws don't work.

We have seen this pattern with the Brady Act. The NRA has enthusiastically embraced a study by Philip Cook of Duke University and Jens Ludwig, now of the University of Chicago, that found no evidence that the Brady Act has led to a reduction in homicide rates.[59] According to the authors, if Brady had a dampening effect on homicide, it would be seen most significantly in the states that did not have background check systems before Brady, as compared to the states that did. Yet the post-Brady homicide trends in the two groups of states were quite similar. The authors acknowledged, however, that their methodology would not account for any disruptive impact of the Brady Act on the trafficking of illegal firearms into the states that already had background check systems.

At least one other study found that Brady has, indeed, substantially affected interstate gun trafficking patterns.[60] Cook and Ludwig themselves reported, in a subsequent version of their study, that Brady had reduced interstate trafficking of guns from the Deep South into Chicago.[61] Not only does the NRA never mention this limitation of the Cook/Ludwig study; it also neglects to note that the two professors attributed the limitations on Brady's effectiveness largely to the fact that its background checks apply only to sales of guns by licensed dealers, not to sales between unlicensed people in the so-called secondary market. Because 40 percent of gun sales occur in the secondary market, exempt from Brady regulation, Cook and Ludwig refer to it as "an enormous loophole that limits the effectiveness of primary-market regulations" like the Brady Act.[62] Later the professors wrote, "Some may argue that the regulation of gun acquisitions is futile. A more likely explanation for why the Brady Act did not do more to reduce gun homicide is that the act exempts the 30%–40% of all gun sales each year that do not involve a licensed dealer."[63] Of course, the NRA does not advocate requiring background checks on all gun sales to close the loophole. It would prefer to use the limitations of the Brady Act to insist that gun control doesn't work.

THE MACHINE GUN STORY

One federal law, however, stands as a powerful counterpoint to the "when guns are outlawed" argument. In 1934 President Franklin D. Roosevelt signed into law the National Firearms Act (NFA), the first significant federal statute regulating guns. The Roosevelt administration pushed for the new law as a response to the rise in violent gangsterism in the Roaring Twenties and into the 1930s.[64] The NFA was passed as an amendment to the Internal Revenue Code and was designed primarily as a taxation statute. It imposes a tax on the manufacture and sale of machine guns and other gangster-type weapons and accessories, like sawed-off shotguns, short-barreled rifles, silencers, bombs, etc. Significantly, the statute also requires machine guns and other such weapons to be registered with ATF and requires buyers of the guns to be fingerprinted, submit to an extensive federal background check, and obtain the permission of their local police department.[65] The NFA, however, does not prohibit law-abiding citizens from owning machine guns. It is, in effect, a comprehensive registration, licensing, and taxation statute, but not a gun ban.

In 1986 Congress banned the future production of machine guns for sale to the civilian market, as a last-minute addition to the infamous Firearm

Owners' Protection Act, a Reagan administration–supported statute curbing the enforcement powers of the Bureau of Alcohol, Tobacco and Firearms.[66] The legislation, however, did allow machine guns already legally owned to be bought and sold subject to the existing NFA registration and taxation requirements. To this day, therefore, it is still possible to legally own a machine gun, if it is properly registered.

The NFA stands as a seventy-five-year-old experiment in comprehensive federal regulation of a specific kind of firearm. If the NRA is right about the futility of gun laws, the nation should continue to face a severe problem of machine gun crime, as it did in the days of Al Capone. After all, machine guns certainly can be valuable tools of the criminal trade. Machine guns, by definition, feature fully automatic fire, meaning that they fire continuously as long as the trigger is depressed until the ammunition magazine (which may contain scores of rounds) is exhausted. A machine gun can fire approximately thirty rounds in about two seconds,[67] an enormous advantage in a gunfight with police. Therefore, if it is true that the determination of criminals to be heavily armed will overcome any gun control laws, then machine gun–wielding criminals should be commonplace. Are they?

Plainly not, according to some of the strongest gun control critics. According to the National Center on Policy Analysis, a libertarian think tank sharply hostile to gun control, "even the illegal use of machine guns by drug dealers and other violent criminals is extremely rare."[68] Gary Kleck found that machine guns are far less of a threat to police officers than other firearms. Kleck found that of 713 police officers killed in the line of duty in the United States from 1983 to 1992, 651 were killed with guns, but only four with fully automatic weapons.[69]

ATF crime gun trace data confirms negligible use of machine guns in crime. Trace data from 1994 showed that machine guns accounted for less than 0.1 percent of all guns traced to crime in that year.[70] In 2000, of forty-six cities doing comprehensive tracing of all their crime guns, in only twelve cities did machine guns account for as much as 0.1 percent of their crime gun traces. Las Vegas was the only city where machine guns accounted for more than 0.1 percent; its count was 0.5 percent.[71] Of course, the evidence would be stronger if we had comparable data on the use of machine guns in crime for the pre-NFA period, but such data does not exist. Nevertheless, all sides in the gun control debate seem to agree that machine gun crime is not a serious problem after decades of tight controls, even though the value of these guns to criminals is obvious.

The apparent success of the NFA suggests that the solution to weaknesses in our gun laws is stronger gun laws. The NFA does not suffer from the same limitations and loopholes that plague other gun control laws. Unlike the Brady Act, the NFA regulates every sale of the guns covered by its provisions, not simply sales by licensed dealers. Unlike the Brady Act, the background checks for NFA weapons have no time limit. In contrast, if a Brady background check is not completed within three working days, federal law allows the dealer to complete the sale anyway. These are known, in the background check business, as "default proceeds." It is not uncommon for the FBI to determine, after a default proceed has occurred, that the buyer is, in fact, a convicted felon or falls into another of the categories of prohibited buyers under federal law. Justice Department figures show that this happened approximately thirteen thousand times in the period 1998–2001.[72] How would you like to be the FBI or ATF agent assigned to retrieve a gun from a buyer who the law already has determined is too dangerous to be sold one?

The situation is exacerbated by the fact that information about the prohibited classes of gun buyers is insufficiently computerized and accessible to the FBI personnel doing the background check to enable an accurate check to be done within three working days. As of January 2006, roughly 25 percent of state felony conviction records were still not computerized and instantly accessible to the background check system.[73] Under the NFA, in contrast, because there are no time limits for the background checks, there is not the same imperative that the records be computer accessible. The absence of time constraints makes manual checks of records possible. In short, under the NFA, background checks take as long as necessary to do them right.

The NFA requirement that machine gun purchasers be fingerprinted also enhances the effectiveness of the background checks. Federal law regulating retail sales of conventional firearms requires that the buyer present only a picture ID such as a driver's license. For handgun sales, the ID must establish the buyer's residence in the state where the gun purchase is being made. The ease of obtaining fake driver's licenses has long plagued gun regulation. Indeed, in March 2001 the General Accounting Office issued a report on an undercover investigation it had conducted into how easy it is to evade background checks with bogus identification documents. In Virginia, West Virginia, Montana, New Mexico, and Arizona, special agents equipped with counterfeit driver's licenses were able to buy seven firearms, including a semiautomatic assault weapon.[74] In effect, the Brady background check is only as effective as the states' safeguards against fake driver's licenses. There is no such problem with fingerprint background checks to purchase machine guns under the NFA.

The NRA itself inadvertently demonstrated the effectiveness of comp-rehensive gun control in a legendary propaganda piece it circulated in the early 1990s. The document was an attack on my employer, the largest organization working for strong gun control laws, which was at the time named Handgun Control, Inc. (HCI), and is now named the Brady Camp-aign to Prevent Gun Violence. The document, titled "Don't Buy HCI Lies,"[75] addressed the machine gun issue. In arguing that Congress did not need to ban production of new machine guns in 1986, the NRA pointed out that machine gun regulation had long included "background checks, fingerprinting, registration, and a $200 transfer tax." It further asserted that "possession of fully automatic firearms [machine guns] has been lawful for more than 50 years and *has never been a crime problem* [emphasis added]." In other words, according to the NRA, the one category of guns that has been subjected to comprehensive regulation "has never been a crime problem."

Ironically, even the National Firearms Act was a victim of the NRA's catch-22. The bill originally proposed by the Roosevelt Justice Department included handguns among the weapons to be regulated. At the urging of the NRA and other gun groups, the bill was weakened in committee, and handguns were removed.[76] If, during the last seventy years, handguns had been subject to comprehensive NFA regulation, there is every reason to believe that countless lives would have been saved. Of course, there may be sound policy objections to imposing on handguns the same tight controls we impose on machine guns. But the "criminals will always get guns" argument is not one of them. Based on the machine gun regulatory experience, there should at least be a presumption that a strong, well-administered licensing and registration system can be as effective for other firearms as it has been for machine guns.

ARE "OUTLAWS" THE ONLY PROBLEM?

The argument that "when guns are outlawed, only outlaws will have guns" is based on two premises that are central to the argument against gun control laws. First, the world can be neatly divided into "outlaws," or criminals, on one hand, and "law-abiding people" on the other. Second, the gun violence problem is entirely one of criminals acquiring guns to undertake criminal activity. To this point in our discussion of the argument, these premises have gone unquestioned. We have taken for granted that the gun violence problem in America is largely a problem of intentional violence committed by people who are easily identifiable as criminals. Is this an accurate picture of gun violence? Or is the picture more complicated?

One obvious complication is that most fatal gun violence has nothing to do with criminals. Most gunshot deaths in America are inflicted with guns owned by, in the NRA's parlance, "law-abiding citizens." These are, by definition, the people most likely to obey the law.

For example, in every year since 1981, more Americans have died from gun suicides than from gun homicides.[77] In 2005, for instance, over seventeen thousand Americans took their lives with guns.[78] More people kill themselves with guns than by all other methods combined.[79]

Several years ago, I was debating an NRA official at the William & Mary Law School, and I cited the figure that over thirty thousand Americans lose their lives every year to "gun violence." During the Q&A session following the debate, one audience member took me to task because I did not disclose that most of those deaths were suicides. He thought it highly misleading that I would refer to gun suicides as "gun violence." In his view, the gun violence problem is strictly a problem of criminals using guns.

I suppose it is possible to simply define away a huge part of the problem by stipulating that gun violence means use of guns by criminals. Surely, however, this is a highly artificial approach. If the incidence of suicide can be reduced by public policies that limit access to guns by depressed teenagers or others at risk, then why shouldn't suicide be considered part of the gun violence problem? Obviously, the claimed determination of criminals to overcome any obstacle to gain access to guns is irrelevant to the suicide problem. We saw earlier that the use of guns in suicide attempts makes them far more likely to succeed than if other means are chosen. Can gun control laws make guns less accessible to the suicidal and, by doing so, save lives?

Before I starting working on the gun issue, I tended to think of suicide as strictly a mental health issue and to assume that it was preventable only by alleviating whatever mental illness was producing the urge to self-destruction. There is no question that some people are so determined to kill themselves that they are destined to succeed regardless of whether a gun is available. However, suicide often is an impulsive act, motivated more by a passing crisis than by severe mental illness. Dr. David Hemenway of the Harvard School of Public Health has summarized the striking evidence that suicide attempts do not often follow extensive deliberation and, if unsuccessful, may never be repeated. He writes,

> Many suicides appear to be impulsive acts. Individuals who take their own lives often do so when confronting a severe but temporary crisis. In one small study of men who survived self-inflicted intentional gunshot

wounds to the face, few attempted suicide again. In another study of nearly lethal suicide attempts, 24 percent of attempters reported spending less than five minutes between the decision to attempt suicide and the actual attempt. In yet another study of self-inflicted gunshot wounds that would have been fatal without emergency treatment, none of the thirty attempters had written a suicide note, and more than half reported having suicidal thoughts for less than twenty-four hours. In two years of follow-up, none of the thirty attempted suicide again. As the lead researcher put it, "Many patients in our sample admitted that while they had originally expected to die, they were glad to be alive, and would not repeat the destructive behavior, despite the continued presence of significant medical, psychological and social problems." [citations omitted][80]

Given that suicide attempts with guns are far more likely to be completed than with other means and that the suicidal impulse is often temporary, it stands to reason that access to guns will increase the risk of suicide. With guns around, there is likely to be no second chance.

Sure enough, Hemenway reports that ten studies in the previous twenty years have examined the relationship between gun ownership and suicide in the United States, "and all find that firearms in the home are associated with substantially and significantly higher rates of suicide."[81] In the last chapter we noted one of these studies, by Dr. Arthur Kellermann and his colleagues. Kellermann looked at over eight hundred suicides that occurred during a thirty-two month period in two urban areas: Shelby County, Tennessee, a predominately poor black community, and King County, Washington, a predominately upper-middle-class white community. After controlling for several variables bearing on suicide risk, including alcohol consumption and use of medication for mental illness, the study showed that the presence of a gun in the home was associated with an almost fivefold increase in the risk of suicide. Dr. Kellermann also found that this association was even greater for persons with no history of depression or mental illness.

Other studies have documented the tragic association between guns in the home and the risk of suicide by adolescents. The presence of guns is a particularly high suicide risk factor for adolescents with no apparent psychiatric disorder.[82] Is there much doubt that many lives, particularly young lives, have been lost to suicide because a gun was readily available to people who merely wanted to stop the intense, but temporary, pain of being spurned by a loved one, or losing a job, or failing in school, or some other passing trauma?

Of course, it is a separate question whether gun control laws can prevent suicide. The research is encouraging. One study found that after the District of Columbia enacted its handgun ban in 1976, there was an abrupt 23 percent decline in firearm suicide, with no increase in suicide by other means.[83] Even far less extreme controls may have a preventive effect. Several studies have found that strict state gun control laws, none of which were as restrictive as the D.C. handgun ban, are nevertheless significantly associated with lower levels of suicide.[84] Indeed, one study found that such modest handgun restrictions as waiting periods, reporting of handgun sales to the government, and permits to purchase handguns each were correlated with lower suicide rates.[85]

Particularly promising are laws designed to require gun owners to make their guns inaccessible to young people. Research shows that "safe storage practices"—storing household guns locked, unloaded, and separate from the ammunition—reduce the risk of suicide among adolescents and children.[86] This suggests that laws requiring gun owners to safely store their guns may prevent adolescent suicides. As of 2001 eighteen states had enacted such child access prevention (CAP) laws to impose criminal penalties on gun owners who are negligent in their storage of guns. A study published in the *Journal of the American Medical Association* showed that CAP laws were associated with an 8 percent reduction in suicide rates for youth aged fourteen to seventeen, which translates into 333 suicides prevented in that age group since Florida enacted the first CAP law in 1989.[87] Those who may minimize the significance of this result should ask themselves if they would feel differently if they knew their child was among the 333 suicides that did not happen. This life-saving success, of course, did not depend on criminals obeying gun laws, but on compliance by presumably law-abiding gun owners.

Perhaps the most striking study of suicide and guns was done by Dr. Garen Wintemute of the University of California–Davis and his colleagues and published in the *New England Journal of Medicine*.[88] Wintemute looked at death rates among the 238,292 persons who purchased a handgun in California in 1991, compared to death rates in the general population. He found that in the first year after the purchase of a handgun, handgun purchasers were over four times more likely to commit suicide than persons in the general population and that this increased risk was entirely attributable to an increased risk of suicide with a firearm. This increased risk of suicide for handgun buyers persisted for at least six years. He also found that in the first week after the purchase of a handgun, the rate of suicide by firearm was fifty-seven times as high as the suicide rate in the general population. This is the best evidence yet developed to indicate that some people buy handguns with the intention of killing themselves.

In 1991 California had a fifteen-day waiting period for handgun purchases (it has since been shortened to ten days, applicable to all gun purchases). Given the temporary nature of suicidal impulses in many individuals, Wintemute's findings suggest that the waiting period alone likely saves lives. A cooling-off period to prevent suicides and impulsive homicides was part of the original justification for proposals for a federal mandatory waiting period. However, as finally passed into law, the Brady Act included no such waiting period. For the first five years after enactment (1993–1998), law enforcement authorities had five business days to conduct a background check on handgun buyers. This, however, was not a true waiting period because the purchase could be completed if the check took less than five business days to complete. In 1998 the "permanent provisions" of the Brady Act kicked in, and the National Instant Criminal Background Check System (NICS) became applicable, not just to handguns but to all firearms. Under NICS, the FBI has three business days to complete the background check, but 95 percent of the checks are completed within two hours.[89] Obviously, there is no cooling-off period under federal law; indeed, a major rationale for NICS is to ensure that the background checks are done, as the name makes clear, "instantly." The suicide evidence suggests that there is life-saving value in a waiting period, not simply to ensure a high-quality background check, but also to make it more difficult for someone with passing suicidal thoughts to gain access to the most lethal means of converting those thoughts into action.

Apart from suicides, unintentional shootings are another category of gun violence that appears to have little to do with criminals (although, I suppose, it is possible for criminals, as well as law-abiding citizens, to make mistakes with guns). We have already seen that accidents with guns are far more likely to be fatal than accidents involving other dangerous products; this is particularly true if gun accidents are compared with accidents involving other products purchased as weapons. However, gun accidents would appear inherently more preventable than gun suicides or homicides, even though, of course, gun suicides and homicides often can be prevented. Unintentional shootings are, by definition, not subject to any substitution effect; that is, unlike suicides and homicides, there is no basis for saying that if the perpetrator of an unintentional shooting had been denied access to a gun, he would have unintentionally hurt himself or someone else by some other means. The causal connection between the gun and the infliction of injury is, therefore, far more direct in unintentional shootings, there being no doubt that the injury would not have been inflicted if the shooter did not have access to a gun.

Although unintentional shootings represent a far smaller percentage of gun deaths than homicides or suicides, they nonetheless account for a significant loss of life. Between 1965 and 1998, over sixty thousand Americans died from accidental shootings, more Americans than were killed in the Vietnam War.[90] While the rate of accidental shootings has declined in recent decades, an average of twelve hundred Americans still died each year from gun accidents in the 1990s, or over three people a day.[91] For every person who dies in a gun accident, about thirteen are injured seriously enough to be treated in hospital emergency rooms.[92] These figures likely understate the number of deaths and injuries from unintentional shootings. As experts have pointed out, medical examiners in some states typically classify as homicides or suicides all shootings where the shooter intentionally pulls the trigger, regardless of whether the shooter intended to harm the victim.[93] Where the shooter inflicts injury because he does not know his gun was loaded, the incident is nevertheless not classified as "unintentional" or "accidental."

Gun accidents often victimize the young. Between 1991 and 2000, an average of 159 American children younger than fifteen died each year from unintentional shootings,[94] and over two thousand were injured. In other industrialized countries, these tragedies are virtually nonexistent. The unintentional gun-related death rate for children under age fifteen in the United States is nine times greater than the combined rates for twenty-five other industrialized countries.[95]

In arguing against gun control laws, the NRA and the gun industry often point out, quite correctly, that the accidental firearm death rate has been declining over time. The U.S. accidental death rate for firearms declined 44 percent between 1970 and 1994.[96] The NRA attributes the decline to its own "voluntary firearms safety training, not government intrusion,"[97] while offering no evidence that a higher percentage of gun owners receive such training now than in earlier periods or that the training is more effective now than before. David Hemenway cites other likely factors, including a rising American standard of living, improvements in emergency medicine, increasing suburbanization, and a sharp decline in the number of hunters, particularly young hunters who are at highest risk for accidental shootings.[98] The trend also is toward a lower percentage of households with guns: from approximately 48 percent in 1973 to 35 percent in 2001.[99] Whatever the reasons for the decline in accidental shootings, the trend is hardly a good reason to oppose policies that will accelerate the trend and save even more lives. Should the government not have required cars to have air bags because mandatory installation of seat belts had already reduced auto deaths?

If the NRA is right and "voluntary" safety training accounts for the decline in accidental gun fatalities, wouldn't even more accidents be prevented if the training were mandatory for every gun owner? If cars are sufficiently dangerous to require safety training in order to drive, then aren't guns sufficiently dangerous to require such training of prospective gun owners? Or is the NRA in favor of purely voluntary driver education for driver's license applicants? Mandatory training that included a safe storage component could be especially important in reducing the risk of gun accidents involving young people. Operator manuals provided by manufacturers with new guns typically advise gun owners to store their guns locked and unloaded, with the ammunition stored separate from the gun. Research shows that compliance with this advice substantially lowers the risk of unintentional shootings involving adolescents and children.[100] Why shouldn't safe storage be part of mandatory gun safety training?

Child access prevention laws, shown above to be an effective strategy against teen suicide, also are promising in their potential to prevent accidental shootings by children and teens. During the first eight years it was in effect, Florida's CAP law was associated with a 51 percent decline in the rate of unintentional firearms deaths to children under fifteen years old, which translates to fifty-two young lives saved.[101] Although this dramatic effect has not been observed in other CAP law states, this may be owing to Florida's stiffer penalties for violations (felony versus misdemeanor), its far higher rate of unintentional firearm deaths of children before the law was passed, and the unique publicity given the law because it was the first of its kind in the nation.[102] The Florida experience suggests that CAP laws can save lives by communicating a serious message, backed by serious penalties, that storing a gun accessible to a child is very dangerous behavior. Again, the success of these laws requires compliance by law-abiding gun owners, not criminals.

Required safety training and CAP laws seek to prevent unintentional shootings by altering the behavior of gun owners. Injury prevention specialists teach us, however, that more deaths and injuries from a dangerous product can be prevented by changing the product itself, rather than focusing exclusively on changing the behavior of the user. In this regard, the most illustrative success story has been the automobile.

Until the 1950s, federal policy toward auto accidents consisted of trying to instill good driving habits in the general population and punishing bad drivers. The focus was entirely on the driver, not the car. This orientation reflected the influence of the auto industry, which sought to deflect attention from its own lack of interest in making its cars safer by promoting the idea that injuries from auto accidents were entirely the fault of bad drivers. Research into auto design by engineers and physicians began to change that perspective. This led to a series of design innovations, including padded dashboards, shatterproof windshields, collapsible steering columns, additional brake lights, seat belts, and air bags. In the second half of the twentieth century, the number of motor vehicle fatalities per mile driven dropped more than 80 percent. There appears to be little evidence that drivers became significantly more careful. Rather, the dramatic drop in auto deaths appears largely related to safety improvements in cars.[103]

Similarly, safer guns likely would save more lives and prevent more injuries than an exclusive focus on the behavior of the gun user. If guns truly were regulated as consumer products, and safety features were made mandatory, many unintentional shootings could be prevented. One study sought to assess the percentage of unintentional shooting deaths (and shooting deaths where the intent was undetermined) that would be preventable if certain safety devices were placed on guns.[104] The researchers studied three possible safety improvements: loaded chamber indicators, magazine safeties, and "personalization" technology.

A loaded chamber indicator alerts the user of a pistol that the gun is loaded, but it is included in only about 10–20 percent of new pistol models. A magazine safety prevents a pistol from being fired when its ammunition magazine is removed, but many pistols do not have this feature. This device is designed to prevent unintentional shootings that occur when a user thinks he has unloaded the gun by removing the magazine, forgetting that there may be a round left in the gun's firing chamber. A personalized gun can be fired only by an authorized user, thus preventing use by children, teenagers, and others.

The study found that of the shooting deaths examined, 20 percent were preventable by a loaded chamber indicator, 4 percent by a magazine safety, and 37 percent by personalization.[105] The authors emphasized that the deaths would not *necessarily* have been prevented, but they *could* have been prevented by these design changes. Again, if the law required these devices, their risk-reducing benefits would depend on compliance not by criminals, but by gun manufacturers, whom the gun industry constantly assures the public are absolutely law abiding.

REFRAMING THE GUN VIOLENCE ISSUE

We have seen that expanding the concept of gun violence beyond the use of guns by "outlaws" both changes the debate and the range of policy options for preventing gun deaths and injuries. If the objective is reducing the number of gun suicides and accidents, the debate over whether gun laws can prevent access to guns by hardened criminals is transparently irrelevant. Moreover, if the gun violence problem were defined as a problem of "gun death and injury," as opposed to a problem of "gun crime," it would dramatically alter our beliefs about who is at the greatest risk of gun violence and where they live. Most Americans assume that gun violence in America is a problem largely of California and the urbanized states of the East and Midwest, with rural states in the West and South largely exempt.

Which state has the higher rate of guns deaths (that is, deaths per 100,000 residents, not simply total deaths)? New Jersey or Montana? New York or Mississippi? Massachusetts or Alaska? Montana's gun death rate is over three times higher than New Jersey's. Mississippi's is over three times higher than New York's. Alaska's is six times higher than Massachusetts's.[106] How can this be true? Because there is a largely ignored gun suicide epidemic in rural America. Indeed, in many rural counties, the incidence of suicide with guns is greater than the incidence of murder by guns in major cities.[107] "Americans in small towns and rural areas are just as likely to die from gunfire as Americans in major cities," says Charles Branas of the University of Pennsylvania School of Medicine. "The difference is in who does the shooting."[108]

It will also come as a shock to gun control opponents that the ten states with the highest gun death rates in the nation are rural states with among the weakest gun control laws, whereas the six states with the lowest gun death rates are urban states with among the strongest gun control laws. This is not to say that weak gun laws necessarily mean higher gun death rates or that strong laws necessarily mean lower death rates. As with city-by-city comparisons, state-by-state comparisons reflect many factors other than gun laws. But state comparisons do illustrate that framing the gun violence issue as purely one of criminal conduct with guns has a profoundly distorting impact on the debate. The NRA benefits greatly from the widespread assumption that communities with the worst gun violence problems also have the strongest gun control laws. That assumption is destroyed as soon as "gun violence" is redefined to include all gun deaths and injuries, not just those inflicted by criminals. As we have seen, there is substantial reason to believe that background checks, waiting periods, CAP laws, mandatory safety training, and consumer protection regulations can reduce gun violence as so defined.

Alas, however, our elected officials are a long way from viewing the gun violence problem as anything but a gun crime problem. In the fall of 2004, new legislation was passed by Congress to prevent youth suicide, now taking about four thousand young lives every year. Named for Garrett Lee Smith, the twenty-one-year-old son of Senator Gordon Smith (R-Oregon) who killed himself in his college dorm room, the new law expands counseling services and other efforts to identify kids at risk for suicide. As Dorothy Samuels of the *New York Times* lamented, however, nothing in the legislation addressed the need to protect suicidal young people from access to guns. "Fear of the gun lobby is such," she wrote, "the subject never came up."[109] Although political cowardice was no doubt an important factor, I suspect that even those in Congress willing to stand up to the NRA would have regarded a debate over guns to be out of place when the subject is teen suicide. Even when policymakers summon the courage to discuss gun violence, the equation of gun violence with gun crime continues to frame the issue.

FIGURE 2.3

STATE FIREARM DEATHS AND DEATH RATES PER 100,000 (2005)

State	Deaths	Age-Adjusted Rate	State	Deaths	Age-Adjusted Rate
Hawaii	28	2.18	Pennsylvania	1352	10.77
Massachusetts	224	3.41	Texas	2490	11.02
Rhode Island	39	3.57	Indiana	705	11.09
New Jersey	434	5.10	Colorado	535	11.44
New York	1019	5.18	Virginia	888	11.49
Connecticut	187	5.31	Georgia	1064	11.76
New Hampshire	88	6.50	Maryland	657	11.82
Iowa	201	6.67	North Carolina	1119	12.78
Vermont	44	6.69	Missouri	752	12.86
Minnesota	361	6.91	Kentucky	548	12.94
Maine	109	7.63	Oklahoma	468	13.18
Nebraska	135	7.68	Wyoming	71	13.44
Illinois	1019	7.90	West Virginia	261	13.72
Wisconsin	474	8.45	Idaho	195	13.81
Washington	567	8.73	South Carolina	589	13.82
Delaware	75	8.85	New Mexico	267	13.91
North Dakota	61	9.01	Arkansas	439	15.59
Kansas	257	9.19	Arizona	934	15.67
California	3453	9.46	Mississippi	455	15.97
Ohio	1116	9.59	Alabama	736	16.02
Utah	227	9.73	Tennessee	976	16.09
Florida	1838	9.98	Nevada	390	16.22
South Dakota	82	10.19	Montana	161	16.96
Oregon	402	10.61	Alaska	116	17.38
Michigan	1074	10.63	Louisiana	858	18.63

Source: Office of Statistics and Programming, National Center for Injury Prevention and Control, Centers for Disease Control.

ARE GUN CRIMINALS ALWAYS "OUTLAWS"?

We have seen that a fundamental premise of the argument that "When guns are outlawed, only outlaws will have guns" is that the gun violence problem is entirely one of criminals acquiring guns to undertake criminal activity. We also have seen that this premise works only by artificially excluding from the gun violence problem any mention of suicides and unintentional shootings. Even if we narrowly define the problem to be one of gun crime, however, the argument depends on a second, and equally artificial, premise: that the world can be neatly divided into "outlaws" on the one hand and "law-abiding people" on the other.

Of course, it is trivially true that anyone who commits a gun crime is an outlaw, in the sense that they, by definition, have defied the law. Gun control opponents seek to prove something more: that gun criminals are outlaws in the sense that they are so determined to be armed, so defiant of our criminal laws, and so easily able to dip into the vast pool of illegal guns, that gun control laws can have no effect on their behavior or their access to guns. Much energy, therefore, has been invested in trying to show that because violent gun criminals, particularly murderers, have long criminal records, they are fundamentally different than the rest of us and, essentially, incapable of being deterred by gun laws. Pro-gun lawyer and writer Don Kates, for example, has made a career of debunking what he calls "the myth that ordinary people murder."[110]

According to some studies, most homicide offenders have serious prior criminal records. One Justice Department study showed that 67 percent of homicide defendants in the largest urban counties have at least one felony arrest; 54 percent have at least one felony conviction.[111] A later study of Illinois arrest records for a ten-year period showed that although persons arrested for homicide were far more likely to have previous felony convictions than the general population, nevertheless only 42 percent of homicide arrestees had prior felony convictions in the previous ten years.[112]

Even if a majority of persons arrested for homicide had a previous serious criminal record, it is unclear how that fact would support a critique of gun control laws. Indeed, if it is true that murderers commit other crimes before they kill, this would support a policy of ensuring that every gun purchase, whether from a licensed dealer or a private citizen, be preceded by a criminal background check. As we have seen, there is strong evidence that such a policy of universal background checks, supplemented by required registration of gun transfers, would prevent substantial numbers of violent criminals from obtaining guns.

There is, of course, a flip side to the data showing that a majority, or near majority, of gun homicides are committed by offenders who already have a criminal record. It means that many gun homicides are committed by people who have *no* criminal record until they pull the trigger. These are not the hardened career criminals who are most likely to have multiple potential illegal sources to acquire guns. They are, nevertheless, dangerous individuals who were able to arm themselves by exploiting weaknesses in existing gun laws. Absent those weaknesses, they might have committed a violent act, but it would not have been with a weapon of the same lethality as a gun.

The school shootings that so horrified the nation were not committed by hardened criminals with ready access to a pool of illegal guns destined to be unaffected by strong gun laws. We have already seen that the Columbine killers armed themselves by exploiting the loophole allowing guns to be sold at gun shows with no questions asked. A year earlier, thirteen-year-old Mitchell Johnson and eleven-year-old Andrew Golden killed four girls and a teacher and wounded eleven others at their middle school in Jonesboro, Arkansas, with guns they had taken from Golden's grandfather, a wildlife conservation officer. They took rifles displayed in a gun rack hanging on the wall, pistols that were "hidden all over the house," according to the grandfather, and boxes of shells stacked on top of the kitchen refrigerator.[113] However, when they broke into Golden's father's house, they were unable to get the high-powered rifles locked in his safe and had to be satisfied with three guns that weren't locked up.[114] Is there a message here too obvious for even the NRA to miss? The guns that were secured were off limits. The guns that weren't secured ended up being murder weapons. Arkansas had no CAP law to require guns to be secured away from kids. There is no federal or state requirement that guns have internal locks or be otherwise personalized to bar use by juvenile thieves and other unauthorized users. Had such laws existed, Johnson and Golden might well have acted out their violent fantasies, but not in a way that inflicted mass carnage on their classmates. The guns they used were easy targets of opportunity. The opportunity was created by the too-casual storage of guns by a law-abiding father and grandfather and by the failure of gun manufacturers to make design changes to reduce the risk of misuse.

Consider also the 1997 shooting at the Empire State Building by a Palestinian English teacher who had a "restless aspiration" to murder a list of enemies he associated with Zionism.[115] Ali Hassan Abu Kamal arrived in New York on Christmas Eve in 1996. He then traveled to Melbourne, Florida, stayed there in a motel for two weeks, used the motel's address to obtain a photo identification card from the Florida Department of Highway Safety and Motor Vehicles and, that same day, used the ID to buy a Beretta pistol.[116] The next month Kamal opened fire on spectators on the 86th Floor Observation Deck, one of America's most-storied urban destinations. He killed one person and wounded six others before turning the gun on himself. (This shooting should be remembered the next time the NRA argues that terrorists use box cutters, not guns.)

Why would Kamal travel to Florida to buy his gun? Why not make the purchase in New York? Kamal obviously was deterred by New York's licensing system, which would have required him to be fingerprinted, undergo an extensive background check, and obtain a license from the police department. This was a textbook example of the weak gun laws of one state undercutting the strong gun laws of another state. New York Mayor Rudy Giuliani was furious: "He just shows up in Florida, gets a residence in a motel, walks in and walks out with a gun that could kill 14 people in three or four seconds. That's just absurd."[117] (During Giuliani's later presidential campaign, when he was in full "pander mode" toward the NRA, he somersaulted on the issue, arguing that gun control was better left to individual states.)[118]

Kamal had no practical access to New York City's underground market in guns. But he knew which state had weak gun laws. Kamal also was able to exploit Florida's weak laws because of an inexcusable loophole in federal law. The Gun Control Act requires that an alien must be in residence in one location for ninety consecutive days before legally buying a firearm. But the ATF, despite having broad authority to issue regulations to enforce the statute, had never imposed a requirement that an alien actually prove he had been resident in this country for ninety days. To its credit, the Clinton administration moved quickly after the Empire State Building shooting to close this loophole, requiring that aliens seeking to purchase guns present documents substantiating their ninety-day residency, such as utility bills or a lease agreement,[119] documents Kamal would have been unable to provide.[120]

Like the school shooters, Kamal was not an experienced criminal easily able to navigate the world of illegal guns. His access to guns could have been frustrated by sensible national gun regulation. The NRA's notion that anyone who commits a violent gun crime would necessarily have armed themselves despite strong gun laws is a gross oversimplification of who commits gun crimes and how they get their guns.

"When guns are outlawed, only outlaws will have guns" is, then, fallacious on several levels. Taken literally, it is simply irrelevant to a range of policy proposals that would regulate guns, but not outlaw them. To the extent that it expresses the view that gun laws cannot be effective because criminals will not obey them, it is fallacious because the success of gun laws in limiting access to guns by criminals does not depend on the willingness of criminals to obey them. Finally, the argument is based on two implied premises, both of which are untrue. The first premise—that gun violence is a problem only of criminals using guns in criminal activity—is contradicted by the evidence that most gun deaths involve shootings by law-abiding citizens in suicides and accidents. The second premise, that the world can be neatly divided into law-abiding citizens (who obey gun laws but are not the problem), and outlaws (whose access to guns is unaffected by gun laws), is both untrue and unpersuasive as an argument against gun control. It is untrue because some who use guns in violent acts are not outlaws until they pull the trigger and stronger gun laws would have likely blocked their access to guns. It is unpersuasive, because even if every gun crime *were* committed by a hardened criminal with a long rap sheet, this would argue *for*, not *against*, a system by which every gun transfer is subject to a criminal background check and registration of the transfer, a system that has been working since the Depression to limit criminal access to machine guns.

3.

"BUT WHAT YOU REALLY WANT . . ."

ALTHOUGH THIS ARGUMENT may never be bumper sticker ready, it is as ubiquitous as "Guns don't kill people . . . " and "When guns are outlawed . . . ." No gun control debate would be complete without the assertion, by opponents of gun laws, that to endorse whatever proposal is under discussion is to take the first step down a slippery slope toward more Draconian gun restrictions and, ultimately, toward confiscation of all guns.

There may be no other public policy issue where the slippery slope argument is as frequently used. Wayne LaPierre of the NRA invoked the argument as a key reason to oppose a waiting period for handgun purchases:

> This brings us back to the real intent behind waiting periods. Waiting periods are only a first step. Regardless of what they promise to do or not to do, they are nothing more than the first step toward more stringent "gun control" measures. Some people call it "the camel's nose under the tent," some call it "the slippery slope," some call it a "foot in the door," but regardless of what you call it, it's still the same— the first step.[1]

Six years after the passage of the Brady law (which, as we have seen, did not enact a waiting period), the NRA made it clear what was at the bottom of the slippery slope—the end of private ownership of firearms: "The plan is now obvious to all who would see: First Step, enact a nationwide firearms waiting period law. Second Step, when the waiting period doesn't reduce crime, and it won't, enact a nationwide registration law. Final Step, confiscate all the registered firearms."[2]

The NRA asserts that waiting periods are a bad idea for many reasons: for example, they may interfere with the legitimate exercise of self-defense, they don't curb gun violence, and so forth. In contrast to these arguments, the slippery slope argument asserts that a proposed policy change (e.g., waiting periods) should be resisted, not because the policy change is itself a bad idea, but rather because it will lead to the adoption of some other policy (e.g., confiscation of all guns) that *is* a bad idea.

WHY THE NRA NEEDS THE SLIPPERY SLOPE

Although slippery slope arguments are commonly used in other public policy debates, they are especially important to the gun lobby for several reasons.

First, because it is so obviously difficult for the pro-gun forces to persuasively argue that such reasonable and popular measures as waiting periods, background checks, licensing and safety training, registration of gun sales, curbs on large-volume gun sales, mandatory consumer safety standards, etc., are objectionable in their own right, it becomes essential to argue that they will ultimately lead to policies that have far less popular support and may be more difficult to justify. For example, given the reality that gun traffickers buy large numbers of guns from dealers and that few law-abiding gun owners really need to buy more than one handgun per month, the benefits of a national law restricting large-volume sales appear to substantially outweigh any inconvenience to ordinary gun owners. For this reason, the NRA's strategy is to suggest that the real problem with such laws is that they set a dangerous precedent that would lead to far greater restrictions in the future. Thus, the NRA argues that "one gun a month" could be changed to "one per year," "one per lifetime" or "none ever."[3] This is classic slippery slope argumentation. Since the NRA knows it is on weak ground if the issue is whether large-volume handgun purchases should be prohibited, it recasts the issue to be whether the government should have the power to ban all gun purchases.

Second, the NRA must sell the slippery slope argument to convince gun owners and sportsmen that they have an important stake in the gun control fight. As noted previously, polls consistently show that gun owners, and even those who identify themselves as members of the NRA, actually support gun control proposals, like registration, that are anathema to the gun lobby's leadership. This must be quite discomfiting to the NRA. If the NRA's core constituency does not view gun control as a threat to gun ownership, the foundation of the organization's political power will weaken. It is essential to the NRA's long-term viability that any gun control proposal be viewed by millions of Americans as an attack on a valued personal possession. Indeed, the NRA's strategy is to go even further—to portray even modest gun control as an attack on a way of life for which the gun is both an important tool and, more important, a powerful symbol.

As one NRA leader put it some years ago, "You would get a far better understanding if you approached us as if you were approaching one of the great religions of the world."[4] This is not a frivolous comparison. There is an unquestionably religious fervor about the beliefs of many pro-gun partisans. It is grounded in various articles of faith that form the catechism of the NRA: that law-abiding citizens are under constant risk from attack by predatory criminals, that the safety of every person and family depends on the ability of individuals to defend themselves with firearms, that the government cannot be trusted to provide security to individuals and families, that democratic institutions cannot be counted on to protect our liberties as Americans, that those institutions are at constant risk of subversion by tyrannical elements, and that tyranny is kept at bay only by the potential for insurrection by an armed populace intent on maintaining liberty. In the NRA's world, these are eternal truths. They are not themselves proper subjects for empirical testing or debate, but rather are a priori verities according to which the world is interpreted and understood.

To the true believers, the gun is an object of religious devotion. It is seen as the wellspring of individual liberty and the guarantor of a free society. The hallowed place of the gun is reflected in the holy text of the gun rights movement: the Second Amendment to the Constitution. According to the NRA, the Second Amendment is really the "First Freedom" because the gun is the ultimate means for a free people to secure and protect all other rights. Although the NRA's misuse of the constitutional text awaits a fuller treatment in a later chapter, suffice it to say that, for the faithful in the gun rights world, the amendment is biblical in its importance. Lest the reader think that the religion analogy is overdrawn, it is worth remembering that when the NRA was most in need of a revival—after the Oklahoma City bombing when its antigovernment virulence took on frightening implications—it chose as its leader Charlton Heston, an actor whose most famous role was Moses in *The Ten Commandments*! Heston himself spoke of the "sacred stuff" that "resides in that wooden stock and blued steel" of the rifle. "When ordinary hands can possess such an extraordinary instrument," he said, "that symbolizes the full measure of human dignity and liberty."[5]

Frequently gun control is referred to—alongside issues like abortion and gay rights—as a "cultural" issue. It is fashionable in some quarters to refer to the cluster of cultural issues as "God, guns, and gays." Describing it in such terms immediately elevates the stakes in the gun debate because it suggests that gun control proposals may be seen as attacks on a set of core beliefs that define many Americans, particularly Americans in rural areas for whom guns embody important values of self-reliance and personal liberty. For the gun lobby, it is strategically critical to raise the stakes in this way. If the gun debate is seen as addressing only the efficacy of specific, practical proposals to reduce death and injury, then the NRA is on shaky ground because even its own members do not have strong objections to many such proposals. However, if the gun debate is seen as fundamentally about larger issues involving the value systems of millions of gun-owning Americans, then the NRA is able to radicalize and mobilize those Americans who see their values as under attack. Gun control is then seen as an attack on gun-owning Americans and how they live their lives.

One of Charlton Heston's strengths when he was the NRA's president was his ability to frame the gun issue as part of a larger cultural struggle. In an angry, theatrical oration at Harvard Law School in 1999, he exclaimed, "As I have stood in the crosshairs of those who target Second Amendment freedoms, I've realized that firearms are not the only issue. No, it's much, much bigger than that." He went on to declare that "a cultural war is raging across our land."[6] The speech then turned into a rant against political correctness, the rights of transvestites, bilingual education, black separatism on college campuses, violent song lyrics, grade inflation, sexual harassment laws, and other grievances that made the "cultural struggle" worth fighting. The real audience for the speech was not Harvard Law students, but conservative gun owners everywhere. Heston's message was that the NRA cause was about defending the values of ordinary Americans against attack by Eastern elitists. He was showing them that he was willing to take their cultural war right to the heart of the enemy.

The NRA's congressional allies understand well the importance of making the gun issue about culture and values. In the summer of 2006 House Republicans unveiled their legislative priorities, calling them the "American Values Agenda." One of the bills would have made it more difficult for ATF to revoke the licenses of gun dealers who violate the law. How, it may be asked, is protecting lawless gun dealers an American value? I'm not sure how the House Republicans would respond, but it seems clear that they would go to great lengths to cast the debate as about gun ownership as a core American value, not about whether it makes sense to curb the power of ATF to crack down on lawbreaking dealers. The NRA issued a press release applauding the Republican leadership "for including Gun Ownership Rights in their 'American Values Agenda.'"[7]

For the gun lobby, then, the gun debate needs to be a debate about banning all guns. The slippery slope argument is the NRA's primary means of achieving this goal. As writer Osha Gray Davidson put it, "The religious fervor of many gunowners when it comes to firearms restrictions also has its roots in a less mystical and more pragmatic concern: the fear that all gun-control laws lead inexorably to the complete confiscation of all firearms."[8] We have already seen that one of the NRA's great successes has been to associate the words "gun control" in the public mind with the idea of banning gun possession. This is the power of the slippery slope argument.

Before dissecting the argument, an obvious question comes to mind. Given that the persuasive power of the slippery slope seems to spring from gun owners' fears of gun banning and confiscation, what is the impact of the Supreme Court's Second Amendment decision in *District of Columbia v. Heller*? If a ban on private ownership of guns is now unconstitutional, as determined in *Heller*, is there anything left of the slippery slope argument? As discussed later in this chapter, *Heller* may well have a profound effect on the argument over time, with far-reaching implications for the gun control debate going forward. To fully understand the potential impact of *Heller*, however, we must first analyze the gun lobby's use of the slippery slope argument, and its weaknesses, before *Heller*.

The slippery slope argument in the gun context actually takes several forms. First, the argument is made that because gun control proponents really want to eventually ban all guns, their proposals of more modest controls are really a sham. Second, it is claimed that, regardless of what gun control proponents actually want, the adoption of modest gun restrictions will lay the logical and historical groundwork for the eventual end of gun ownership in America.

WHAT DO GUN CONTROL ADVOCATES WANT AND WHY SHOULD IT MATTER?

Opponents of gun control spend an inordinate amount of time and energy in pursuit of the "smoking gun" evidence that advocates of gun restrictions really want to ban all guns, or at least all handguns. With respect to handguns, some gun control organizations are quite open about their goal of ending the sale of handguns to the civilian market entirely.[9]

For the gun control advocate seeking to overcome the slippery slope argument, these groups present a problem. They can be effectively cited as evidence that the ultimate goal of gun restrictions is to ban all guns. But the size and influence of these groups pales in comparison to the largest organization advocating stricter gun laws—the Brady Campaign to Prevent Gun Violence, formerly known as Handgun Control, Inc. (HCI), and, before that, as the National Council to Control Handguns. The Brady Campaign does not support banning all guns, or even all handguns, and says so publicly every time it is asked and often when it is not asked. I know because I have worked in the Brady organization for most of my professional career. Our position on gun banning was explained to me on my first day on the job, and it has remained the same ever since. Sarah Brady said it in her 2002 book, *A Good Fight*: "My stand is pretty simple. I believe that law-abiding citizens should be able to buy and keep firearms. And I believe there are sensible standards that we can and should insist upon when it comes to gun ownership."[10]

It is fair to say that the Brady Campaign's position that it does not support a handgun ban drives the NRA around the bend. Brady's position gives it far more credibility when it argues for reforms like waiting periods and background checks, allows it to find common ground with broader constituencies like the police, and generally has much to do with its dominance as an NRA opponent. Consequently, the NRA and other gun control opponents are positively obsessed with showing that the Brady organization is, to put it bluntly, lying. This has created a cottage industry of looking in every nook and cranny of published and unpublished material for any shred of evidence that gun banning is the Brady group's hidden agenda.

The most ambitious effort to expose the imagined hidden agenda of the Brady group was presented by Florida State University professor Gary Kleck in *Armed: New Perspectives on Gun Control*, a book he published with longtime pro-gun lawyer Don Kates. Kleck contributed a lengthy chapter entitled "Absolutist Politics in a Moderate Package: Prohibitionist Intentions of the Gun Control Movement." It is an odd subject for a criminologist at a major university to explore. The intentions of a particular gun control group have nothing to do with the use of guns in crime, the value of gun control laws, the net effect of guns on society, or any other criminological or public policy issue related to firearms. Rather, it is a natural subject for an advocate seeking to discredit his opponents.

In thirty-six pages of text, Kleck is able to cite only a single quotation— from *twenty-five years earlier*—of a Brady official stating that handguns should be banned. The quotation is from Pete Shields, who became chair of the National Council to Control Handguns in 1978. In a 1976 *New Yorker* interview Shields said, "Our ultimate goal—total control of handguns in the

United States—is going to take time. My estimate is from seven to ten years. The first problem is to slow down the increasing number of handguns being produced and sold in this country. The second problem is to get handguns registered. And the final problem is make the possession of *all* handguns and *all* ammunition—except for the military, policemen, licensed security guards, licensed sporting clubs, and licensed gun collectors—totally illegal."[11]

Well, there you have it. A description of how the slippery slope will work, from the very person who will apply the grease. And Pete Shields seems to confirm the NRA's worst fear about registration: that it will lead directly to a ban. As we will see, the word "registration" has been known to induce near-seizures in the true believers. For them, the idea of the government having a list of who owns guns is a nightmare scenario.

At most, Pete Shields's statement shows that he favored a handgun ban in 1976. As we will see below, Shields explained in his aptly titled 1981 book *Guns Don't Die—People Do*, that he changed his view shortly thereafter.

Pete's son, Nick, was fatally shot with a handgun at the age of twenty-three. He was the last victim of the notorious "Zebra" killers, who terrorized the Bay Area in California in the early 1970s. His son's death was the catalyst that caused Pete to give up his job as a DuPont Chemical executive and devote his life to preventing other innocent Americans from suffering similar tragedies. Shields attributed his early support for a handgun ban to the desire—common among those who lose loved ones to gun violence—for "a magic wand you can wave over the problem and make it disappear."[12] But the more he learned about the issue and the more he considered alternative solutions, he began to move away from the ban position, which he feared was "inflexible and unworkable."[13]

Kleck concedes that "HCI changed its policy of open advocacy of handgun prohibition" by 1978 and has not publicly advocated a handgun ban since that time.[14] By Kleck's account then, it was HCI's public position that handguns should be banned for only the first two years of the organization's forty-year history. According to Kleck, however, the organization really never changed its position at all. It just decided to keep its gun-banning agenda quiet. If Kleck is right, the Brady group has been awfully good at keeping secrets. It has kept its true program under wraps for four decades, with neither current nor former employees (which number in the hundreds) ever blowing the whistle.

Kleck's project, then, is to blow the cover off the Brady conspiracy. What evidence has his sleuthing uncovered of the Brady group's secret agenda to ban guns?

First, he cites the organization's open acknowledgment of an "incrementalist strategy," quoting Sarah Brady as predicting "that passage of the Brady Bill will soften up Congress for more. 'Once we get this,' she said, 'I think it will become easier and easier to get the laws we need passed.'" [15] Apparently, for Kleck, it is highly probative that the Brady organization has refused to take the position that the Brady Act is the only reform needed to prevent gun violence. Of course, given the scope and complexity of gun violence in America, such a position would be patently absurd. The Brady Act is a modest measure that closed a loophole in federal law that was allowing criminals to buy guns over the counter at licensed gun dealers. Arguing that additional reforms are needed to save more lives is hardly evidence of a secret intention to ban all guns. Would we have required the proponents of seat belts to refrain from advocating additional safety devices for cars (like air bags) lest they be forced to acknowledge their secret intention to ban all cars?

It also is worth noting that there has been nothing secretive about the Brady organization's support of measures beyond the Brady Act. Kleck asserts that "by 1994 . . . after the Brady Act was passed, HCI had expanded its goals to include registration." [16] Actually, the organization actively and openly supported registration long before the Brady Bill was passed. The Brady group has long had an extensive agenda of needed legislative reforms. Because it obviously is very difficult to achieve enactment of all the needed reforms in a single bill, the group has worked for more limited legislation that would achieve only a portion of the needed changes in the law. Thus, as Kleck says, the path to change has been "incrementalist, with each legislative victory leading to a push for further controls." Yes, it's true. When the Brady group has achieved needed reforms, it has not closed its doors and announced that it has accomplished everything necessary to prevent senseless gun violence. It has, in fact, rededicated itself to passing additional laws, and strengthening existing ones, to save even more lives. How is this evidence of a secret agenda to ban guns?

Whereas Kleck suggests that Brady's incrementalism is evidence of its secret desire to ban handguns, supporters of a handgun ban do *not* apparently believe that the way to accomplish a ban is through an incrementalist strategy. Indeed, they have been openly critical of the Brady group because they believe that its incrementalism frustrates progress toward a handgun ban. A year before the Brady Bill passed, Josh Sugarmann of the Violence Policy Center, a longtime supporter of banning handguns, criticized the effort in its behalf and expressed his fear that "the Brady bill had become equated with gun control itself": "The danger of this is that enactment of a national waiting period could result in Congress, the press and the public viewing the problem as solved, leaving the issue of gun control to founder for the near future—probably for years. And as firearms violence continues unchecked, the bill will then serve as just another NRA example of how 'gun control' doesn't work."[17]

We now know that Sugarmann was wrong in predicting that gun violence would continue "unchecked" after the enactment of the Brady Bill. Instead, the use of guns in violent crime has dropped dramatically, a trend that began in the first year Brady went into effect. We also know the gun control issue did not, as Sugarmann predicted, "founder for the near future" after the Brady Bill was passed; indeed, the federal assault weapon ban was passed in the very next year. This progress in Congress came to a halt with the elections of 1994 and the ascendancy of Republican majorities in the House and the Senate. The important point is that those who want to ban handguns obviously do not believe in a slippery slope from the Brady Bill to a handgun ban. Instead, they appear to believe that modest, incremental measures lead to absolutely nothing.

Second, Kleck notes that the Brady organization has not opposed specific gun bans that have been proposed or enacted. He cites the enactment of various local laws banning handgun possession, which the group did not oppose.[18] Nor has the Brady group called for repeal of handgun bans in cities like the District of Columbia. Does this mean that the group is lying when it says it does not support a handgun ban? Does the group's refusal to support handgun bans logically require it to oppose them or to call for their repeal?

The question must be considered in light of the purpose and mission of the Brady organization, which is to prevent gun deaths and injuries. If the Brady Campaign believed that local gun bans actually increase gun deaths and injuries, it would be odd for the group not to oppose them. Since no such evidence exists, no inconsistency is suggested by its failure to oppose them or to advocate their repeal.

Moreover, for the Brady Campaign to advocate the repeal of local gun bans, which typically have enormous popular support in the community, the group would have to question the judgment of local officials and voters about the gun policies they believe are necessary to address their particular needs and circumstances. If a city believes it needs to resort to a handgun ban to protect its citizens from violence, it may be simply an exercise in humility for gun control advocates to refrain from second-guessing that judgment. Again, assuming the absence of evidence that local handgun bans actually increase gun violence, it seems entirely sensible for believers in moderate gun control measures to neither support local handgun bans nor oppose them. Conversely, the Brady group opposes some pro-gun local and state laws that it believes increase the risk of gun violence—such as laws mandating gun ownership or weakening restrictions on carrying concealed weapons. Its opposition to these local and state laws is entirely consistent with its neutrality on local gun bans because it believes the pro-gun laws increase gun violence, whereas the gun bans do not have that effect.

It is fair to say that the Brady organization's refusal to support a policy of banning future production of handguns is not based on evidence that a handgun ban would be ineffective in saving lives. It is founded, rather, on the organization's view of the appropriate limits on government power to deny citizens the choice to possess handguns—a product that many millions of Americans believe, rightly or wrongly, is critical to their personal security. A general ban on handguns necessarily involves government substituting its judgment for that of the individual on the question of personal handgun ownership. While the Brady group consistently has advised the public that bringing a gun into the home increases the risk of harm to gun owners and their families, it is an entirely different matter to cede that decision to the government. It is one thing to believe that an individual's choice to own a handgun may be dangerous and to attempt, through public education and persuasion, to influence him not to make that choice. It is quite another to advocate making that choice illegal, thus bringing to bear the coercive power of the criminal law. Instead, Brady has advocated legislation to "keep guns out of the wrong hands," an approach that has been roundly criticized by more radical gun control groups on the ground that much gun violence is perpetrated by people with no signs of having the "wrong hands." Though many obviously will disagree with Brady's philosophy, it is hardly evidence of a hidden agenda.

Indeed, the Brady approach bears useful similarities to the current national consensus on alcoholic beverage policy. There is little dispute about the cost to our nation—in lives and money—of widespread alcohol abuse. There is also little dispute that America's experience with Prohibition was disastrous. This is not because Prohibition was altogether ineffective from a public health standpoint; indeed there is evidence that it caused alcohol consumption and cirrhosis to decline substantially.[19] Rather, Prohibition was a failed experiment because it was such a radical extension of government power into the individual choices of Americans that it produced other unintended and destructive consequences, such as an explosion of black markets and organized, violent criminal activity. Indeed, Prohibition brings to mind Pete Shields's words about a general handgun ban—"inflexible and unworkable."

For decades now, the American policy approach to alcohol abuse has been not prohibitory, but educational and regulatory. Many millions of dollars in public and private money have been spent to discourage over-consumption, youth drinking, drunk driving, and other destructive behaviors. At the same time, the production, sale, and use of alcohol is regulated in various ways, including labeling requirements, dram shop laws, and drunk driving laws. But the nation has learned, through difficult experience, that there are limits to the power of government to deny individuals a product they value highly. When applied to alcohol, this is regarded as a perfectly defensible position and adherence to educational and regulatory strategies is seldom seen as evidence of a hidden agenda to return to Prohibition. It is an equally defensible position when applied to guns.

According to Kleck, since Brady and other gun control advocates believe that "guns cannot provide any significant benefit in the form of defensive use" and that "gun availability increases . . . harms" such as crime, suicide, and gun accidents, then "the logical implication is that we should limit gun availability as much as we can, and should pursue gun prohibition as soon as it is attainable."[20] Of course, no one argues that guns cannot be used successfully in self-defense. But the gun control community has pointed to research showing that a gun in the home is far more likely to kill or injure the homeowner, friends, and acquaintances than to be used in self-defense.[21] If we examine the self-defense benefits versus the risks of guns from a societal standpoint, a similar disproportionality emerges. According to the FBI, in 2007 there were 10,086 gun homicides in the United States, of which only 198 were justifiable homicides by private citizens (as opposed to police).[22] And, as we have seen, gun homicides are less than 50 percent of total gun deaths.

If gun control advocates are convinced by this research that guns kill far more people in homicides, suicides, and accidents than they save through successful self-defense uses, does this empirical conclusion logically commit them to the position that guns should be banned? Clearly not. It is entirely sensible to believe that the easy availability of guns has a net destructive impact on society without believing that the appropriate solution is for the government to deny individuals the choice to buy guns. Again, such a radical interference by government in the choice of individuals to own a product that they believe is essential for the defense of their homes and families is likely to have adverse, unintended consequences. It also may be possible to avoid those consequences while reducing misuse of guns through less radical legislative reforms, combined with public education to persuade, but not coerce, individuals to refrain from buying guns or to get guns out of their homes. Again, the analogy to other products is instructive. Even if it were true that an alcohol-free society would result in a net saving of lives and avoidance of suffering, this conclusion does not necessarily mean that Prohibition should be resurrected. Is there any doubt that a tobacco-free society would be a healthier society? Yet few seriously argue that the government should ban all tobacco products.

The gun lobby will protest that Brady and other advocates of moderate controls are being hypocritical because they do advocate bans of certain kinds of guns. For example, the Brady group has long sought federal bans on ownership and sale of "Saturday Night Specials"—the small, easily concealable, low-quality handguns that have always had a special appeal for young street criminals—and semiautomatic assault weapons, which are military-style guns designed for high-capacity firepower in combat situations. In 1994, with the support of the Clinton administration, a federal assault weapon ban was enacted into law, but with a ten-year "sunset" provision. The NRA, with a wink from President George W. Bush, who said he supported the ban but did nothing to cause the Republican-controlled Congress to renew it, was able to successfully frustrate efforts to extend the ban's life in 2004. Given the willingness of gun control advocates to substitute the government's judgment for that of the individual on the ownership of Saturday Night Specials and assault weapons, isn't it hypocritical for those same advocates to discover limits on government power when it comes to handguns?

The charge of hypocrisy and inconsistency misses the point. The argument made by gun control advocates for banning certain narrow classes of guns is that those guns are materially *different* from other guns—either in the degree of danger they pose when in the wrong hands or in their value in the right hands or both. For example, the case against civilian ownership of assault weapons is that they have a unique set of features designed to maximize the shooter's capacity to discharge large numbers of rounds without pausing to reload in a combat setting. Such features include large-capacity magazines containing scores of rounds, pistol grips on rifles and shotguns (enabling the shooter to stabilize the gun while "spray-firing" from the hip), and barrel shrouds (to protect the shooter's hand from a barrel made hot by rapid fire). While quite useful in military scenarios, or to criminals in firefights with the police, such features have little utility (and, indeed, pose special dangers) in legitimate sporting or self-defense situations.

The NRA, of course, vehemently disagrees that semiautomatic assault weapons are materially different from other guns (especially other semi-automatics). The point is that the advocates of a ban on assault weapons premise their argument on the claim of such a difference. Every national law enforcement organization supported a ban on such guns precisely because the police, based on their experience in the streets, believe assault weapons to be a far greater danger to the public, and to themselves, than conventional firearms. No major police organization favors a general ban on handguns. The effort to persuade state legislatures, and the U.S. Congress, to ban assault weapons has been effective only to the extent that legislators have been persuaded that there is a material difference between assault weapons and conventional firearms. Regardless of the merits of the dispute over the nature of assault weapons, it cannot be said that gun control advocates and police organizations are being hypocritical or inconsistent in arguing that the government should not permit people to have the choice to buy assault weapons, while not insisting that government power be employed to deny individuals the choice to buy other guns.

The evidence offered by Kleck of the Brady group's secret agenda to ban guns is thin indeed. There is, however, no doubt about the good professor's determination to say whatever is necessary to undermine the credibility of the Brady Campaign. He even makes reference to a document, circulated widely on the Internet over ten years ago (and, apparently, still available today), that appeared to be a confidential internal Handgun Control, Inc., memo "for use by Lobbyists or Senior Officers only" and "not for general circulation." The memo purported to set out a summary of the minutes of a December 17, 1993, meeting and described the group's "Five Year Plan," including an "eventual ban on handgun possession." It stated excitedly, "We think that within 5 years we can enact a total ban on possession at the federal level."

The document, of course, was a complete fabrication. It stated that the material in the document was sent to various individuals on the group's board of directors, including Pete Shields. Pete, however, had passed away some months before. After summarizing the document, Kleck comments that it was "almost certainly a hoax."[23] Could it be any more obvious that his real intention is to plant the idea that the document may actually have been real? Is Professor Kleck generally in the habit of referring to "almost certain" hoaxes in his writings? Kleck's reference to this hoax document shows the desperation of gun control opponents to show that the Brady group cannot be trusted when it says it does not favor a handgun ban.

The real question, though, is whether any of this should matter to the public policy debate. Even if an eventual handgun ban were what the Brady Campaign "really wants," would that be a good reason to oppose less radical gun control proposals like licensing gun owners and registering gun sales? Should large-volume gun sales to likely traffickers be permitted because Brady has a hidden agenda? Would it justify continuing to exempt guns from consumer safety regulation? If there is convincing evidence that such measures would save lives, would it be rational to oppose them simply because some of their advocates "really want" (or even openly want) to ban handguns? Shouldn't the slippery slope issue turn not on what gun control supporters "really want," but on whether support for these modest measures logically compels support for more radical measures like a handgun ban?

Don Kates, Gary Kleck's collaborator, draws upon the auto regulation analogy in this context: "Gun control advocates disingenuously ridicule gun owners for fighting regulation of guns similar to what they readily accept for cars. But drivers too would adamantly oppose controls if they were promoted by people who believed that automobiles are evil instruments no decent person would want to have and that anyone who does desire them must be warped sexually, intellectually, educationally, and ethically."[24]

Notice that Kates suggests that gun owners oppose gun regulation that is similar to auto regulation. This is factually incorrect. As we have seen, even NRA members actually support gun licensing and registration. Notice also his assertion that gun control supporters look down on gun owners as "warped sexually, intellectually, educationally, and ethically." This is an extreme example of the pro-gun strategy of portraying gun control as an attack on gun owners and the way they live. Indeed, a recurring theme of Kates's writings is the "gun owner as victim"—the notion that gun owners are a persecuted and despised minority.

Is it true, as Kates argues, that drivers would oppose the requirement that they be licensed and that their cars be registered simply because some advocates of licensing and registration saw cars as intrinsically evil and car owners as "warped"? Would drivers oppose federal safety standards for cars because some defenders of such standards were "car haters"? It seems doubtful. Apart from whether drivers *would* oppose regulation of cars because of the "car-hating" motives of some regulation proponents, the real question is *should* they oppose regulation on that ground? The answer must surely be "no." If regulation of autos and drivers would prevent accidents and save lives, and if regulation would not, in some sense, lead to banning cars, then drivers should support regulation even if some pro-regulation groups "really want" to ban cars. The same is true for guns and gun regulation.

If a slippery slope argument based on what gun control advocates "really want" is invalid, then what slippery slope arguments might be more valid?

WHEN IS A SLIPPERY SLOPE REALLY A FLIGHT OF STAIRS?

The metaphor of the slippery slope suggests that, once we are committed to supporting one, presumably desirable, policy (the top of the slope), we will inevitably end up supporting another, presumably objectionable, policy (the bottom of the slope). The most slippery of slopes would be those in which the endorsement of the desirable policy at the top leaves us with no rational basis to oppose the undesirable policy at the bottom. Once we step onto the slope, logic leads us inexorably to the bottom because all the possible brake points turn out to be completely arbitrary. This style of slippery slope argument typically raises the question, "Where do you draw the line?" as a way of suggesting that, once we are on the slope, any line drawing is arbitrary.

As I have noted, in the core slippery slope argument of the gun lobby, the bottom of the slope is a ban on gun ownership, or at least handgun ownership. It should be immediately clear that the alleged slippery slopes that lead to a broad gun ban are not "logical slippery slopes"; that is, it is not difficult to find logical distinctions between a gun ban and the policy being proposed. I earlier quoted the NRA as claiming a slippery slope from a national waiting period to registration of all guns to eventual confiscation of the registered guns. But it should be immediately obvious that there is a logical distinction between a waiting period and registration and between registration and confiscation. It is perfectly rational for a policymaker to endorse a waiting period and registration of gun sales because they will reduce gun deaths and injuries and yet oppose confiscation of guns as an extreme governmental intrusion on the individual choice of law-abiding citizens to own a product they obviously value. The path from a waiting period to gun confiscation seems more like a staircase than a slippery slope. Once we take the first step, we are not logically and inexorably committed to take any further steps. Rather, each step requires its own individual assessment of risks and benefits, and we are free to consider them before taking the next step to a new and different policy.

For some alleged slippery slopes, the apparent arbitrariness of possible lines drawn at various points on the slope incorrectly suggests that there is no rational distinction between the proposal at the top of the slope and the proposal at the bottom. This is the fallacy of the NRA's objection to one-gun-a-month laws. According to the NRA, once the government imposes a limit on handgun purchases of one per month, that limit could easily be "one per year" or "one per lifetime" or "none ever." It is true that the line between "one per month" and "one per forty-five days" seems arbitrary. The line between "one per forty-five days" and "one per sixty days" seems equally arbitrary. Does this mean that there is no rational basis to endorse "one per month" and oppose "one per sixty days," or for that matter, "one per year" or "one per lifetime"? Clearly not. The point of restrictions on large-volume sales is to disrupt gun trafficking while preserving the ability of legitimate buyers to purchase handguns. Whereas "one per month" interferes with legitimate gun purchases only to the extent necessary to achieve the antitrafficking objective, "one per sixty days" arguably imposes an additional burden on legitimate gun purchasers (although a small one) not necessary to diminish gun trafficking. Although reasonable people can disagree about where to draw the line, certainly a reasonable line can be drawn. It is fallacious to argue that because there is an element of arbitrariness between any two lines along the slope, no restrictions on large-volume sales should be imposed and gun trafficking should continue unabated.

It would be similarly fallacious to argue that no waiting periods should be imposed on handgun purchases to deter suicides and allow time for effective background checks because there is no rational distinction between a waiting period of five days versus six days, or six days versus seven days, etc. If the NRA's arguments were valid, our roads would be without speed limits, since a speed limit of fifty-five miles per hour could not be defended as materially different than one of fifty-six mph, and one of fifty-six mph is not materially different than one of fifty-seven mph. The arbitrariness of any particular speed limit does not render irrational the task of setting a speed limit and should not mean that we must tolerate the deaths and injuries that would result from the absence of any speed limit.[25]

This is not to deny that there are some very slippery slopes in the gun control debate. For example, it may be claimed that once we recognize the necessity of mandatory background checks on people buying guns from licensed gun dealers, then there is no rational basis for not extending those background checks to purchases of guns, through gun shows or classified ads, from unlicensed sellers. If the objective is to prevent the sale of guns to criminals, it should not matter whether the seller is a licensed dealer or an individual at a gun show claiming to be selling only his "personal collection."

Arguably the NRA itself stepped on the background check slippery slope in the early '90s when, as a ploy to slow the Brady Bill's gathering momentum in Congress, the organization endorsed the concept of a computerized "instant check," as an alternative to the Brady Bill's provision of five business days to conduct the background checks on gun dealer sales. Of course, at the time the NRA came up with this idea, a computerized instant check was no check at all because the records to be checked had not been computerized.[26] But once the NRA conceded the desirability of background checks at licensed dealers (thereby undercutting its claim that "criminals don't buy guns at gun stores"), it became more difficult for the gun lobby to argue against background checks for other sales. The NRA arguably stepped on the background check slippery slope when it first claimed to support laws barring sales of guns to convicted felons. If it makes sense to deter gun sales to felons by making these transactions a criminal offense, then would it not make even more sense to do criminal background checks to prevent the sales in the first place?

Strictly speaking, the background check slippery slope may not be a logical slippery slope because it may be possible to imagine a rational basis for supporting background checks at gun stores, but not at gun shows. As noted before, the NRA has tried to argue that gun show background checks would have an adverse effect on gun shows themselves. There is no question, however, that supporting background checks for dealer sales strongly undercuts the basis for opposing background checks for other sales. If this is not a logical slippery slope, it is pretty close to one.

Although the background check slope may be treacherous, it pretty clearly does not function in the way users of slippery slope arguments intend. It does not make us oppose the proposal at the top of the slope, whether that be banning gun sales to convicted felons or requiring background checks at licensed dealers. Why? Because the proposal at the bottom of the slope—background checks for all gun sales—does not seem undesirable at all, especially if you think banning gun sales to felons or requiring background checks at licensed dealers are good ideas.

Since the NRA needs the debate to be about banning guns, if the slippery slope argument does not lead to a broad ban on guns at the bottom of the slope, then the argument is not of much use to the gun lobby. There certainly is no logical slippery slope from background checks for all gun sales to a general gun ban. A universal background check system, if it functions properly, would block sales to high-risk individuals, while permitting sales to the NRA's "law-abiding citizens." The dilemma for the NRA is this: The logical slippery slopes in the gun debate don't lead to a gun ban. And the path from modest gun control measures to a gun ban is more akin to a staircase than a slippery slope.

FACTUAL SLIPPERY SLOPES

To this point in the discussion, we have considered only what I have called "logical slippery slopes"—that is, arguments that support of the proposal at the top of the slope logically compels support for the proposal at the bottom. There is, however, another category of slippery slope argument. In this second form of argument, the opponent of a proposal maintains that it should not be adopted because to do so would increase the likelihood that the next step would be taken, which would make a third step more likely, and so on. I call these "factual slippery slopes" because they amount to factual predictions about what proposals will be adopted. Here the "flight of stairs" metaphor seems more appropriate than the "slippery slope" because each proposal on the slope can be logically distinguished from the others and a rational basis can be given for refraining from taking the "next step." But, it is claimed, because each step increases the likelihood of the next step, ultimately leading to an undesirable last step, the first step should not be taken at all.

To gun control opponents, the most fearsome factual slippery slope usually involves government registration of guns as a key element. Recall that the NRA objected to a waiting period for handgun purchases because it would lead to registration that would, in turn, lead to confiscation of the registered guns. The idea here is that once the government has records of who owns what guns, confiscation of those guns from the registered owners will be made far easier. Pro-gun writers, anxious to dispel the notion that the "knock on the door" fears of gun advocates reflect only their own paranoia, have sought to carefully explain just how gun registration can lead to gun confiscation.[27]

Some general observations about factual slippery slope arguments counsel extreme caution before they are treated as good reasons to oppose moderate gun control measures because they may make it more likely that radical measures will be adopted in the future.

First, factual slippery slope arguments are inherently susceptible to the post hoc fallacy.[28] In offering examples of factual slippery slopes in action, it is not enough to be able to point to a succession of gradual reforms through time. The factual slippery slope is one in which each incremental reform has some causal connection to the incremental reform that followed it. Each reform must have an impact that increases the likelihood that the next reform will be undertaken, such as by removing a barrier to further reform. The causal connections between the incremental reforms are not established simply by evidence that one reform followed the other in time. Absent these causal connections, presumably the undesirable reform at the bottom of the slope would have occurred regardless of whether less radical reforms had been implemented or not.

For example, pro-gun writers frequently invoke the history of British gun laws as an example of how moderate gun laws can lead to an eventual handgun ban.[29] In 1997 Britain passed the Firearms Amendment Act banning the possession of all handguns of .22-caliber and above and those able to fire more than one shot at a time. The statute was enacted as a direct result of the massacre in the Scottish town of Dunblane a year and a half earlier, in which a gunman used handguns to kill sixteen schoolchildren and their teacher. Under the new law, handgun owners would receive compensation for the guns they turned in and face prosecution for the guns they kept.

It is true that this handgun ban was preceded by a licensing and registration system. However, the British licensing and registration system had been in place since 1920, *over seventy years before the handgun ban was enacted.* Although other gun laws were enacted in the interim, the only guns that were banned during that period were short-barreled shotguns and machine guns. These "gangster" weapons were banned in 1936, two years after America cracked down on these guns by passing the National Firearms Act (NFA). Would Great Britain have banned handguns in 1997 if the licensing and registration system had not been in place? Or would the Dunblane massacre have brought about the ban even if the prior gun laws had never been enacted? Given that Britain had licensing and registration for over seventy years before it banned handguns, it is highly speculative to argue that such a system eventually led to or caused the 1997 handgun ban. The fact that a handgun ban eventually followed licensing and registration in Britain does not itself demonstrate that such controls make gun banning more likely.

Even if a causal connection could be established in Britain, other examples could be cited in which licensing and registration have not led to a handgun ban or gun confiscation. The NRA cites New York City as another example of "registration leads to confiscation," but actually New York's gun laws prove the opposite. The city adopted a licensing and registration law governing rifles and shotguns in 1967, under Mayor John V. Lindsay.[30] Confiscation allegedly arrived in 1991, but even the NRA's own description of the 1991 law makes it clear that it only applied to "certain semiautomatic rifles and shotguns," that is, assault weapons.[31] The New York City assault weapons ban required registered assault weapon owners to surrender their assault weapons, render them inoperable, or move them out of the city. It would appear that the police were in pretty good position to enforce the ban against continued possession, given that the guns already were registered.

As explained earlier, however, legislation restricting assault weapons was passed only because its proponents were successful in arguing that assault weapons are fundamentally different than conventional firearms in terms of both their risks in the hands of criminals and their utility for lawful purposes. The question for the NRA is: If there is such a slippery slope from registration to confiscation, why hasn't New York City banned continued possession of *all* the rifles and shotguns that are registered, instead of just the small minority of them that qualify as assault weapons? (During the early 1990s ATF estimated that about 1 percent of the guns in circulation were assault weapons.) To the extent that the New York City experience teaches anything, it is that the registration of guns does *not* necessarily lead to their confiscation.

Many other examples can be offered of registration laws that have been on the books for decades, without prompting any move toward banning civilian gun possession or confiscating guns. The State of Pennsylvania, for example, has maintained records of handgun sales since 1931.[32] The Pennsylvania State Police currently maintains a database of persons who lawfully purchased handguns in Pennsylvania. Although in theory Pennsylvania's database would make it easier to confiscate guns should the state enact such radical legislation, nothing about Pennsylvania's registration of handgun sales has moved the state even close to doing so.

Other states with some form of registration include New Jersey, Massachusetts, Michigan, Missouri, Maryland, and California.[33] Not one of those states has banned, or tried to confiscate, all handguns or long guns. Despite the fact that the authorities in those states have a pretty good idea of who owns the guns, all have been able to resist the temptation to demand their surrender.

Conversely, examples can also be cited of gun bans that were enacted without being preceded by any registration system whatsoever. The federal assault weapon ban, in effect for ten years beginning in 1994, banned an estimated two hundred pistols, rifles, and shotguns. None of those guns were subject to a federal registration system at the time they were banned. Thus registration appears neither necessary nor sufficient to bring about an eventual gun ban.

The machine gun registration system created by the NFA raises particularly interesting slippery slope issues. Under the NFA, since 1934, the federal government has had a record of every owner of a legal machine gun. The NFA remained in undisturbed form until 1986, when Congress passed the NRA-supported Firearms Owners Protection Act, which severely weakened federal gun laws (more on that later) but featured one redeeming provision. Gun control forces in Congress were able to add an amendment, known as the "machine gun freeze." It banned future manufacture of fully automatic machine guns for the civilian market, as well as prohibiting transfer and possession of machine guns not already legally owned when the act went into effect.[34] Its effect was to freeze the number of machine guns in circulation, while continuing to subject the "grandfathered" machine guns to the licensing, registration, and taxation provisions of the NFA.

The NRA would no doubt argue that the NFA experience shows that a licensing and registration system can eventually lead to a gun ban. The unanswered question, though, is: Would machine guns have been banned if the licensing and registration system had never been enacted? As we have seen, all signs are that the NFA system was quite successful in curbing machine gun use in crime. Had it not been enacted, it is quite plausible to believe that machine gun crime would have been far greater in the years following the thirties, thus leading to public pressure for a complete ban. Absent the NFA, civilian possession of machine guns might have been banned decades earlier than 1986. Again, a factual slippery slope is not established simply by showing that licensing and registration were followed in time by a ban. In the machine gun case, licensing and registration may not have caused the eventual ban; they may have postponed it.

Notice what did *not* happen in 1986. Even though the NFA enabled the government to know the identity of every legal machine gun owner, Congress did not move to confiscate those registered weapons nor bar their continued possession in any way. Even today, over seventy years after the beginning of machine gun licensing and registration, the government has done nothing to confiscate registered machine guns. As long as you comply with the licensing, registration, and taxation provisions of the NFA, it is entirely legal to own, buy, and sell a machine gun made before May 19, 1986, when the machine gun freeze went into effect.

Pro-gun law professor Eugene Volokh has described some of the "mechanisms" by which gun registration laws may make gun bans more likely to be enacted.[35] In addition to making confiscation easier, Volokh suggests that registration may alter public attitudes about gun ownership, discourage gun ownership itself, and thus reduce the natural constituency to oppose confiscation, create political momentum for confiscation, and make confiscation seem less radical a step. Volokh's speculations are all quite plausible, but they are speculations nonetheless. It is just as plausible that registration will have none of these effects. Instead, gun registration, like auto registration, may simply be regarded by the public as an appropriate regulatory and law enforcement tool applied to a dangerous product, with no tendency to generate support for banning the product itself. Other than speculation of the Volokh variety, all we have to guide us is real-world experience. As we have seen, the U.S. experience has been that gun registration systems have *not* been precursors to gun bans or confiscation, both because registration has not led to gun bans and because gun bans have not been preceded by registration.

To borrow Professor Volokh's term, there are at least three "mechanisms" at work to make it unlikely that registration of guns would lead to confiscation in this country. First, to return to the staircase analogy, it is a big step from keeping government records of guns to preventing the general populace from owning them. As we have discussed, it is a big step logically and philosophically because gun bans and confiscation necessarily involve the government in making the final judgment about whether ordinary citizens can own guns. The public has understood this for decades, which accounts for its consistent opposition to a handgun ban at the same time it consistently supports registration, as well as many other gun restrictions. I doubt, for example, that over seventy years of state police gun record-keeping in Pennsylvania has made most Pennsylvanians feel that it would not be a big deal to take the next step of banning handguns in that state.

Second, as the NRA is fond of pointing out, we are a nation of gun owners. Although the percentage of gun-owning American households has declined gradually, it is still around 35 percent, with 22 percent of households having a handgun.[36] This is a huge constituency likely to strongly oppose broad gun bans.

The relatively high incidence of gun ownership also distinguishes the United States from nations like Great Britain. Oddly, this point is made by two authors—Joseph Olson and David Kopel—in the midst of arguing that the British experience shows the realistic danger of the slippery slope. They note that only about 4 percent of the British population owns guns, "a much smaller interest group" to resist a general gun ban than is present in the United States.[37] Even if the incidence of American gun ownership continues to decline—a life-saving sociological trend over the long run—it is likely to continue to be a substantial force impeding any serious move from gun control to a gun ban. Interestingly, although the gun-owning constituency stands as a formidable political barrier to a handgun ban, it is not a barrier to registration. Although only 34 percent of American gun owners favor legislation restricting handgun ownership to law enforcement, 61 percent favor mandatory registration of handguns.[38]

The most powerful mechanism working against the gun lobby's fear that registration would lead to confiscation is, well, the gun lobby itself. As one who has struggled for some time for even modest gun control reforms against the intransigent opposition of the NRA, I view the likelihood that pro-gun forces could eventually become so weak as to be overrun by a radical, gun-banning agenda as fanciful, to say the least. To return to the Keystone State, Pennsylvania has more NRA members than any other state. I doubt whether the ardor of the NRA partisans for their guns has been diminished one iota by the fact that they are registered with the state police. Professor Volokh and others can suggest as many sophisticated scenarios as the creative mind can devise, but as long as there is a committed minority of single-issue gun voters, there is little prospect that Pennsylvania, or any other state for that matter, will slip down the slope (or tumble down the stairs) to a general gun ban. To put it bluntly, it is absurd for any serious policymaker to oppose registration or other gun control proposals on the ground that they eventually will cause the end of private gun ownership in America. To the NRA's objection that registration will lead to confiscation, it is entirely rational to respond: No it won't *because you won't let it!*

Of course, I am not arguing here that the power of the NRA is a social good because it protects against the enactment of a gun ban. On the contrary, it should be plain by now that far too many innocent Americans have lost their lives as a direct result of the NRA's influence. But if the NRA's slippery slope argument turns on the likelihood that modest gun controls will make a gun ban more palatable to politicians, then it seems clear, though admittedly paradoxical, that the stronger the NRA's capacity to make the argument, the weaker the argument becomes.

The problem, of course, is that the NRA and the single-issue gun voters who are its base of support also exert enormous pressure on politicians to oppose even the most sensible reforms. That brings us to the most potent argument against the pro-gun slippery slope argument. We have seen that the factual slippery slope consists essentially of raw speculation that gun restrictions will lead to a gun ban, with little real-world evidence of such a causal effect. The gun lobby, however, uses that speculative fear to argue against gun control measures *that have benefits that are not speculative at all.*

If Congress had agreed with the NRA argument that the Brady Bill should be defeated because it was the first step toward a gun ban, since 1994, 1.5 million convicted felons and other illegal gun buyers would have been able to buy guns over the counter. For those who oppose a general gun ban, the real slippery slope question posed by the Brady Bill is: Was the risk that the Brady Bill may eventually lead to such a ban so concrete and severe that we should have been willing to tolerate the continued sale of guns to many thousands of criminals every year? In other words, allowing the slippery slope argument to dictate gun policy has a cost, and it likely is a cost in death and serious injury from gunfire.

There is, in fact, a close connection between the slippery slope argument and the argument that gun control is ineffective. It is fair to say that the persuasive power of the slippery slope argument to a policymaker will depend, in large part, on his or her beliefs about the effectiveness of licensing, registration, and other proposals in treating the gun violence problem. If he or she is convinced that licensing and registration will save countless lives, he or she is likely to respond to a slippery slope argument with a demand for much more than mere speculation that such life-saving measures will eventually lead to a gun ban.

Whatever form the slippery slope argument takes then, it turns out to be misguided as a reason to oppose gun restrictions that are easily justifiable in their own right. If the argument is based on what gun control advocates "really want," it is based on a false premise because the evidence is overwhelming that the nation's leading gun control advocacy group, the Brady Campaign, does not "really want" a broad gun ban. Moreover, even if the gun control community were united in supporting a broad gun ban, why would this fact alone justify opposition to far more modest measures that would save lives and prevent grievous injuries?

If the argument is, rather, that supporting limited gun control measures like licensing and registration will, by force of logic, dictate support for a far-reaching gun ban, then the argument falls of its own weight. There is an obvious logical distinction between proposals like licensing and registration, which still permit law-abiding citizens to make the choice to own guns, and gun bans, which substitute the judgment of the government for that of the individual on the issue of gun ownership.

Finally, if the argument is that the adoption of limited gun control measures will operate to increase the likelihood that a broad gun ban eventually will be adopted, then it fails for lack of historical evidence that when modest gun restrictions are adopted, they actually have the predicted causal impact. Although examples can be found of gun bans being adopted many years after more modest restrictions became law, the cause-and-effect relationship between these events is highly, and perhaps inherently, speculative. This is especially true of the asserted connection between registration of guns and gun bans, given the examples of registration systems that have not been followed by gun bans, as well as gun bans that were not preceded by the adoption of registration systems.

In the final analysis, the slippery slope argument asks policymakers to forgo the life-saving benefits of sensible gun control policies because it is possible to dream up some hypothetical scenario in which such policies may increase the likelihood of a gun ban. This is sheer folly. In no other area of policymaking would we allow such rank speculation to defeat proposals that have concrete and demonstrable benefits.

The fact is that virtually all progress toward alleviating societal ills is incremental in nature. Seldom does the first step turn out to be sufficient. Instead, it often simply reveals the necessity for the next step. Taken to its logical conclusion, the fear of the slippery slope would have a paralyzing effect on policymaking on a wide range of issues. Surely the automotive industry could have argued (and likely did argue) that once the federal government starts mandating safety features in cars like padded dashboards and shatter-resistant glass, it is taking the first steps on a slippery slope toward a host of expensive safety mandates that someday would make cars unaffordable for most American families. If policymakers had been persuaded by such an argument, the next steps, like seat belts and air bags, never would have been taken and many thousands of lives would have been lost.

With guns as well, the fear of slipping down the imaginary slope is simply too costly, in needless deaths and shattered lives, to allow it to block movement toward sanity in our gun laws.

HAS THE SUPREME COURT FLATTENED THE SLIPPERY SLOPE?

We have seen that the slippery slope argument, in all its forms, never made sense as a reason to oppose sensible gun laws that will save lives. Does it make even less sense now that the Supreme Court, in the *Heller* case, has erected a constitutional barrier to laws banning the possession of guns in the home for self-defense?

Even after *Heller*, there is no doubt that the gun lobby will try to frame gun control as a cultural issue, portraying gun control advocates as elitists who have nothing but contempt for gun owners and their values. While campaigning, Barack Obama made a comment at a San Francisco fund-raiser about "bitter" people who "cling to guns" to "explain their frustrations," which became an instant hit as an NRA T-shirt ("I'm a Bitter Gun Owner and I Vote"). The search for evidence that advocates of reasonable gun restrictions "really want" to ban guns will continue.

But it is difficult to believe that this message will resonate with the same force among gun owners in the post-*Heller* era. If what gun control advocates "really want" was ever important, it seems far less important after *Heller*. Before *Heller* there was every reason to believe that the political system, disproportionately influenced by single-issue pro-gun voters, would ensure against a general gun ban. After *Heller*, the legal system now has erected a second barrier by declaring gun ownership a constitutional right. Even if the gun control agenda were to ban guns for law-abiding citizens (a gross misrepresentation, as we have seen), it would be an agenda that is now, in Justice Scalia's words, "off the table."

Heller also now stands as an additional barrier to the effective use of logical and factual slippery slope arguments against modest gun laws. Before *Heller*, it was already easy to draw a logical distinction between regulating guns and banning them. After *Heller*, an additional distinction emerges, based on the new meaning given the Second Amendment. Moreover, the gun lobby's examples of factual slippery slopes—gun regulation leading to gun bans—become even less relevant. Even if it were true that this occurred in places like New York City, in none of those cases did the courts recognize a constitutional barrier to banning guns.

After *Heller*, we may see the factual slippery slope argument assume a somewhat different form. Instead of arguing that regulation of guns will lead to eventual confiscation, the gun lobby may assert that each new restriction will lead to another restriction, which will lead to another restriction, and so on, until the burden and expense of gun ownership will be so great as to amount to a de facto gun ban, even if no law banning guns is ever passed.

It is hard to imagine that this "de facto gun ban" argument will ever generate the emotional response from gun owners that the gun lobby has long provoked with the "slippery slope to confiscation" argument. For one thing, Americans, including gun owners, have personal experience with extensive regulation of dangerous products—for example, automobiles, pharmaceuticals, alcohol—that has not amounted to a de facto ban on the products. Second, in states with extensive laws regulating the sale and possession of guns, like California and New Jersey, there are still lots of guns and gun owners. Some of those gun owners no doubt complain about overregulation, but they have no argument that the existing restrictions amount to a de facto gun ban. Third, the *Heller* decision itself suggests a constitutional limit on the burdens that can be placed on gun possession.

After *Heller*, opponents of gun laws will be free to argue to courts that the particular law at issue, judged in the context of other preexisting regulation, puts such a severe incremental burden on gun possession for self-defense in the home that it infringes the *Heller*-created right.

Over the long term, therefore, *Heller* should lead to a weakening of gun owner activism against modest gun control proposals like mandating background checks on private gun sales at gun shows and elsewhere. This is particularly true given that large majorities of gun owners support a wide range of gun controls on their merits. Indeed, even leaders in the gun rights movement have acknowledged this likely effect. In a revealing discussion on public radio in Los Angeles a few days after the *Heller* ruling, Chuck Michel, a lawyer who has long represented the NRA and other pro-gun groups, was asked about *Heller*'s effect on gun registration and licensing. He responded, "The problem has always been that registration and licensing led to confiscation and I . . . still think registration and licensing is . . . problematic in multiple respects . . . , but I think that now . . . there are a lot of people in the gun control movement who are really gun . . . banners. They're in favor of civilian disarmament. These folks are never going to get their way now as a result of this [Heller] opinion, so *I think licensing and registration is . . . going to be . . . tougher to criticize* [emphasis added]." Moments later, Michel realized the implications of what he had said, as the NRA talking points suddenly kicked in. "Well, let me just first clarify," he said as his life as a gun lobby lawyer passed before him, "so I don't get overly criticized by the members of the NRA who may be listening, you can't license a civil right. So, I'm not talking about a license to own a gun or have a gun. There are certain types of licensing which will survive and others that won't."[39] Nice try. But Michel had committed the classic "gaffe," as famously defined some years ago by columnist Michael Kinsley. He had told the truth by accident. Because *Heller* has taken a general gun ban "off the table," what some gun controllers "really want" has become less relevant, making it more difficult for the NRA to successfully argue against licensing and registration.

By the same token, *Heller* may enhance the efforts of gun control advocates to frame the debate in terms of public safety, not cultural norms. It will help them force their opponents to explain why reforms like background checks for private sales, curbs on multiple sales, greater enforcement power for ATF, and consumer safety standards for guns can't work, or cause greater problems than they solve. If the debate can focus on the pros and cons of specific proposals, free from the distraction of the gun ban issue, gun control may well be on a new path to victory.

Heller also may make it harder, over the long run, for politicians to hide behind the slippery slope argument when opposing sensible gun laws. The argument has long furnished easy political cover for politicians anxious to curry favor with the gun lobby by opposing even modest reforms like the Brady Act. *Heller* may put greater pressure on legislators to explain their opposition to such measures without resorting to imaginary threats of gun confiscation.

The positive impact of *Heller* on gun control efforts likely will take years to yield tangible results. The degree of its impact also will depend on future cases on the constitutionality of gun laws. *Heller* addressed the application of the Second Amendment to the District of Columbia, a unique political entity that is a hybrid of federal and local power. *Heller*'s immediate impact is to render a handgun ban unconstitutional in the District. Because the District is a federal enclave, it is now clear that Congress also cannot constitutionally ban handguns (not a likely prospect anyway). However, the Supreme Court expressly refused to address in *Heller* the further question of whether the new Second Amendment right also applies to state and other local gun laws.[40]

The Bill of Rights—the first ten amendments to our Constitution—originally applied only to restrain federal legislation and imposed no restrictions on state laws or, by extension, to local governments, which generally derive their legislative powers from states. However, the Fourteenth Amendment, enacted following the Civil War, provides that no state shall "deprive any person of life, liberty or property, without due process of law."

The Supreme Court, in a series of rulings interpreting the due process clause, decided that certain provisions of the Bill of Rights are so fundamental to the liberty guaranteed by due process that they are "incorporated" as restrictions on the states and their local governments. Thus, the state of Georgia, and the city of Atlanta, cannot infringe freedom of speech any more than can the federal government. However, the Second Amendment is one of the provisions of the Bill of Rights that has *not* been incorporated against the states.

This incorporation issue is surely the next important Second Amendment battleground, likely destined for resolution by the Supreme Court in the next few years. How it is ultimately decided will have a lot to do with the impact of *Heller* on the slippery slope argument. If the Supreme Court were to confine application of the new Second Amendment right to the District of Columbia and the federal government, it would leave the states and local governments free to ban handguns, at least under the federal Constitution. (Forty-two states have broadly worded "right to bear arms" provisions that have been applied to protect an individual right unrelated to the militia in their state constitutions.[41] However, at least one local handgun ban has been upheld under such provisions,[42] and they have done little to weaken the power of the slippery slope argument.) If the courts fail to incorporate the Second Amendment as a restraint on the states, this would allow the gun lobby to continue to create the specter that gun control advocates, and their political allies, will use an incrementalist strategy to ban guns, one city and one state, at a time. In short, although *Heller* should diminish the steepness of the slippery slope regardless of the incorporation issue, the slope likely can be flattened only if the new *Heller* Second Amendment right eventually is applied to the states and their localities.

Heller is the greatest gun rights victory in our constitutional history, yet it could actually end up strengthening the effort to pass sensible gun control laws by undercutting one of the core gun lobby arguments against those laws. But will it also be a strong legal precedent supporting constitutional attacks on a broad range of gun control laws? And, by giving guns a special constitutional status enjoyed by no other dangerous product, will the ruling help the gun lobby overcome the analogies to automobiles and other products used by gun controllers to support strengthening our gun laws?

A final reckoning of *Heller* must fully consider its legal implications and their impact on the gun debate. That awaits a later chapter.

4.

"AN ARMED SOCIETY
IS A POLITE SOCIETY."

THIS VENERABLE SLOGAN uses a dose of sarcasm to express a bedrock principle of gun control opponents: if law-abiding citizens are armed, they will collectively deter crime because criminals will not risk a confrontation with an armed defender. To the extent that deterrence fails in individual cases, so the argument goes, the armed citizen will have the means to successfully resist a criminal attack, which only will serve to enhance the deterrent effect. "Self-defense works," writes Wayne LaPierre of the NRA, because "criminals fear armed citizens. . . . The survival instinct is not exclusive to law-abiding citizens, it is just as basic to criminals."[1]

Unlike the arguments we have previously dissected, the "armed society" argument is not only *against* gun control; it also is *for* guns. It unambiguously claims that the more law-abiding citizens are armed, the lower will be the incidence of crime, including violent crime. Thus, gun ownership by the law abiding is seen as a positive social good. To the extent that gun control laws function to discourage gun ownership, they are seen as crime enhancing. Under this theory, public policy should encourage private gun ownership, including permitting gun owners to carry their guns in public places in order to maximize the deterrent and protective effects of guns. Kennesaw, Georgia, has taken this idea to its logical limit. It requires its adult citizens to own guns.[2]

JUST HOW POLITE ARE WE?

By its terms, the argument makes a societal claim: that societies with a well-armed populace will be more "polite"—that is, experience less crime

105

and violence—than societies that have fewer legal guns. From the outset, the argument faces a formidable problem. American society is quite well armed, but not very polite. As gun control advocates have long, and rather effectively, pointed out, if guns made us safe, we would be the safest nation on earth. In fact as we have seen, the violent crime rate in America is not dramatically different from that in other Western democracies.[3] As we also have seen, violent crime in America is far more lethal than in other countries. If we look at the least "polite" crime of all—homicide—the United States leads the rest of the industrialized world by a wide margin. Finland ranks second, and the U.S. age-adjusted homicide rate is 2.5 times greater than Finland's. Indeed, the U.S. homicide rate is over 3.5 times that of Northern Ireland's, with its bloody history of religious warfare. It is five times that of Canada and Australia.[4]

FIGURE 4.1

AGE-ADJUSTED HOMICIDE RATES IN HIGH-INCOME NATIONS (1995–1998)

	Nation		Homicide rate per 100,000
1.	United States	(1995-1997)	8.2
2.	Finland	(1996)	3.3
3.	Northern Ireland	(1996-1997)	2.3
4.	Scotland	(1996-1997)	2.2
5.	Belgium	(1993-1994)	1.8
6.	New Zealand	(1994-1996)	1.7
7.	Australia	(1995)	1.6
8.	Canada	1996-1997	1.6
9.	Italy	(1994-1995)	1.4
10.	Netherlands	(1996-1997)	1.3
11.	Singapore	(1996-1997)	1.2
12.	Denmark	(1994-1996)	1.2
13.	Sweden	(1996)	1.2
14.	Norway	(1995)	1.0
15.	Israel	(1996)	1.0
16.	France	(1995-1996)	1.0
17.	Austria	(1996-1998)	1.0
18.	Germany	(1996-1997)	1.0
19.	Ireland	(1994-1996)	0.8
20.	Spain	(1995)	0.8
21.	Luxembourg	(1996-1997)	0.6
22.	England/Wales	(1996-1997)	0.6

Source: World Health Organization Data presented in Hemenway, *Private Guns, Public Health*, 46.

Yet, by any measure, the United States has the highest rate of gun ownership in the industrialized world.[5] If "an armed society is a polite society," how can this be? In the gun lobby's simple world of good guys versus bad guys, it should necessarily be true that the more gun saturated a society, the greater the deterrent effect on criminals and the lower the incidence of crime. According to the NRA's account, criminals prey on the unarmed because they want to reduce the risk of getting shot. The greater the likelihood that any prospective victim will be armed, the less likely the criminal will attack at all. The United States, the nation that presents its criminals with the greatest risk of encountering a prospective victim who is armed, should have the lowest crime rates in the world. It seems pretty clear that an armed society is not necessarily a polite society at all.

I am not arguing here that higher rates of gun ownership cause higher rates of crime, violent crime, or homicide.[6] Such causation is difficult to show because so many other factors bear on the incidence of crime. For instance, simple cross-national comparisons of gun availability and crime do not control for the degree to which various countries impose legal restrictions on firearms. It also is difficult to sort out whether high levels of gun ownership lead to high crime rates or whether high crime rates lead to high levels of gun ownership. Even the most sophisticated study of firearm availability and homicide rates across high-income nations—which showed that where guns are more available, there are more, not fewer, homicides—was careful to make no claims about causation.[7] I am using international comparisons here not to make a causal link, but to deny one. The idea that more guns means less crime because of a society-wide deterrent effect of gun ownership simply cannot explain the plain facts about gun availability and crime in the industrialized world.

Perhaps because the homicide rate in the United States is so dramatically high versus other high-income nations, gun advocates are determined to show that nations can have many guns and low homicide rates or can have few guns and high homicide rates. According to pro-gun lawyer Don Kates, for example, "Norway, with the highest gun ownership rate in Western Europe, has the lowest murder rate—far below England's."[8] And "Holland, with Western Europe's lowest rate of gun ownership, has a 50 percent higher murder rate than Norway."[9] I have no doubt numerous other country pairings could be made illustrating the point that the prevalence of gun ownership in a country does not necessarily correlate to the incidence of homicide or other violent crime. The proposition that greater gun availability necessarily means greater violence, or even lethal violence, is a straw man that gun advocates like Kates take great pleasure in knocking down, again and again. The central policy issue is whether the enactment of specific restrictions on firearms will prevent violence. Whether violence necessarily increases with the number of guns available in a society provides little guidance on that central issue. This is shown by briefly examining the NRA's two favorite examples of countries where legal ownership of guns is common and crime is low—Switzerland and Israel.

WHAT SWITZERLAND AND ISRAEL HAVE IN COMMON

In his book, *Guns, Crime, and Freedom,* the NRA's Wayne LaPierre claims that Switzerland "has a higher rate of firearms possession than the United States" and yet in 1990 had only thirty-four firearm-related homicides.[10] According to LaPierre, this shows "that there is no causal effect between firearms possession and crime. Indeed, just the opposite seems to be the case: a thoroughly armed people is relatively crime free; it is the ultimate deterrent to crime."[11]

In this brief passage, LaPierre manages to commit multiple errors, both factual and logical. First, it is not true that Switzerland has a higher rate of firearms possession than the United States, although it appears to have a higher rate of gun possession than other European countries, with the possible exception of Norway.[12] Second, LaPierre refutes the idea that "firearms possession causes crime," even though the case for sensible gun control laws has never turned on a showing that there is a causal link between gun possession per se and crime. For the gun control issue, the critical gun-crime causal link, as we saw in chapter 1, is between gun use in crime and the lethality of crime, not between gun possession and crime. Gun laws that reduce the use of guns in crime will save lives, whether the prevalence of gun ownership is relatively high or relatively low.

Finally, and of greatest importance, LaPierre confidently asserts that Switzerland's low number of homicides is owing to the deterrent effect of a well-armed society, without accounting for Switzerland's strong gun laws. Pro-gun advocates repeatedly misrepresent the circumstances of gun ownership in that country. If you believed their accounts, you would think that the Swiss government issues a machine gun to every citizen for his or her personal use. In point of fact, Switzerland has a functioning militia system (of the kind originally contemplated by the framers of our Second Amendment) in which every able-bodied male citizen is enrolled for required military training from the ages of twenty to forty-two. Privates and lower-ranking noncommissioned officers are issued a 5.56 assault rifle, while officers and higher-ranking noncommissioned officers are issued semiautomatic handguns. Twenty rounds of ammunition are also issued.

Although these weapons are to be kept in the homes of the militiamen, they are intended only for military use, as defined by the government. The weapons and ammunition are required to be stored under lock and key, with the ammunition in a sealed container. The guns and ammo must be presented for regular inspections and failure to store them securely is severely punished by the military justice system.[13] In describing the Swiss system, LaPierre makes much of the fact that fully automatic rifles are supplied by the government "free of charge," without mentioning that they are subject to government regulation that goes much further than registration and actually makes Swiss citizens subject to regular government inspections of the guns.[14] Can you imagine the fury of the NRA's opposition to any suggestion that guns in the homes of U.S. citizens be subject to government inspection?

The Swiss can also possess their own private firearms, but they are subject to a licensing system of a kind the NRA would surely denounce as totalitarian. Prior to 1997 the system was implemented by agreement of the Swiss cantons, which are comparable to American states. Anyone wishing to acquire a handgun had to obtain a license, which would be denied not only if the applicant had a criminal record but also if he "gives cause to believe that he might become a risk to either himself or a third person."[15] This was a highly restrictive system in which the government had discretion to deny a license even to persons who, in the NRA's world, are "law-abiding citizens." In 1997 the Swiss Parliament adopted a federal licensing law that went into effect in 1999 and incorporates the same restrictive standards of the earlier canton laws. The federal law applies to purchases of both handguns and long guns from a gun dealer. Subsequent transfers between private citizens have to be documented and the parties must retain the paperwork for ten years.[16]

Wayne LaPierre asserts that the Swiss experience proves that "a thoroughly armed people is relatively crime free,"[17] when it may prove only that a society can be well armed and crime free *only if its guns are tightly controlled.* He notes that Great Britain and Switzerland have similar homicide rates, despite their vastly different rates of gun ownership,[18] but fails to mention a salient similarity: *they both have restrictive gun laws.*

Few would think Switzerland and Israel have much in common, but to the gun partisans Israel also qualifies as a crime-free utopia thanks to its well-armed populace. It is true that the homicide rate is lower in Israel than in the United States, but its civilian gun ownership rate also is well below that of the United States.[19] As in Switzerland, Israel has a system of near-universal military service in which nearly every adult—male and female—

serves in the armed forces at one time or another.[20] Much of the population is armed in connection with active or reserve military service. Nevertheless, as CNN Jerusalem bureau chief Walter Rodgers notes, "Israel has incredibly strict gun control laws. Try to buy a handgun, and you'll face perhaps a 3-month waiting period, police, medical and psychological checks and hard-to-win approval from the Interior Ministry."[21] Licenses are given on a "show-need, case-by-case basis."[22] As in Switzerland, gun ownership is not a citizen's right: in fact, the government decides who will own a handgun. Such a system would be anathema to the NRA. Finally, although gun advocates can point to some instances in which armed civilians have stopped terrorist attacks in Israel, it is absurd on its face to argue, based on that nation's experience, that an armed populace necessarily deters violence. Israel is, for unique political reasons unrelated to gun ownership, a society plagued by acts of horrific violence committed by persons obviously undeterred by the prospect of armed response by Israelis.

The key point obscured by the pro-gun commentators is that in both Switzerland and Israel the government has a pervasive role in the private possession of guns. It is beyond strange that the pro-gun advocates choose these two countries to make their case that "more guns means less crime" because their experience just as persuasively demonstrates that "more gun control means less crime."

DO MORE GUNS EQUAL LESS CRIME?

International comparisons, therefore, do little to bolster the theory that gun ownership deters crime. America's infatuation with guns has not made it a noticeably polite society, when stacked against other high-income nations. But, the gun advocates may respond, that's because gun control laws prevent law-abiding Americans in high-crime areas from owning more guns. Where gun control laws are weak, and law-abiding people own many guns, so the pro-gun argument goes, crime is low because criminals know their potential victims likely are armed. According to the NRA's Sandra Froman, "As lawful firearm ownership increases in a community, violent crime decreases. Criminals still prefer to prey on the weak, and they don't like armed victims."[23]

Does this theory even remotely resemble reality? Actually, no. Let's look first at the relationship between gun ownership and homicide rates. Researchers at the Harvard School of Public Health looked at this relationship in all fifty states and found that people living in "high-gun states" were *more likely* than those in the "low-gun states" to become homicide victims.[24] Although these results were primarily the result of higher gun-related homicide rates in states with higher rates of firearm ownership, non-gun-related homicide rates were also higher in states with more guns.[25] This association remained strong even after the researchers controlled for other factors that could affect homicide rates, such as poverty, urbanization, unemployment, per capita alcohol consumption, and violent crimes other than homicide.

The relationship is striking if you look at the states with the highest rates of gun ownership versus the states with the lowest. Residents of the extreme high-gun states (Louisiana, Alabama, Mississippi, Wyoming, West Virginia, and Arkansas) were more than *2.5 times* more likely to become homicide victims than those in the extreme low-gun states (Hawaii, Massachusetts, Rhode Island, and New Jersey).[26] In the NRA's world, Arkansans must be safer than residents of the Garden State because Arkansas criminals are cowering in fear of law-abiding Arkansas gun owners, whereas Jersey criminals have little to fear because New Jersey gun control laws have disarmed the law-abiding population. The facts show instead that the NRA's world is make-believe.

Again, it is important to keep in mind what we are using these statistics to prove. The Harvard study makes no claim that higher rates of gun ownership "cause" higher rates of homicide, only that there is a positive association between the two. The researchers say they cannot rule out "reverse causation," that is, the possibility that higher homicide rates in states like Arkansas may have led to increased gun acquisition in such states.[27] But even assuming that such reverse causation could be shown, what would this mean? It certainly would provide no support for the Wayne LaPierre view that more guns mean less crime. If LaPierre were correct, then the association between high homicide rates and high gun ownership could not exist for long because murderous criminals would begin, at some point, to be deterred by the realization that they were increasingly likely to be confronted by law-abiding gun owners. The Harvard study shows, rather, a strong association between high levels of gun ownership and high homicide rates over a nine-year period. If the question is whether a well-armed populace deters criminals from engaging in lethal violence, the statistical evidence provides a compelling reason to believe the answer is no.

What about crimes other than homicide? If criminals fear law-abiding gun owners, then areas with a high incidence of gun ownership should experience fewer property crimes such as burglary. The first systematic evidence on this question, assembled by Philip Cook of Duke University and Jens Ludwig, then of Georgetown University, actually found that residential burglary rates tend to *increase* with the prevalence of guns in a community.[28]

Their study controlled for various non-gun factors bearing on burglary rates, such as per capita income, prisoners per capita, the poverty rate, and alcohol consumption.[29] Not only did widespread gun ownership not have a net deterrent effect, but a 10 percent increase in gun ownership actually increased burglary rates by 3 to 7 percent. According to Cook and Ludwig, the most plausible explanation for this effect is that guns are extremely valuable loot for burglars.[30] Whatever burglars' fear of law-abiding gun owners, apparently it is overcome by the prospect of scoring a piece with no bodies on it.

But isn't it possible that the prospect of being confronted by an armed citizen may lead burglars to avoid homes when they are occupied, thus reducing the risk of violence arising from burglaries? Pro-gun researchers have long been excited by figures purporting to show that the percentage of "hot" burglaries (meaning those of occupied homes) is far higher in Canada and some European countries than in the United States. The gun enthusiasts attribute this to differences in gun possession rates.[31] Cook and Ludwig find these comparisons "entirely unpersuasive" because they fail to control for other obvious differences between the countries that could also account for the lower percentage of hot burglaries in the United States.[32] For instance, when burglars are arrested in the United States, they are subject to more certain and severe punishment than are those in other countries—another potent incentive for burglars to avoid contact with victims to reduce the risk of apprehension.[33] In any event, the analysis by Cook and Ludwig of U.S. data from the National Crime Victimization Survey (NCVS) shows that hot burglary victimizations tended to increase, not decrease, with gun prevalence. They conclude, "If anything, residences in a neighborhood with high gun prevalence are at greater risk of being burglarized, hot and otherwise."[34] That doesn't sound very polite to me.

There is, therefore, not much in the way of statistical evidence to support the theory that criminals are deterred by the prospect of confrontation with armed citizens. The deterrence theory also poses a logical conundrum. The theory says that criminals avoid prospective targets who are armed because they fear being shot. If this is true, then why aren't armed criminals deterred from attacking other armed criminals? Why do armed drug dealers have anything to fear from other armed drug dealers? Why do armed gangs have anything to fear from other armed gangs? Indeed, why isn't being an armed criminal a relatively safe way to make a living? Gary Kleck reports studies showing that street gang members are 8.8 times more likely to own handguns than other youths, and 19 times more likely to be homicide victims.[35] Drug dealers are 3.7 times more likely to own a handgun, and 6 times more likely to be homicide victims.[36] Why doesn't their gun possession deter attacks on these criminals? Does the deterrence theory suggest that criminals fear armed law-abiding citizens more than other armed criminals? If it does, there seems to be something quite wrong with the theory.

Rather than being deterred from criminal acts by the potential of confronting armed victims, it seems at least as likely that criminals will simply ensure that they are better armed than their potential victims. In one prisoner survey, 62 percent of respondents who used a gun to commit the crime for which they were incarcerated reported that the possibility of encountering an armed victim was "very important" or "somewhat important" in their decision to employ a gun.[37] The proliferation of guns in a community does not cause criminals to choose another line of work; it rather causes an arms race in which the criminals make sure they are not left behind.

Surveys show that most people do not believe they would be safer if there were more guns in their community. As to non-gun owners, over 80 percent say they would feel less safe if more people in their community acquired guns; only 8 percent would feel safer.[38] Even more striking, for gun owners, about half would feel less safe with more guns.[39] Obviously there are gun owners who may think their own gun makes them safer, but are less than comfortable about their neighbors owning guns.

I sometimes wonder if advocates of the deterrence theory really believe it themselves. If the NRA really believes in the crime-deterring effect of gun possession, then why does it repeatedly have its annual meetings in convention centers that don't allow guns? Why would the NRA put its members at a greater risk of crime in this way? And when NRA-supported legislators vote to ease restrictions on carrying concealed weapons, they do so after walking through metal detectors that prevent the law-abiding public from bringing guns into legislative offices. How could the NRA's elected true believers subject themselves and their staffs to such an unsafe environment? The answer can't be that it is important to keep out the armed bad guys. The premise of the NRA's argument is that the bad guys will always find ways around efforts to separate them from their guns but will be deterred from using them by fear of the armed citizenry. Indeed, if the deterrence theory is taken seriously, it is not at all clear why the NRA should be comfortable with metal detectors at airports. Doesn't the theory imply that the best way to prevent a recurrence of 9/11 would be a plane full of pistol-packing law-abiding citizens?

The fact is that when our society really wants to ensure that a particular group of people, a place, or an event is safe and secure, we do everything we can to keep the guns out. The greater our fear of violence, the greater are our efforts to exclude guns. The best illustration of this is from the gun industry itself. Several years ago, the National Shooting Sports Foundation (NSSF), an industry trade association, began a program it called Project Childsafe, which involved a van touring the country handing out free gunlocks. The NSSF started the program as an image booster after manufacturers were targeted by lawsuits charging that they had failed to incorporate locks in their guns to prevent access by children. On the door of the van were the words "This vehicle contains NO firearms."[40] Say what? The premise of the deterrence theory is that criminals will avoid potential victims who might be armed but will search out victims they know are not armed. If the theory is right, the NSSF is issuing an engraved invitation to criminals to attack the Project Childsafe van and its occupants. In reality, the legend on the van means that even the gun industry itself understands that when complete safety is the goal, the guns must go. It also is an obvious admission that if the van carried guns its cargo would be far more likely to be stolen than to be used to fend off a criminal.

The NSSF also sponsors the largest industry trade show—the annual SHOT Show. One of the NSSF's rules for attendance at the SHOT Show is "For attendee and exhibitor safety, no personal firearms and/or ammunition is allowed."[41] If guns carried by law-abiding citizens into restaurants, movie theaters, sports stadiums, and shopping malls make us all safer, as the gun lobby insists, why does this principle not apply to gun trade shows as well? If "attendee or exhibitor safety" is threatened by guns at the SHOT Show, then isn't my safety threatened by the carrying of concealed weapons in public places in my community?

The deterrence theory will be debated for years to come, but it will always be somewhat detached from reality. As we will see, many pro-gunners actually argue that we need more guns in schools, bars, courthouses, churches, airports, and pretty much everywhere else. For most of us, however, such views are the reductio ad absurdum of the deterrence theory.

HONK IF YOU'VE SHOT A CRIMINAL

Even if law-abiding gun ownership is not much of a general deterrent to crime, it may still prevent individual crimes. The gun lobby has long been obsessed with proving the obvious: that guns can be used successfully in self-defense against a criminal attacker. "The Armed Citizen," a longtime column in the NRA's monthly magazine, is devoted to reporting heroic uses of guns to defend the innocent against predatory criminals. To the extent that guns are used to prevent particular crimes that would have

FIGURE 4.2

VAN USED BY THE NATIONAL SHOOTING SPORTS FOUNDATION'S PROJECT CHILDSAFE

Source: www.gunguys.com (June 21, 2006).

been completed in the absence of armed resistance, it may argue for public policies that promote widespread gun ownership. If guns are frequently used in self-defense, this may also argue against gun control laws that appear to place additional costs and other burdens on gun ownership.

I've made reference before to the notably repetitive nature of the arguments and language used by pro-gun advocates, whether on radio talk shows, in letters to the editor, in op-ed pieces, or elsewhere. It is as if they are programmed to say the same things, in the same way, regardless of the forum or the opponent. You read it first in the NRA's publications and on its website. Then you hear it, virtually word for word, out of the mouths of NRA members and fellow travelers. The NRA has legions of these Stepford advocates. They are spookily "on message."

Even certain statistics are burned into the brains of the NRA's hard-core believers. If you ask any delegate to the NRA's convention how many times Americans use guns each year for self-defense, you will get the same answer every time: 2.5 million.[42] They may not know the source of the figure or how it was derived. But they know it like they know there are twenty-four hours in a day. The more it is repeated, the truer it becomes for them.

The number is, in fact, mythical. It is based on a 1995 telephone survey done by Gary Kleck and his Florida State colleague Marc Gertz. They surveyed five thousand individuals, asking each person if he had used a firearm in self-defense and, if so, under what circumstances and with what effect. They reported only sixty-six incidents of self-defensive gun use. From those sixty-six incidents they extrapolated to estimate 2.5 million defensive gun uses each year in the general population.[43]

Thus, in Kleck's survey, slightly more than 1 percent of the respondents reported a defensive gun use. The fact is that such a tiny percentage of the population will say just about anything. Harvard's David Hemenway gives an amusing illustration. In a random telephone survey like Kleck's, conducted in 1994, more than fifteen hundred adults were asked, "Have you yourself ever seen anything that you believe was a spacecraft from another planet?" Ten percent said yes. These 150 people were then asked, "Have you personally ever been in contact with aliens from another planet or not?" Six percent, or nine people, said yes.[44] If we extrapolate to the entire U.S. population, as did Kleck, we could conclude that 1.2 million American adults have seen ET! Most reasonable people would think that a gross overestimate. I am not suggesting that defensive uses of guns are figments of the imagination, only that it is risky business to estimate millions of annual defensive uses based on a handful of positive answers to a survey, particularly, as we will see, given the built-in incentives for a falsely positive response.

There is far more reliable data that enables us to determine how far off Kleck is. The NCVS, conducted by the U.S. Bureau of the Census for the Justice Department, twice every year surveys a nationally representative sample of 59,000 households to estimate the incidence of crime in the United States. That's 59,000 households surveyed twice every year, as opposed to Kleck's 5,000 individuals surveyed once. Residents of each of the households aged twelve or older are interviewed over a period of three years. Respondents who report an attempted or completed victimization answer detailed questions about the incident, including whether they did or tried to do anything about the incident while it was going on. Victims who say they took action are then asked to describe what they did. The survey then follows up with an additional question: "Did you do anything (else) with the idea of protecting yourself or your property while the incident was going on?" Victims who respond "yes" are again asked to describe their activities.[45] The questioning certainly gives crime victims every opportunity to volunteer their use of guns in self-defense.

The NCVS paints a picture radically different than Kleck's. Criminologists at the University of Maryland looked at the NCVS results from the years 1987 through 1990. After excluding uses of guns by police, they estimated an annual average of approximately 52,000 civilian defensive uses of firearms.[46] Estimates for defensive uses for other years based on the NCVS have ranged as high as 120,000 per year.[47] A far cry from Kleck's 2.5 million.

Finding the flaws in Kleck's estimate has become a growth industry for gun violence scholars. The first problem they note is the nature of the question asked in Kleck's survey. The question was whether, within the past five years, the respondent or a member of his household "used a gun, even if it was not fired, for self-protection or for the protection of property at home, work, or elsewhere." If the answer was yes, they were then asked whether any of the incidents happened in the past twelve months. Unlike those surveyed by the NCVS, Kleck's respondents were not first asked whether they had been victimized by a criminal act. The Kleck question is far more open-ended and allows the respondent to resolve the obvious ambiguity in the phrase "used a handgun for self-protection." This ambiguity creates a serious risk of "false positives," that is, reports of self-defensive gun use that involved something other than the legitimate use of a gun to repel a criminal attack. As the Maryland researchers point out, "Persons who have used firearms to settle arguments might believe that they have prevented assaults."[48] After all, in a survey of prison inmates, 63 percent of those who fired guns during crimes described their actions as self-defense.[49]

There is an obvious potential for gun owners to give biased and inaccurate claims of self-defensive gun use. Particularly for handgun owners, who are far more likely to have bought their guns for self-protection than for sport, the claim of successful self-defense is the ultimate justification of their purchase. This natural bias is enhanced by the intense admiration the gun culture, and the general public, bestows upon those who use guns against criminals. For example, in November 2005 radio talk shows were ablaze with the story of Susan Gaylord Buxton, an Arlington, Texas, grandmother who used her .38 pistol to confront a "bald-headed, muscle-bound burglar crouching in her front-hall coat closet," as the incident was described by the *Dallas Morning News*.[50] The 911 tape of the incident captured Ms. Buxton screaming in the background, "How dare you come in my house, you lousy son of a bitch!" When the burglar tried to grab her gun, she shot him in the thigh. "If you can't protect your own home," she told the *Morning News*, "then life's not worth living."[51] Grandma Buxton became an instant star in the gun culture, with the NRA's own talk show host, Cam Edwards, using her story to show how the gun is the "equalizer" for senior citizens against the criminal element.[52]

I am not here intending to minimize Ms. Buxton's actions, which apparently were carried out with no small degree of courage. I offer this incident only as an example of the kind of positive public reaction to reports of gun use against criminals that could easily encourage gun owners to exaggerate their own self-defense achievements when asked. Even in communities evidencing some degree of public disapproval toward gun ownership per se, there would likely be a natural tendency for the gun owner to want to demonstrate the wisdom of his choice to buy a gun (and perhaps the absence of foresight by his neighbors) by claiming that his weapon had actually protected his home and family. Although Kleck's survey included questions to determine whether the defensive gun use was "genuine," these questions were asked after the respondent had already committed himself to the claim that he used a gun for self-protection. The risk of self-justifying answers was high.

Scholars have noted that, in any survey designed to show the incidence of a relatively rare event, even a small percentage of respondents giving falsely positive responses can produce estimates far in excess of the actual incidence of the event. Kleck surveyed five thousand people and found only sixty-six reported incidents of firearm self-defense. As David Hemenway has put it, Kleck's search is "for a needle in a haystack."[53] To achieve huge overestimates of defensive gun use in a survey, the bias toward exaggerating one's gun use has to be dominant among only a few respondents.

Kleck claims that the NCVS systematically underestimates defensive gun uses because the NCVS surveyors make it clear they are government employees and respondents fear that they will be putting themselves in legal jeopardy by describing their gun use to the government.[54] This would be true, of course, only if the respondents fear that their gun use or possession is, in fact, illegal. It would not be a reason to believe that the NCVS undercounts defensive gun uses by law-abiding citizens, only that it undercounts such uses by law violators.

Putting aside for a moment the interesting question of whether illegal defensive uses of guns should count, the fear of legal jeopardy would have to be pervasive among gun owners to reconcile Kleck's data with the NCVS results. "To preserve the 2.5 million self-defense gun estimate," writes Hemenway, "Kleck and Gertz are forced to claim that nineteen of every twenty people with a genuine self-defense use do not report it to the NCVS (and virtually no one without a genuine self-defense use in the time frame does report one)."[55] This seems improbable, especially since, as Hemenway also points out, there is no reasonable basis to believe that information given the NCVS could be used to prosecute someone for a crime. The Census Bureau interviewers are not permitted to report the information received to other authorities, nor has it been reported to other authorities, nor has any respondent ever been subjected to punishment for the answers given.[56]

Kleck's survey data yields absurd results that, as Dr. Douglas Weil puts it, "bear no resemblance to what we know about the real world."[57] According to Kleck's survey, women defend themselves with a firearm in 40 percent of all sexual assaults, even though all other available data shows that a firearm is used for protection in fewer than one in a hundred incidents of sexual assault.[58] According to Kleck's estimates, a firearm is used for protection in 80 percent of burglaries when a victim is at home, despite the fact that fewer than 40 percent of households have guns. "For this finding to be true," Weil notes, "burglars must have an uncanny knack of victimizing only households in which the owner has a gun."[59] Kleck's survey also yields an estimate that about 200,000 criminals are shot each year by their intended victims, though we know from other data that the total number of shootings of *all* kinds is less than 200,000 per year.[60] We also know that, according to the FBI, there are fewer than 300 justifiable self-defense firearm homicides by civilians every year.[61] Given the inherent lethality of firearms, is it plausible to believe that civilians use guns in self-defense 2.5 million times per year, but fewer than 300 attackers die?

Telephone surveys may be fine for sampling public opinion or for other purposes. They appear to be utterly unreliable for estimating the frequency of a comparatively rare event, like the use of guns in self-defense.

Finally, by his own admission, Kleck's survey "made no effort to assess either the lawfulness or morality" of the respondents' reported defensive uses of guns.[62] It turns out that a high number of claimed self-defensive gun uses likely are reckless and illegal.

Researchers from the Harvard School of Public Health did their own telephone surveys and then had the individual reports of firearm self-defense analyzed by a panel of courtroom judges. The judges found 51 percent of the claimed self-defense uses to be "probably illegal."[63] Even more revealing, three respondents accounted for 58 percent of the total defensive uses, claiming fifty, twenty, and fifteen self-defense incidents each in the previous five years.[64] A single eighteen-year-old male reported six incidents in which he used a gun in self-defense. It seems that there are more than a few "make my day" defensive gun uses being counted. Somewhat understating the matter, the Harvard researchers observed that "many reported self defense gun uses from a respondent creates a suspicion that the uses may be aggressive rather than defensive."[65] Gary Kleck may be right that the questionable legality of the gun user's conduct may cause the NCVS to somewhat undercount claimed self-defensive uses of firearms. For the same reason, however, the telephone surveys tend to count claimed gun uses that are not socially desirable and should not be encouraged.

For Kleck, though, the calculation of defensive gun uses is but the prelude to his clincher statistical argument—that guns are used to defend against crimes far more often than to commit them. Based on his estimate that there are about "500,000 to 700,000 incidents in which criminals used guns to commit crimes," he reaches the startling conclusion that guns are used defensively by crime victims four to five times more often than they are used by offenders to commit crimes.[66]

The Kleck/Gertz survey was conducted in the spring of 1993 and, according to the Justice Department, there were over 1 million violent crimes committed with guns in 1993, not 500,000–700,000, as estimated by Kleck.[67] Even using the Justice Department figure, the Kleck/Gertz survey means that crime victims use guns defensively more than twice as often as guns are used to commit violent crimes. Whatever the exact ratio, it is now received wisdom in pro-gun circles that guns are used far more often in self-defense than in crime. When conservative ABC News reporter John Stossel set out on *20/20* to explode the myth that "guns are bad," he confidently asserted that "guns are used twice or three times as often for defensive uses as they are to commit crimes."[68]

If this were true, it would mean criminals are even dumber than we thought. Apparently, they frequently commit crimes with weapons less lethal than guns and are met with resistance by gun-wielding victims. Assuming that this situation persists year after year (and Kleck does not suggest otherwise), it must mean criminals do not respond to this risky situation by starting to pack heat. Obviously, if criminals started to use guns in greater numbers, then the ratio of self-defense to criminal use would move closer to 1:1. Nor does it mean that criminals turn away from crime, because we have already seen that a well-armed citizenry does not deter crime. Instead, criminals apparently continue to assume the risk that their knives or fists will encounter their victims' guns. Kleck's estimates suggest that there are many criminals who actually are bringing a knife to a gun fight. Not very bright. And these are the same criminals who the NRA says are so clever and resourceful that they will always find ways to get guns?

What is the true ratio of criminal use to self-defensive use of guns? The most methodologically sound way to measure the ratio would be to use the same survey to estimate both the number of the gun crimes and the number of self-defense uses of guns (something Kleck did not do). Using the NCVS to estimate both, the Maryland researchers determined that, during the period they studied (1987–1990), *guns were used in crime ten times more often than they were used for protection.*[69] Using their own 1996 telephone survey for both gun crimes and self-defense uses, Harvard's David Hemenway and Deborah Azrael estimated that *the number of gun crimes exceeded the number of self-defense uses by a ratio of between 4 to 1 and 6 to 1.*[70] In short, the available evidence indicates that guns are used in crime far more often than they are used to defend against crime. Will John Stossel admit that he misled the public? I'm not holding my breath.

THE IMPOLITENESS OF GUN-OWNING HOMES

For gun advocates, the debate over gun ownership begins and ends with the question: If a criminal is coming through your sliding glass door, what would you do?[71] Call 911? Threaten him with a kitchen knife? Hit him with a baseball bat? I have been confronted with this line of questioning myself, more than a few times. It is an example of an advocate effectively using the time-honored technique of framing the issue in a way that ensures he will win the day. If we confine ourselves to the scenario in which a home invasion crime is in progress, the argument for having a gun for self-defense becomes quite persuasive. An NRA poster published some years ago asked women, "Should you shoot a rapist before he cuts your throat?" The question, of course, supplies the answer. If the gun control issue is defined in this way, it compels the conclusion that the primary goal of our public policy should be to avoid interfering with the ability of that prospective victim to shoot the rapist before he cuts her throat.

There is now an established body of research into how guns kept in homes are actually used. Instead of using surveys, this research uses the alternative approach of studying official reports of crimes and shootings that actually occurred. Public health researchers have used this technique to uncover some remarkable results. The studies establish that the "criminal coming through the sliding glass door" is not the only scenario for gun use to be considered; indeed, it is a far less likely scenario than others in which the gun plays a far less salutary role. The studies also show that just as gun-owning societies are not very polite, neither are gun-owning homes.

First, guns are rarely used successfully against home intruders. In one study, a team of researchers headed by Dr. Arthur Kellermann of Emory University worked with the Atlanta police department to review every case of unwanted home entry in Atlanta during a three-month period. They found that a firearm was used in self-defense in only 1.5 percent of the cases (3 cases out of 198).[72] Two brandished the gun but did not fire; the third fired but missed. None of the three defenders suffered injury; one suffered a property loss. There also were three cases in which the gun kept in the home was stolen by intruders who left undetected, and another in which the victim lost the gun during a scuffle with the intruder.[73] The study suggests that many guns kept for self-defense are simply not used for that purpose, even when the need arises.

Gun partisans would insist that even if the statistics are true, they mean only that too many gun owners are listening to the advice of safe storage advocates (and, for that matter, gun manufacturers) and are locking away their guns and making them insufficiently accessible. The trouble is that the gun kept loaded and unlocked in the nightstand may be more accessible for use in self-defense, but it also is more accessible for use in other scenarios most gun owners would strongly wish to avoid.

In a separate study, Kellermann and his colleagues examined all fatal and nonfatal gunshot injuries involving guns kept in the home during a specific time period in Memphis, Tennessee, Seattle, Washington, and Galveston, Texas. For every time a gun in the home was used in a self-defense or legally justifiable shooting, there were four unintentional shootings, seven criminal assaults or homicides, and eleven attempted or completed suicides.[74] Thus, guns kept in the home were used to injure or kill twenty-two times more often in criminal assaults, accidents, and suicides than to injure or kill in self-defense. For fatal shootings alone, the ratio rises to 43 to 1.[75]

A survey of over nineteen hundred individuals by the Harvard School of Public Health asked detailed questions about gun victimization and self-defense uses of guns. The survey found that thirteen respondents reported having had a gun displayed against them in the previous five years, while only two respondents reported using a gun in self-defense at home.[76] Most of the hostile gun uses involved brandishing of guns against women by spouses or other intimates. Clearly, the issue is not as simple as "What will you do when the criminal is coming through the sliding glass door?" Other questions are equally relevant. What will you do when your curious ten-year-old finds your gun in a box under your bed? What will you do when your depressed teen is able to unlock your gun rack? Will you be tempted to gain the upper hand in an angry argument by reaching for the gun yourself?

Other work by public health researchers has attempted to determine whether the mere fact of having a gun increases the risk of homicide in the home. Arthur Kellermann and his colleagues investigated this question using the case-control method.[77] They obtained lists of persons killed in their homes in three urban counties in Tennessee, Washington State, and Ohio (the cases) and then compared them with persons of the same sex, race, and approximate age living in the same neighborhood (the controls). Since the households with homicide victims more commonly contained an illicit-drug user, a person with prior arrests, or someone who had been involved in a fight in the home, the researchers controlled for those factors. They found that "keeping a gun in the home was strongly and independently associated with an increased risk of homicide" and that "virtually all of this risk involved homicide by a family member or intimate acquaintance."

Much of the debate over Dr. Kellermann's work concerns whether it proves that a gun in the home actually causes an increase in the risk of homicide or whether it simply means that people who are exposed to a high risk of homicide tend to acquire guns. Gary Kleck has argued, for instance, "Virtually all known factors that increase the risk of homicide victimization could also increase the likelihood that persons exposed to those factors would acquire a gun for self-protection."[78] But Kellermann did control for a number of independent risk factors for homicide and still found that the homes of homicide victims were substantially more likely to have guns. Other case-control studies have yielded similar results. One found that keeping a gun in the home is associated with an increased risk of homicide for women, particularly at the hands of a spouse, an intimate acquaintance, or a close relative.[79] Another found that the purchase of a handgun is associated with an increased risk of homicide victimization.[80]

Regardless of whether the case-control method demonstrates that gun ownership causes an increased risk of homicide, these studies at least suggest that gun ownership does not reduce the risk of homicide. A more recent case-control study found that a gun in the home does not reduce the risk of a non-gun homicide, while it increases the risk for gun-related homicide.[81] As the authors point out, "This runs contrary to the notion that keeping a gun at home makes household members less likely to be killed by intruders." Just as gun-owning nations are not more polite and gun-owning states are not more polite, neither are gun-owning households. If the criminal coming through the sliding glass door is the only relevant scenario and a gun in the home is an effective defense, then homicide victims should be less likely to have a gun in the home, not more likely, as Kellermann found.

The best available evidence, therefore, tells us that a gun in the home (1) does not reduce the risk of homicide or burglary; (2) can be used for self-defense but is rarely used for that purpose, even in cases of home invasion; and (3) is far more likely to victimize those who live in the home, or their acquaintances, than to be used to shoot intruders. It can therefore be said, with some confidence, that bringing a gun into the home is usually a very bad idea. These facts do not necessarily lead to the conclusion that our public policy should bar gun ownership. As with consumption of alcohol and cigarettes, to a great degree the government should allow individual citizens to make their own mistakes. But our public policy should at least ensure that people know the truth about guns in the home, just as the risks of alcohol and cigarettes should be widely known. And it is blinding us to the truth to insist that the only relevant risk is being unarmed as a criminal approaches in a darkened bedroom.

TAKING IT TO THE STREETS

If guns in the home deter crime, as the NRA insists, then it stands to reason that gun carrying by law-abiding citizens in public places would deter even more crime. After all, homicides and robberies more commonly occur outside the home. Thus, the logical extension of the deterrence theory is to encourage the legal carrying of guns in public places.

There is, of course, a self-evident distinction between guns in the home and guns in public. As we have seen, the risks from the decision to bring a gun into the home are borne largely by those who live there. This, of course, does not mean that the public has no legitimate interest in that decision. A gun in the home can make visitors to the home victims as well as residents. Bullets have been known to penetrate external walls and injure those in nearby homes. Almost by definition, however, the public has a more direct interest in gun carrying in public. The risk from an individual's decision to carry a gun in public is borne almost entirely by strangers who had no say in that decision and, if the carrying is concealed, have no knowledge of the decision.

Take the case of Kelli McCormack Brown and Dawn Larson, two health educators who were out for dinner with college friends at an Indianapolis restaurant in November 1997. Little did they know that another diner, Thomas Neuman, had a loaded .32-caliber derringer concealed in his shirt pocket. Neuman's valid Indiana concealed weapons permit proved no insurance against carelessness. When he bent over to retrieve a broken necklace, the gun fell out of his pocket, struck the floor, and discharged a single bullet that struck Ms. Brown's hand before it penetrated Ms. Larson's arm.[82] One bullet. Two injuries. Obviously it could have been much worse.

To add a heavy measure of irony to the incident, the two women were in Indianapolis to attend the annual meeting of the American Public Health Association (APHA). The next day APHA held a press conference to renew its call for stricter gun control. The local prosecutor's office, however, dismissed the shooting as "a freak accident, an unfortunate incident in which, luckily, no one was fatally injured."[83]

Was it a freak accident that Indiana law allowed Thomas Neuman to bring a concealed handgun into a crowded restaurant? The law exposed Ms. Brown, Ms. Larson, and everyone else in that restaurant to a risk of potentially fatal harm of which they were entirely unaware and could do nothing to guard against. It is one thing for a gun owner like Neuman to create such a risk in his own home. It is quite another for him to take the risk with him wherever he goes.

The distinction between guns in private homes and guns carried in public places, until recently, has been reflected in state concealed weapon laws. Traditionally, states have imposed far greater restrictions on the carrying of concealed weapons in public than on the ownership of guns per se. Until the 1990s, in fact, most states either banned the carrying of concealed weapons or at least had restrictive permitting systems. Most states vested law enforcement authorities with great discretion to deny permits to carry concealed weapons, even for applicants who did not have a criminal record. Such discretionary systems recognize that a clean criminal record is no guarantee that an applicant is a responsible, law-abiding person. For example, a Massachusetts police chief told his local newspaper that it is important to be able to weed out applicants who may have clean criminal records but are closely associated with gangs and may be involved in buying weapons for them.[84]

For the NRA, however, allowing police this kind of discretion is an unacceptable limitation on the right of self-defense in public places and an open invitation to criminals to victimize law-abiding citizens without fear of retaliation. The NRA embarked on a campaign in the states to push "shall issue" concealed weapon laws, in which authorities would be forced to issue concealed weapon permits to anyone who wanted them and did not have a criminal record. The campaign was regrettably successful. By 2006 thirty-four states had adopted "shall issue" concealed carry weapons (CCW) permit laws. Alaska and Vermont already allowed the carrying of concealed weapons without any permit at all. In only fourteen states were concealed weapons either banned or subject to strict permitting that gave police discretion over who was allowed to carry hidden handguns in public.

The CCW issue is a singular illustration of the NRA's power to dominate state legislatures in utter defiance of the popular will. A May 1995 poll of Louisiana voters found 60 percent of them opposed to legislation to weaken that state's CCW law.[85] A year later Louisiana became a "shall issue" state. A February 1995 Texas poll found that 62 percent of Texans were opposed to legislation allowing law-abiding citizens to carry concealed weapons in public.[86] Texas enacted just such a law that same year. A November 1994 Michigan poll found 76 percent opposition to relaxing that state's CCW law.[87] After several failed attempts, the NRA finally succeeded in ramming a "shall issue" bill through the Michigan legislature in 2001.

In April 1999 the NRA suffered a humiliating public repudiation of its CCW campaign, when Missouri voters defeated an NRA-sponsored referendum to enact a "shall issue" law. The NRA spent $4 million on the issue in Missouri, nearly five times the amount spent by its opponents, and still lost. Only four years after Missouri citizens made their views clearly known (by voting, not by answering a pollster's questions), the Missouri legislature passed the very statute the voters had rejected. A state senator serving in the Army National Guard in Guantanamo Bay, Cuba, who flew back to Missouri for the vote, cast the deciding vote.[88] He was later reprimanded by the military.[89] When it comes to twisting arms in a state legislature, the gun lobby is not to be trifled with.

If you take a seat in a movie theater, ready to see the latest blockbuster, would it make you feel more or less safe to know that several of your fellow law-abiding citizens are packing heat? How about in a restaurant? In a bar? In a stadium during a football game? In church? At your doctor's office? At your son's little league baseball game? At your child's school? Surveys show that most people take a dim view of being in places where others have hidden handguns in their clothes, purses, or cars. A national survey by the Harvard Injury Control Research Center asked, "Some states have recently changed their laws concerning gun carrying. . . . If more people in your community begin to carry guns, will that make you feel more safe, the same, or less safe?" Sixty-two percent said "less safe," and only 12 percent said "more safe."[90]

Another Harvard survey in 1999 asked whether "regular citizens should be allowed to bring their guns into (a) restaurants, (b) bars, (c) college campuses, (d) hospitals, (e) sports stadiums, and (f) government buildings? Generally *more than 90 percent of the respondents answered "no" to each location*.[91] Yet the NRA's "shall issue" CCW laws are designed to ensure that greater numbers of ordinary citizens will carry hidden handguns in those locations. Gun advocates are now seriously engaged in active campaigns to change "shall issue" laws to allow CCW license holders to carry guns into places that have heretofore been off-limits, including schools, workplace parking lots, national parks, and, believe it or not, airports. Even where surveys have asked questions making explicit reference to allowing only law-abiding citizens who have passed safety-training courses to carry concealed weapons, the respondents still disliked the idea. A 1996 survey by the National Opinion Research Center asked, "Do laws allowing any adult to carry a concealed gun in public provided that they pass a criminal background check and gun safety course make you feel more safe or less safe?" Fifty-six percent of respondents replied "less safe," and 36 percent said "more safe."[92]

I suppose the NRA would interpret these results as reflecting an ungrateful public's ignorance of the added safety and security being afforded by the handgun carriers in our midst. The polls certainly reflect how alien the NRA's worldview is to the rest of us. First, most people obviously think the deterrence theory is pure bunk. Second, most people recognize that the world is not so easily divided into well-defined categories of good guys and bad guys, particularly on the basis of a criminal background check. Third, most people understand that it is a big deal to entrust someone with a hidden handgun and the right to carry it virtually everywhere. Indeed, we treat it as a big deal to allow police to carry handguns in public. No "shall issue" law in the nation comes close to mandating the extensive and continual training undergone by the police in marksmanship, gun safety, shooting scenarios, and proper application of the rules of deadly force. Even with this extensive training, law enforcement officers are generally bonded by their employers and insured to pay for the risk that they may do harm to others through accidents or mistakes in judgment.

The public's instincts on the CCW issue are borne out by experience. The NRA claims that its opponents have been discredited on the CCW issue because they hysterically claimed there would be "blood in the streets" and "Dodge City gunfights" in "shall issue" states, when nothing of the kind has occurred. It's not clear how much blood would have to flow to impress the NRA, but it is not difficult to find case after case of mayhem, and near-mayhem, involving the "law-abiding citizens" who have been given concealed weapon permits. I could probably devote the next twenty pages to describing these incidents, but restraint is clearly called for. Permit me, however, to share a few examples—my own version of the NRA magazine's longtime feature, "The Armed Citizen":

- Clinton Grainger of Seattle, who had received his CCW license a year before, brought a Glock 19 handgun and 15 rounds of ammunition to the Northwest Folklife Festival. After he got into an altercation with another man, he fired a single bullet that passed through the man's nasal cavity, went through a second victim's wrist, and lodged in a third victim's leg. Grainger was a diagnosed schizophrenic who had been enrolled in a methadone maintenance program.[93]
- Charles Johnson, a concealed carry licensee, took three guns into Doctors Hospital in Columbus, Georgia, where his mother had died of natural causes. He shot an intensive care nurse and an administrative assistant inside the hospital and shot a seventy-six-year-old man in the parking lot.[94]
- A road rage incident in Orange County, Florida, between Louis Davis and Victor Vilchez, both holders of concealed carry licenses, resulted in an exchange of gunfire in a residential neighborhood. Davis, who was taking his six- and eleven-year-old daughters to elementary school, began firing at Vilchez, who returned fire. Davis dropped his daughters off and continued to pursue Vilchez until Vilchez crashed into a passing vehicle.[95]
- Enraged by the fireworks set off at a neighbor's party, Terrence Hough Jr., a Cleveland, Ohio, concealed carry license holder, confronted his neighbors with a handgun. He opened fire on the guests, killing three and wounding two others. Police seized twelve other firearms from Hough's home.[96]
- Tulsa, Oklahoma, resident Harold Glover, who became a CCW permit holder shortly after that state's law went into effect, shot and killed Cecil Herndon at a day-care center, as 250 children looked on. Glover and Herndon argued about who would take their four-year-old grandson home, when Glover pulled out his .357 magnum and shot Herndon in the chest. Glover claimed that Herndon had threatened him with a pocketknife, but authorities determined that Herndon was not acting in a "life-threatening" manner.[97]
- Five men, all holding valid concealed weapon permits, got into an argument outside Big Willy's Saloon in Baldwin, Pennsylvania. Shots were fired, and five people were injured, two critically. Five guns were recovered at the scene.[98]
- Seventy-six-year-old Clay "Junior" Wallace, an Arkansas CCW permit holder, shot and killed Robert Qualls, sixty-five, after an argument over new sewer service for the town of Black Oak. The two men had been arguing inside Vera's Café and went outside to settle the argument with

fists. After being knocked to the ground twice, Wallace pulled out a .38-caliber revolver and shot Qualls twice in the stomach, killing him.[99]

- One day after his wife filed for a protective order against him after months of domestic abuse, Carlton Evans of Seattle applied for and was granted a Washington State concealed weapons permit. Less than two months later Evans killed his wife and baby.[100]
- Robert Herndon, a Florida CCW holder, gunned down popular Aventura, Florida, surgeon Dr. Bradley Silverman outside his office. Florida's concealed weapons statute allowed him a permit even though he had been twice charged with assault (the charges had been either dropped or reduced to a misdemeanor), had threatened his neighbors with a gun, and had voluntarily committed himself to a mental institution.[101]
- Naveed Afzal Haq, who had been issued a concealed carry license despite his history of mental illness and a pending charge of lewd conduct, opened fire at the Jewish Federation of Greater Seattle, killing one woman and wounding five others.[103]

Remember, these are the people who, according to the NRA, are supposed to be making this a more polite society by lawfully carrying hidden handguns in public. How could "law-abiding citizens" cause such havoc? According to Wayne LaPierre, "Good people make good decisions. That's why they're good people."[104] Of course, it is obvious that some people we thought were "good" do, in fact, make bad decisions. When they make those decisions with guns in public places, there is big trouble.

People who carry concealed weapons outside the home also can endanger public safety without ever pulling the trigger. One of the least-noticed problems posed by more handguns in public places is the increased risk of theft, particular theft of guns from cars. In 2002 research by the *Orlando Sentinel* found that 193 of 680 guns reported stolen in Orange County were taken from parked cars.[105] By definition, stolen guns become part of the illegal market. It stands to reason that increasing the number of people who carry hidden handguns inevitably increases the number of targets of opportunity for thieves eager to traffic their newly found guns to violent criminals.

Of course the proponents of concealed carry can no doubt cite their own list of instances where truly law-abiding citizens thwarted a criminal attack with a hidden handgun. The issue, however, is not whether concealed weapons can be successfully deployed in self-defense in public places. After all, the "may issue" states recognize that some concealed carry of firearms can be justified. The issue is whether it is good public policy to require the police to issue CCW permits to anyone who can pass a criminal background check or whether the police should have the freedom to assess the risk that the permit applicant will be subject to violent attack, as well as the risk that the applicant himself will misuse the gun.

Accurately separating the good guys who should get a license from the bad guys who should be denied has proved to be challenging. A *Los Angeles Times* exposé showed that, in the first five years the Texas "shall issue" law was in effect, more than four hundred people were licensed despite prior criminal convictions and more than three thousand other licensees had been arrested.[106] It took some digging for the *Times* to uncover these facts. Texas authorities do not release the names of licensees who run afoul of the law.

In 2006 the South Florida *Sun-Sentinel* obtained the database of Florida CCW holders just before the effective date of a new law sought by the NRA barring disclosure of those names. When the newspaper compared the names to available criminal records, it found the CCW holders included over 200 people with active arrest warrants, 128 people with domestic violence restraining orders against them, and 1,400 people who had pled guilty or no-contest to felony charges.[107] Among the "law-abiding citizens" who the state of Florida issued licenses to carry concealed weapons were:

- Adel Ahmad, a Tampa pizza deliveryman, who kept his CCW license for four years even though he was wanted by police for shooting and killing a teenage boy over a stolen order of chicken wings.
- Lyglenson Lemorin of Miami, who was a valid CCW holder in 2006 when he was arrested with six other South Florida men on terrorism conspiracy charges involving a plot to blow up buildings in Miami and Chicago, including the Sears Tower.
- Nathaniel Ferguson of Lake Mary, who still had a concealed weapons license after he pleaded no contest to attempted manslaughter charges for shooting a woman in a parking lot outside a Seminole County bar.
- Barry Cogen of Sunrise, who was arrested for aggravated stalking *the day after he obtained his concealed weapons permit in 2005.*
- Robert Rodriguez of Tampa, a bar owner who held a CCW permit in 2005 *despite having been arrested 22 times between 1960 and 1998.*

The underlying premise of "shall issue" laws is that there is a public benefit to increasing the number of citizens without criminal records who carry guns because prospective criminals will be deterred by the prospect of armed resistance. Given that the number of high-risk licensees will always be a minority of the total number of licensees, it may be that the deterrent effect of all those law-abiding people carrying loaded handguns will outweigh the added risk from sometimes putting guns in the hands of dangerous people and turning them loose on the streets. We have seen, however, that the available evidence provides no support for the deterrent value of gun ownership per se. Nevertheless, there have been some dramatic claims of crime deterrence made on behalf of "shall issue" concealed carry laws. That brings us to the saga of John Lott.

MORE GUNS, A LOTT OF CRIME

The August 2, 1996, edition of *USA Today*, under the headline "Fewer Rapes, Killings Found Where Concealed Guns Legal," reported the results of a new "comprehensive" study showing that "shall issue" concealed carry laws were associated with substantial decreases in homicides, rapes, and aggravated assaults. The study, by economists John Lott and David Mustard of the University of Chicago, was imposing indeed: it analyzed crime statistics in the nation's 3,054 counties from 1977 to 1992. It was unveiled six days later at a conference hosted by the Cato Institute, a Washington, D.C., libertarian think tank with a long history of opposing gun control. Later published in the January 1997 *Journal of Legal Studies*, the Lott/Mustard study made the remarkable claim that had all states adopted "shall issue" laws by 1992, 1,500 murders would have been avoided annually, along with 4,000 rapes, 11,000 robberies, and 60,000 aggravated assaults.[108] Lott then published a book based on his study, audaciously entitled *More Guns, Less Crime.*

The Lott study was an adrenaline shot for the NRA's concealed weapons campaign. For the first time, the gun lobby and its allies could give a quasi-scholarly veneer to its claim that criminals would be deterred by the fear of gun-carrying law-abiding citizens.

From the beginning, however, other researchers found Lott's work deeply flawed. As with Kleck's estimate of defensive gun uses, there has been a feeding frenzy of scholarly criticism. More than a dozen researchers have attacked Lott's study in at least eight published articles.[109]

First, like Kleck's survey, Lott's study yields results that make no sense in terms of what we know about crime, and even in terms of the deterrence theory itself. For example, we would expect that the deterrent effect of carrying concealed handguns in public places to be greatest for predatory crimes between strangers occurring in public places, like robbery. Yet Lott's data showed the strongest deterrent effects of "shall issue" laws were for crimes that are less likely to involve predatory criminals in public places, such as rape, aggravated assault, and murder. Most rapes, for instance, are committed in homes by someone known to the victim. Aggravated assaults also usually involve people who know each other.[110] Yet Lott's study found greater deterrent effects of concealed carry for those crimes than for robbery.[111] Indeed, other researchers using Lott's data have found no statistically significant impact on robbery rates at all from "shall issue" laws.[112] The absence of an effect on robbery does much to destroy the theory that more law-abiding citizens carrying concealed guns in public deter crime.

Just as puzzling is Lott's finding that "shall issue" laws, while decreasing the incidence of murder and rape, actually increase the incidence of property crimes, like larceny and auto theft. Lott concluded that criminals who were deterred from committing violent crimes by the prospect of an armed victim switched to property crimes not involving contact with victims.[113] But as one researcher asked, "Does anyone really believe that auto theft is a substitute for rape and murder?"[114]

Because all of the "shall issue" laws have minimum age requirements for carrying concealed weapons, their beneficial effect should be felt primarily among adults, if those laws deter murder as Lott concludes. But other researchers using Lott's data have found that, if anything, "shall issue" laws have resulted in an *increase* in adult homicide rates.[115] Researchers also have found, within Lott's data, wild disparities in results between states, and within states, that are difficult for the deterrence theory to explain. Professors Dan Black and Daniel Nagin did a reanalysis of Lott's data revealing that, following the enactment of "shall issue" laws, "murders decline in Florida but increase in West Virginia. Assaults fall in Maine but increase in Pennsylvania. Nor are the estimates consistent within states. Murders increase, but rapes decrease in West Virginia."[116] Indeed, the Black/Nagin reanalysis generated estimates that "shall issue" laws were associated with a 105 percent increase in murder in West Virginia, but with a 67 percent decline in aggravated assault in Maine.[117] Only by masking these unexplainable disparities does Lott support his thesis that "shall issue" laws deter violent crime. Black and Nagin also discovered that if the single state of Florida is omitted from the data, the evidence of an impact on homicides and rapes completely disappears.[118] Where is the deterrent effect in all the other states?

Lott's statistical model yielded other results that are simply bizarre. For example, his data suggested that high numbers of middle-aged and elderly black women are associated with high homicide rates, though such people are rarely either perpetrators or victims of homicide.[119] His results also showed that increasing the rate of unemployment and reducing income will significantly *reduce* the rate of violent crime.[120] Such wacky results leave us with little confidence in the validity of any of Lott's findings.

Lott's study is essentially a comparison of crime rates in the states that adopted "shall issue" laws between 1985 and 1992 with those in the states that did not. As multiple scholars have pointed out, the core problem with the study is that the ten states Lott examined that enacted "shall issue" laws during those years were states, such as Maine, West Virginia, Mississippi, Montana, and Virginia, that are more rural than the states that did not adopt those laws, such as New York, New Jersey, California, and Illinois. Lott's study also encompasses a period when a wave of violent crime, particularly homicide, was sweeping the nation. This wave, most criminologists agree, was fueled by the crack cocaine epidemic, and it was concentrated among adolescents and young adults in urban areas. That crime wave peaked in 1993. Unless factors like drug use were controlled for, any study of an anticrime measure enacted largely in rural states during that period would likely show misleadingly positive results relative to the more urban states that did not adopt it. Other researchers have noted that Lott's study did not control for variables like gangs, drug consumption, and illegal gun carrying that could have accounted for his results.[121] Even Gary Kleck has recognized that "more likely, the declines in crime coinciding with relaxation of carry laws were largely attributable to other factors not controlled for in the Lott and Mustard analysis."[122]

If we look at later years, when the urban crime wave receded and violent crime began to plummet nationally, we see a different story emerge about the "shall issue" CCW states. Lott's study period ended in 1992. From 1992 to 1998 violent crime began an impressive decline nationally, and the violent crime rate in the states that did not adopt "shall issue" laws fell twice as fast as in the "shall issue" states.[123] Even more telling, the robbery rate in the states that did not change their laws fell 44 percent from 1992 to 1998, where the robbery rate in the "shall issue" states fell only 24 percent.[124] Again, if the deterrent effect of "shall issue" laws had any validity, it would be the greatest for robbery, leaving Lott grasping for an explanation of how the "shall issue" states could do so much worse in preventing robberies than the states that chose to fight crime in other ways.

The work of Yale professor John Donahue is perhaps the most devastating to Lott. Donahue simply extended Lott's statistical model through 1997, a period during which thirteen additional states, relying in part on Lott's study, adopted "shall issue" laws. Donahue found that "shall-issue laws are associated with uniform *increases* in crime [emphasis in original]."[125] This helps to explain why, during a period of generally decreasing violent crime in the 1990s, the states with "shall issue" laws lagged behind the other states in fighting crime.

Florida is an interesting case in point. The NRA touts the state as having a "model law" that inspired the national movement toward "shall issue" CCW laws.[126] According to the NRA, Florida has issued more concealed weapon licenses than any other state.[127] From 1987, when Florida passed its law, to 2004, Florida's violent crime rate fell over 30 percent, a fact often cited by the gun lobby. Nevertheless, *in every year during the period 1987 through 2004, the state has ranked either first or second in the nation in violent crime.*[128] Yes, Florida's violent crime rate has fallen, but clearly violent crime has fallen at least as fast across the nation. Many factors affect violent crime, but one thing is clear: despite the NRA's "model law," Florida has consistently remained one of the most violent states in the nation. A study of the effect of the Florida "shall issue" law found that increases in the number of concealed weapons permits were associated with *increases* in robbery rates, a finding that the researchers found "decisively undercuts Lott and Mustard's thesis that criminals are deterred from attacking victims in public places because they fear confronting armed victims."[129]

It's safe to say that the research community has left Lott's study in tatters. Lott, however, has been undeterred. When the best-selling book *Freakonomics* reported that other scholars had tried to replicate Lott's results and instead found that CCW laws don't reduce crime, Lott sued one of its authors, economist Steven Leavitt, for defamation and sought a court injunction against continued sale of the book.[130]

Indeed, so committed is he to his "more guns = less crime" conclusion that Lott repeatedly has argued that the solution to school shootings is (believe it or not) more guns in schools. He advocates abandoning our gun-free schools policy and arming the teachers.[131] No longer would violent kids have to get guns from home to murder their classmates. The guns would already be at school.

It's difficult to be more extreme than the NRA on a gun issue, but Lott has done it. After the Columbine shootings, the NRA's Wayne LaPierre endorsed the policy of "no guns in America's schools, period, with the rare exception of law enforcement officers or trained security personnel."[132] Lott has criticized the NRA for being "too defensive" about guns in schools.[133] Not only should teachers be armed, he says, but people with concealed carry permits should be able to bring guns onto school grounds.[134]

THERE'S SOMETHING ABOUT MARY

It turns out, though, that Lott's statistical errors and rank extremism are the least of his problems. He also occupies the realm of the truly weird.

John Lott has had his defenders. Among his most passionate fans was an Internet blogger named Mary Rosh, who identified herself as a former student of Lott's at the Wharton School at the University of Pennsylvania in the early 1990s. He was, according to Mary, "the best professor I ever had."[135] She told an endearing anecdote about "a group of us students who would try to take any class that he taught. Lott finally had to tell us that it was best for us to try and take classes from other professors to be more exposed to other ways of teaching graduate material." How magnanimous of him.

Rosh also had posted on Amazon.com a rave review of Lott's book, *More Guns, Less Crime.* In it, she gushed, "If you want to learn about what can stop crime or if you want to learn about many of the myths involving crime that endanger people's lives, this is the book to get." She found the book "very interesting reading" because "Lott writes very well. . . . He explains things in an understandable commonsense way." She said she had loaned out her copy of the book a dozen times, and "while it may have taken some effort to get people started on the book, once they read it no one was disappointed." Rosh obviously was quite knowledgeable about gun research, pointing out that Lott's book "is by far the largest most comprehensive study on crime, let alone on gun control," because "Lott examined 54,000 observations and the previous largest study looked at 170 observations." She added, "No previous study had accounted for even a small fraction of the variables that he accounted for." I doubt John Lott could have put it better himself.

Actually, I know John Lott could not have put it better himself because it turns out Mary Rosh *was* John Lott. That's right. Professor Lott had created a fictional former student whose raison d'etre was to say admiring things about John Lott on the Internet. Lott sent Mary into pitched battle with his Internet detractors. It all gets downright creepy when you review Mary's musings, knowing that it was Lott himself at the keyboard. For example, at one point Mary expresses her empathy for the unfair suffering inflicted on Lott by his detractors. "I had Lott as a professor in the early 1990s and he was always very nice and fair to people," she wrote. "I can only imagine the type of hell that you all put him through if you were indeed publishing these reports without first at least asking him for comment."

Rosh would be defending her former professor to this day had Lott's ruse not been exposed in 2003 by fellow blogger Julian Sanchez, who, surprisingly, was with the Cato Institute.[136] Sanchez had been one of the bloggers contributing to the online discussion of Lott and his work and had noticed certain oddities in the postings by Rosh. Sanchez, revealing impressive skills as a cyberdetective, compared the IP address on one of

Rosh's comments to the one on an e-mail Lott had sent him from his home. They were identical. Lott was busted. On January 22, 2003, Rosh uttered her last words, an admission that she and John Lott were one and the same. She had lived by the blogosphere, and she died by the blogosphere.

Lott later explained that "Mary Rosh" was "a pen name account . . . created years ago for . . . my children, using the first two letters of the names of my four sons." In perhaps the first understatement ever associated with John Lott, he added, "I shouldn't have used it."[137] Why did he do it? In a letter to *Science* magazine, he explained that he "used a pseudonym" on the Internet because "earlier postings under my own name elicited threatening and obnoxious telephone calls."[138] By referring to Mary Rosh as a "pseudonym," Lott shows an odd detachment from his own actions. As *Science* editor in chief Donald Kennedy responded, "Lott cannot dismiss his use of a fictitious ally as a 'pseudonym.' What he did was to construct a false identity for a scholar, whom he then deployed in repeated support of his positions and in repeated attacks on his opponents."[139] Even if Lott had received "threatening" phone calls (a reality that gun control advocates have long learned to live with), this is not a credible excuse for constructing an imaginary person whose mission in life is to praise the brilliance of John Lott.

It is difficult to get beyond the abject strangeness of it all to come to grips with the implications of Mary Rosh for Lott's credibility as a scientist. To put it mildly, this is not the behavior of an objective scientist seeking to uncover the truth. It is certainly not the behavior of a scholar who can be expected to give due and serious consideration to critiques of his work by other scholars. Rather, Lott clearly sees himself as a participant in a grand ideological struggle in which his role is to promote, by any means necessary (including the invention of fictitious supporters), the idea that more guns make us safer.

The real problem with Mary Rosh is that she was, purely and simply, a fraud. When Lott had Rosh speak, he wanted her readers to believe she was a real person, a knowledgeable, articulate person who gave independent validation of Lott's work. "I believe Lott," he has her say at one point. With every word she said, Lott was intentionally perpetrating a falsehood. If Lott was willing to invent Mary Rosh, what else is he willing to invent in order to support his case for "more guns, less crime"?

THE 98 PERCENT SOLUTION

It turns out that Lott's casual relationship with the truth has taken a far more serious turn.

In the first edition of *More Guns, Less Crime*, published in May 1998, Lott asserted, citing "national surveys," that "98 percent of the time that people use guns defensively, they merely have to brandish a weapon to break off an attack."[140] He had made a similar claim in a July 1997 *Wall Street Journal* opinion piece, in which he cited as sources "polls by the *Los Angeles Times*, Gallup and Peter Hart Research Associates."[141] A similar statement also appeared in his August 1998 op-ed in the *Chicago Tribune*. Lott wrote, "Polls by the *Los Angeles Times*, Gallup and Peter Hart Research Associates show that there are at least 760,000, and possibly as many as 3.6 million, defensive uses of guns per year. In 98 percent of the cases, *such polls show* [emphasis added], people simply brandish the weapon to stop an attack."[142]

This is a startling assertion and an important one in the gun debate. When considering whether to make it easier for greater numbers of people to legally carry hidden handguns in public, it is reassuring for policymakers to hear of seemingly objective data purporting to show that virtually all defensive gun uses involve law-abiding citizens waving guns around at criminals, instead of starting shootouts at the local shopping mall.

The problem is that no polls by the *Los Angeles Times*, Gallup, or Peter Hart address the percentage of self-defense uses that involve firing a weapon. Lott was first challenged on his sources by University of California–Santa Barbara sociologist Otis Dudley Duncan, writing in *The Criminologist* of January 2000.[143] Duncan noted that the surveys that had addressed the issue had yielded results "radically inconsistent with Lott's claim that 98% of defenders 'merely brandish' their weapons."[144] Once challenged, Lott changed his story. In a response to Duncan, Lott repeated the statistic, but this time cited his own telephone survey "conducted over 3 months during 1997."[145] Lott said he would have discussed the survey in the 1998 edition of his book, "but did not do so because an unfortunate computer crash lost my hard disk right before the final draft of the book had to be turned in."[146] Whereas the first edition of Lott's book had cited "national surveys," the second edition, published in 2000, relied on "a national survey I conducted."[147] During 1997 and 1998, Lott's op-ed pieces had cited nonexistent surveys as his source, never mentioning his own 1997 survey.

This was enough to arouse the interest of Northwestern University law professor James Lindgren. Lindgren had been instrumental in bringing about the demise of Emory University historian Michael Bellesiles, author of the prize-winning book *Arming America: The Origins of a National Gun Culture*. Lindgren had challenged the integrity of Bellesiles's use of probate records to support his surprising thesis that gun ownership was far from common in eighteenth- and nineteenth-century America. Bellesiles had been unable to produce all of his underlying data, claiming it had been lost to a flood in his office. Lott's tale of a computer crash seemed eerily similar.

Lott claimed that he surveyed 2,424 people in 1997, but when Lindgren pressed him for any material still in existence on the survey, Lott had nothing.[148] He had no records related to the funding of the survey, the student volunteers he used to do the survey, the expenses of the survey, or the survey instrument itself. As Lindgren commented on his website, "all evidence of a study with 2,400 respondents does not just disappear when a computer crashes."[149] One person, a prominent pro-gun activist, has come forward to say he believes he had participated in Lott's 1997 survey. He claims that after hearing Lott refer to the 98 percent figure in a 1999 speech, he realized that he had participated in whatever survey produced that figure.[150] This would mean that a random sample of 2,400 out of 300 million Americans questioned on a gun issue happened to include one of the most prominent pro-gun activists in the country and that the one person to come forward to corroborate Lott's claim coincidentally is a pro-gun activist.[151] Lott's computer may well have crashed (apparently he told others about the crash at the time), but considerable doubt has been raised about whether the 1997 survey ever occurred.

Lott finally has been disowned by some of his natural allies, such as conservative columnist Michelle Malkin, who has written of Lott's "extensive willingness to deceive to protect and promote his work."[152] *Science* editor in chief Kennedy reminds us of the seriousness of Lott's deceptions. In an editorial on Lott entitled "Research Fraud and Public Policy," Kennedy writes, "Death by shooting is a national public health problem. Sound social science, not cooked data, is what we need to work out the tough problems like the relationship between gun ownership and violent crime."[153]

In the final analysis, the gun lobby is pushing the country toward a high-risk strategy of fighting crime through the proliferation of guns. More guns in more homes. More guns on more streets. More guns anywhere people gather. There is no sound social science supporting this strategy. Its most prominent advocate has been thoroughly discredited.

The nations with more guns are not safer. The states with more guns are not safer. The homes with more guns are not safer.

In an armed society, people are not more polite. They are simply more fearful, and with very good reason.

5.

"WE DON'T NEED NEW GUN LAWS. WE NEED TO ENFORCE THE LAWS WE HAVE."

THIS IS A RELATIVE newcomer to the gun lobby's parade of aphorisms, adages, sayings, and slogans. It was first unveiled during the Clinton administration following the NRA's stinging defeats in Congress on the Brady Bill and the assault weapons ban. The slogan was cleverly designed to communicate the message that President Clinton is a hypocrite on the gun issue because he supports new gun laws but cares nothing about enforcing them once they are enacted. As we will see, the slogan was not nearly as serviceable for the NRA when its guy was in the White House. Though its utility faded during the Bush years, it is still firmly enshrined as a leading talking point for every pro-gun activist and politician. Five years after Clinton left office, then-senator George Allen (R-Virginia), an NRA "A-rated" legislator, dutifully recited it on the floor of the Senate: "The best gun control measures are to enforce existing gun laws, which do more to keep illegal guns out of the hands of criminals than passing new and additional burden[s] on the sale of firearms to honest gun-owners."[1]

As discussed earlier, the NRA has always taken the view that the panacea for criminal gun violence is to severely punish gun criminals after the fact. If the problem is criminals committing violent crimes with guns, the solution is to lock them up for those crimes and throw away the key. For the NRA, punishment is the only prevention. The gun lobby has long assailed the criminal justice system, including its "bleeding-heart, criminal coddling judges and prosecutors," in the words of Marion Hammer, the NRA's Florida lobbyist and former president.[2] So what was new about the NRA's call for "enforcing current laws" instead of passing new ones?

SUPPORT ENFORCEMENT—DESTROY THE ENFORCERS

The new wrinkle was that the NRA's attack involved the alleged failure to enforce *federal* gun laws. The NRA was calling for stronger *federal* enforcement of gun laws by the Clinton administration. What's wrong with this picture?

In his 1994 book, *Guns, Crime and Freedom*, Wayne LaPierre had this to say about the Bureau of Alcohol, Tobacco and Firearms, the agency that enforces federal gun laws: "If I were to select a jack-booted group of fascists who were perhaps as large a danger to American society as I could pick today, I would pick BATF. They are a shame and a disgrace to our country."[3] LaPierre was actually quoting Congressman John Dingell (D-Michigan), who was an NRA board member at the time he made the statement. Dingell said it in 1982. For years, the NRA had been attacking the ATF—not for its failure to enforce the law, but for enforcing the law too aggressively.

The NRA's attack on the Clinton administration and ATF for overly aggressive enforcement reached a fever pitch after the raid on the Branch Davidian compound in Waco, Texas, by ATF and other federal law enforcement agents in February 1993. ATF acted based on evidence that David Koresh and his followers had illegally amassed dozens of machine guns, unlawfully converted by the Davidians from semiautomatic assault weapons. The Feds were attempting to serve a lawful search warrant on Koresh, when his followers opened fire, killing four federal agents and wounding sixteen others. Agents later found forty-eight illegal machine guns in the compound, along with sixty-one AK-47 assault rifles, thirteen shotguns, two .50-caliber rifles, and millions of rounds of ammunition.[4] As is well-known, the initial exchange of gunfire was followed by a fifty-one-day siege, ended by the final operation against the Davidians by federal authorities on April 19, 1993, during which the compound erupted in a horrific fire, killing scores of those inside.

Obviously much could be, and was, criticized about the tactics of federal agents during the Waco operation. But supporters of strong enforcement of federal gun laws could be expected to at least recognize the importance of enforcing the federal machine gun ban, particularly against a group suspected of building an arsenal of illegal machine guns. The NRA, however, would have been quite content to allow Koresh and his followers to flout federal law and continue to stockpile illegal machine guns. According to Wayne LaPierre, the Branch Davidians were simply a "religious cult of men, women, and children, who grew their own food, taught their own children, and pretty much stayed to themselves."[5] The Davidians, LaPierre wrote, were being investigated for "technical violations" of federal gun laws.[6]

FIGURE 5.1
NRA AD, *WASHINGTON POST*, MARCH 1, 1995

LaPierre apparently was untroubled by the murder of federal agents. His message: they brought it on themselves. "The government agents in charge knew there were firearms in the compound—the 'alleged' type of firearms is what the charade was all about. Did they expect to charge the farm house and not a shot be fired?"[7] The plain meaning of this statement is that the NRA condones the murder of federal agents by persons suspected of violating federal gun laws. If the ATF tries to enforce the law against armed violators, it does so at its own risk. This is the same NRA that says we need to more vigorously enforce federal gun laws.

The ugliness of the NRA's post-Waco rhetoric is now the stuff of legend. It called ATF an "unchecked, renegade federal power."[8] It warned that federal "agents clad in ninja black" were launching "heavy-handed raids against law-abiding citizens,"[9] using "reckless, storm-trooper tactics."[10] It ran full-page ads in the *Washington Post* and *USA Today* calling ATF a "rogue agency" with "a tyrannical record of misconduct and abuse of power" that "deserves public contempt." The NRA told its members that ATF agents were engaged in "brutal misconduct" and threatened ATF to back off or be destroyed—"We plan to challenge its existence."[11]

NRA supporters were whipped into an ATF-hating frenzy. On NRA electronic bulletin boards, its members lashed out. NRA board member Harry Thomas sent this threat of violence to Attorney General Janet Reno: "If you send your jackbooted, baby-burning bushwhackers to confiscate guns, pack them a lunch. The Branch Davidians were amateurs. I'm a professional."[12] Another post on the NRA's electronic bulletin board stated, "If the Republicans will not disband the ATF or demand the head of Reno, it might be time for armed conflict over the desecration of the Bill of Rights."[13] The electronic bulletin board featured a recipe for building a homemade bomb with baby food containers and shotgun shells.[14]

In a now-infamous fundraising letter, on April 13, 1995, Wayne LaPierre warned his members about murderous federal agents: "Jack-booted government thugs [have] more power to take away our Constitutional rights, break in our doors, seize our guns, destroy our property, and even injure or kill us. . . . . If you have a badge, you have the government's go-ahead to harass, intimidate, even murder law-abiding citizens. . . . Not too long ago, it was unthinkable for federal agents wearing nazi bucket helmets and black storm trooper uniforms to attack law-abiding citizens. Not today, not with Clinton."[15] Six days later, as NRA members found the fund-raising letter in their mail, Timothy McVeigh bombed the Murrah Federal Building in Oklahoma City. McVeigh acted on the second anniversary of the fire at the Branch Davidian compound. The Murrah Building contained the offices of ATF agents, as well as other federal agencies. When he was apprehended that same day, McVeigh had in his possession a plain white envelope packed with articles on the Waco siege. The articles referred to federal agents as "Gestapo" or "Terrorist Goon Squads," [16] strikingly similar to the Nazi references in LaPierre's fund-raising letter. It is chilling to read the passage in LaPierre's 1994 book condoning the violence against federal agents at Waco, knowing of the violence to come in Oklahoma City.

Later it was discovered that McVeigh had written his congressman complaining about "firearm restrictions" in a letter stamped with an "I'm the NRA" logo.[17] During the siege of the Branch Davidian compound, he traveled to Waco, where he passed out bumper stickers condemning gun control and the enforcers of gun control laws. The bumper stickers featured such slogans as "Fear the government that fears your gun" and "When guns are outlawed, I will become an outlaw."[18] At gun shows, he wore and sold ATF baseball caps, punctured with two bullet holes.[19] McVeigh had completely absorbed the NRA ideology that saw gun control laws as tyrannical and ATF, as their enforcers, as the agents of tyranny. When he committed the worst terrorist act to that point in U.S. history, McVeigh was acting out the hate-filled anti-ATF rhetoric of the NRA.

McVeigh also was acting out the NRA's long-held, but utterly perverse "insurrectionist" view of the Second Amendment, in which the Constitution, the charter of our government, guarantees a right to destroy the government.[20] As an NRA lawyer had once put it in a law journal article entitled, "The Second Amendment Ain't About Hunting," for the NRA the right to bear arms is "directed at maintaining an armed citizenry . . . to protect against the tyranny of our own government."[21] An NRA field representative, somewhat more colorfully, told the *New York Times*, "The Second Amendment . . . is literally a loaded gun in the hands of the people held to the heads of government."[22] The NRA long had asserted the right to use violence as a tool of political dissent. Timothy McVeigh, tragically, took the gun lobby's constitutional theory to its logical conclusion.

The NRA's incendiary antigovernment rhetoric, followed by mass murder by a rabid pro-gun true believer, was too much for some loyal NRA supporters to bear. President George H. W. Bush, who had threatened to veto the Brady Bill in 1991, resigned his life membership in the organization, calling the NRA's statements against federal law enforcement a "vicious slander on good people" and a "broadside against federal agents [that] offends my own sense of decency and honor."[23] Republican leaders in Congress ran quickly from the NRA's legislative agenda, dropping their plans to repeal the 1994 assault weapons ban.

WHICH GUN LAWS SHOULD WE ENFORCE?

You have to give the NRA points for chutzpah. Barely two years after savaging ATF for enforcing federal gun laws, the NRA launched its new campaign to savage the Clinton administration for not enforcing federal gun laws. The same Wayne LaPierre who in 1995 pledged to challenge the existence of ATF in 1997 wrote, "It's a moral crime for Bill Clinton, Al Gore and Janet Reno and a host of Federal officers and prosecutors to fail to enforce the law. It's evil. And when innocent blood flows, it's on their hands."[24]

How can LaPierre believe it is a "moral crime" to fail to enforce the law, when he so easily dismissed the Branch Davidians' illegal machine guns as "technical violations" of the law? It turns out that the NRA is quite selective about the gun laws it wants enforced.

In its zeal to attack the Clinton administration, the NRA focused on the administration's record prosecuting felons caught in possession of firearms. It had long been a criminal violation for a felon to possess guns. Wayne LaPierre charged that President Clinton and Attorney General Reno had "blood . . . on their hands" for failing to prosecute these cases:

> Almost uniformly, the Clinton Administration has refused to use the powerful, existing Federal firearms laws to arrest and prosecute armed, convicted, violent felons.
>
> The result of that refusal to enforce existing Federal law against violent career criminals has created a horrible waste of innocent lives. Thousands of our citizens have been robbed, maimed or murdered because Bill Clinton and Janet Reno have not met their duty to enforce the law.[25]

LaPierre also accused the Clinton administration of failing to prosecute the felons who try to buy guns from dealers but are denied because of Brady background checks. "Under the Brady Act, [Bill Clinton] turns criminals away. He doesn't arrest them."[26]

The critique of the Clinton administration for failing to bring cases based on Brady purchase denials is heavy with irony. It is true that any prospective gun purchaser turned away because of a Brady background check could potentially be prosecuted for falsely claiming on a federal form that he was not a felon or member of any other prohibited class of gun buyers. However, it is only because of the Brady Act (or state background check laws) that those potential criminal cases are even identifiable. Before Brady, those felons and other prohibited buyers would have lied on the federal form and the authorities would never have known. The NRA, of course, fought tenaciously to defeat the Brady Bill and mourned its passage. "When Bill Clinton signed the Brady Bill," the NRA wrote with its usual restraint, "a drop of blood dripped from the finger of the sovereign American citizen."[27] After the bill became law, the NRA gave financial support for multiple lawsuits seeking to strike down the new law, ultimately filing a brief in the U.S. Supreme Court expressly asking the Court to void the entire statute.[28] Yet, without apparent embarrassment, the NRA accused the Clinton administration of having "blood on its hands" because it failed to bring federal prosecutions *that only the Brady Act made possible.*

In charging the Clinton administration with criminal neglect for failing to prosecute "felon-in-possession" cases, the NRA ignored the fact that felons in possession of guns also violate state gun laws and that the vast majority of those prosecutions traditionally had been brought at the state level. Indeed, from 1992 to 1996 combined federal and state gun convictions rose by 22 percent, during a period when gun crime was going down.[29] When it slammed the Feds for not prosecuting every felon-in-possession case, the NRA was really calling for the federalization of gun crime enforcement (i.e., federal prosecution of crimes that previously had been prosecuted by the states). In this regard, its model was a new program in Richmond, Virginia, called Project Exile.

Project Exile, unveiled in February 1997, consisted of a coordinated effort of Richmond law enforcement and the regional U.S. Attorney's Office to prosecute in federal (instead of state) court all cases involving felons in possession of firearms.[30] It was augmented by a massive local advertising campaign sending a message of zero tolerance for gun offenses. In effect, Exile was a sentence enhancement program since the federal penalties for such firearm offenses were more severe than Virginia state penalties. The point was to more severely punish, in federal court, felons caught with guns.

Project Exile immediately attracted a broad range of support, including endorsements by both the NRA and the Brady Campaign (then known as Handgun Control, Inc.). The Brady group saw sentence enhancement as one element in a broad attack on criminal gun violence. However, it quickly became clear that the NRA would exploit Project Exile as a new weapon to fight against gun control laws. The NRA argued for Exile as a cure-all for violent gun crime that, if implemented nationally, would make tighter gun laws entirely unnecessary. The Richmond program became the NRA's new talking point to support its "we don't need new laws, we need to enforce existing laws" message.

The NRA made wildly exaggerated claims about Project Exile's importance. Asserting that it had caused the murder rate in Richmond to decline 62 percent, the NRA said that the program was proof that if we "get tough on criminals, not on our right to own guns . . . crime will disappear."[31] Because of Project Exile, the NRA claimed "drug dealers are reportedly disarming themselves" and "if the law were enforced in a widely publicized, wide-ranging effort, criminals would cease to use and possess firearms."[32]

Several observations about Project Exile are worth making at this point in our discussion. First, the program is based on the premise that a criminal armed with a gun is far more dangerous than a criminal armed with another weapon. If this is not true, why have especially harsh punishments for criminals caught with guns, as opposed to baseball bats? This, of course, is an implicit endorsement of the "instrumentality effect," discussed in chapter 1, that so effectively refutes the claim that "Guns don't kill people. People kill people."

Second, it should be noted that the gun lobby did not dream up Project Exile. It was developed under the direction of the U.S. attorney for the Eastern District of Virginia, then Helen Fahey, *who was appointed by President Clinton.* The NRA had adopted, as its own, a program designed and implemented under the auspices of the Clinton Justice Department in order to bolster the argument that the Clinton administration was not enforcing our gun laws. As we have seen, this kind of hypocrisy seldom gives the NRA pause.

Finally, although the utility of Project Exile is still a matter of debate, a panacea it is not. Although the program sharply increased federal gun convictions in Richmond,[33] almost ten years after Project Exile was announced, Richmond ranked as the fifth most dangerous city in America.[34]

When the NRA says we should "enforce existing gun laws instead of passing new ones," it really means that the Feds should prosecute more criminals caught lying by the Brady Act, and more cases of felons caught with guns, instead of passing new laws. When it comes to enforcement of other gun laws, the NRA's enthusiasm wanes. We have seen, for instance, that the NRA was not bothered by the manufacture of illegal machine guns by the Branch Davidians. Indeed, when gun owners defy laws the NRA has opposed, far from expressing outrage at the lawbreakers, it characterizes the illegality as "civil disobedience." Thus when relatively few California gun owners registered their assault weapons as required by that state's landmark assault weapon law, the NRA ran a cover story in its magazine *1st Freedom* asking, in bold type, "Is Massive Civil Disobedience at Hand?"[35] The article stated, "Through confusion or conscious decision, observers say, tens or even hundreds of thousands of Californians . . . may be quietly disobeying" the assault weapon law. It asked, hopefully, "Could this be the most massive act of civil disobedience in our country's history?" The article assured readers that "ignoring the law of the land is never the advocated position of the National Rifle Association."[36] *Advocated* position?

In the NRA's world, one can be a "law-abiding citizen" and still violate a criminal law, as long as it is a gun control law that the NRA does not like. The NRA is not a proponent of respect for the law in general, only for the laws it supports.

And what about gun law enforcement after President George W. Bush took office in 2000 with the strong support of the NRA? It turns out that federal prosecutions of gun buyers for lying on the federal gun purchase form increased all of 0.1 percent from 2000 to 2003. During those years, 566,000 potential buyers falsely claimed on the federal form that they had clean records and were blocked from buying a gun by the Brady law. Only 2,126, or far less than 1 percent, were charged.[37] During the Clinton administration, the failure to prosecute such people drew charges that the president and Janet Reno had "blood on their hands" because they "turn criminals away" instead of arresting them. When over 99 percent of these criminals were "turned away" and not arrested by the Feds during the Bush administration, what was the NRA's response? Silence. No charges that President Bush is "evil," or that he has "blood on his hands," or that he has committed "moral crimes" against the American people. Just silence.

When the Justice Department's inspector general looked at the dearth of Brady Act prosecutions during the Bush years, he concluded that charges were rarely brought because convictions are difficult to obtain. According to the IG, among other factors, it is "difficult to prove that the prohibited person was aware of the prohibition and intentionally lied" to the dealer.[38] (This no doubt also explains why there were so few such prosecutions in the Clinton years.) Did the NRA respond by urging that the proof standard be changed to put more criminals behind bars? Of course not. With the Clinton administration long gone, the issue of Brady Act enforcement had lost its utility to the gun lobby.

SUPPORT ENFORCEMENT, WEAKEN THE GUN CONTROL ACT

As we have seen, the gun laws the NRA actually wants to be enforced are few and far between. As to other gun laws, which it doesn't like, the NRA not only seems untroubled by defiance of the laws, but it also has devoted itself to weakening the laws and making them less enforceable.

The NRA's greatest victory in this arena was its campaign in the 1980s to weaken the 1968 Gun Control Act, which culminated in a set of amendments labeled the Firearm Owners' Protection Act of 1986 (FOPA). The statute actually protects gun dealers, not gun owners, particularly dealers inclined to break the law.

FOPA, for example, created an extraordinarily high proof standard for ATF to prove criminal violations of the Gun Control Act, as well as to revoke the licenses of law-breaking gun dealers. For both, the government must show a "willful" violation of the law, which requires proof not only that the conduct was intentional, but also that the violator had knowledge that his conduct was unlawful.[39] Before FOPA, courts had interpreted federal law to require only a showing that the miscreant dealer had "knowingly" violated the law.[40] Although this required proof that the law violator "knew what he was doing" and thus precluded enforcement against a violator making merely inadvertent mistakes, the "knowing" standard did not demand evidence that he knew his conduct was illegal. In practice, this has meant that ATF has been able to revoke the licenses of rogue gun dealers only rarely, and then only after years of multiple violations of the law.

Take the case of Valley Gun Shop of Baltimore, Maryland, owned and operated by former NRA board member Sandy Abrams. He took over Valley Gun in 1996 and was charged with violating federal gun laws less than a year later. By 2003 ATF had documented over nine hundred violations of federal law by Valley Gun. At one point, ATF found that more than a quarter of the shop's firearms inventory was missing and unaccounted for. Though the Justice Department had labeled Abrams's store a "serial violator" of federal gun laws, ATF was not able to shut it down until 2006. Given the NRA's credo that law-violators should be harshly punished, it is worth noting that after Abrams began compiling his record as a "serial violator" of the law, he was twice reelected to the NRA's Board.[41]

FOPA also helped protect law-breaking dealers by reclassifying violations of federal firearms record-keeping laws as misdemeanors rather than felonies. Although "record-keeping" sounds inherently unimportant, actually these laws are crucial to ATF's law enforcement function. We have noted before that ATF helps to solve crimes by using the unique serial numbers on guns to trace guns used in crime to identify the first retail purchaser. Of course, this can be done only if the dealer has complied with the record-keeping provisions of federal law.

In addition, a failure to comply with record-keeping laws may be the only avenue to prosecute dealers suspected of selling guns off the books to criminals. In a survey of its own trafficking investigations, ATF found that "failure to keep required records was found in almost half of the trafficking investigations involving [federal firearms licensees], and the FFL making false entries in the records was found in almost a fifth of these investigations. These violations are primarily misdemeanors, despite being associated with investigations involving a high volume of trafficked firearms."[42] Since it is difficult to convince a federal prosecutor to bring misdemeanor cases, dealers caught violating federal law by ATF inspectors routinely escape criminal prosecution. And since "willfulness" is the standard for license revocation, scofflaw dealers often are able to both escape criminal prosecution and continue to sell guns.

FOPA also made it less likely that record-keeping violations will be uncovered by limiting ATF to a single, unannounced inspection every twelve months.[43] Thus, once a dealer has been inspected in a given year, he knows he is "free and clear" for another twelve months. ATF has told Congress that this limitation "enables unscrupulous licensees to conceal violations of the law and is an impediment to ensuring compliance with the provisions of the Gun Control Act."[44]

Just as crippling to ATF's enforcement efforts has been the bureau's chronic problem of underfunding, a direct result of the NRA's influence over congressional appropriations. In 2004 the Justice Department's inspector general found that "most [licensed dealers] are inspected infrequently or not at all," a record owing "in part to resource shortfalls."[45] He concluded that, with ATF's limited manpower, "it would take the ATF more than 22 years to inspect all [federal firearms licensees]."

One of the great oddities of federal gun laws is that the federal record documenting gun sales by licensed dealers is, except under certain limited circumstances, *not in the possession of the federal government at all*. The federal Firearms Transaction Record (Form 4473), which reflects the name and address of the purchaser, along with his sworn declaration that he is not legally prohibited from buying firearms, generally remains in the gun shop. This is akin to a requirement that tax returns remain in the possession of taxpayers, but not the government.

The limitation of federal government access to its own gun records is, of course, the handiwork of the NRA. Its paranoia about anything approaching gun "registration" led to language appearing in every ATF appropriations bill since 1979 prohibiting ATF from maintaining and centralizing gun purchase records.[46] FOPA also included a provision preventing ATF from establishing a database of firearms sales records.[47] In the computer age, tracing a gun using its serial number should take seconds. Instead, crime gun tracing is far more cumbersome and time consuming because the NRA-inspired restrictions make it necessary for ATF to ask the dealer for the information on Form 4473 to complete the trace. In addition, since gun dealers are the custodians of these vital records, physical inspection of dealers is an especially critical part of ATF's enforcement program and FOPA's limits on such inspections are that much more objectionable.

FOPA also was responsible for making gun shows an enforcement nightmare for ATF. Before FOPA, dealers had to have a federal firearms license for each location where they sold guns. This effectively barred dealers from selling at temporary locations, including gun shows. FOPA lifted this limitation and allowed dealers to sell at gun shows within the dealer's state. According to ATF, this has led to "a wide range of criminal activity by [federally licensed dealers] . . . and felons conspiring with [gun dealers] at gun shows."[48] For example, in 1994, ATF caught a California dealer who had sold over seventeen hundred firearms over a four-year period without maintaining any records. Many of the sales were at gun shows, with the guns ending up in the hands of gang members in Santa Ana and Long Beach. The guns have since been recovered in investigations of violent crimes, including homicides.[49]

In addition to allowing sales by licensed dealers at gun shows, FOPA made it easier for sellers at gun shows (and elsewhere) to avoid the licensing requirements altogether. The Gun Control Act had required anyone "engaged in the business" of selling firearms to obtain a federal license. FOPA created a new definition of "engaged in the business" that allowed unlicensed sellers to sell their "personal collection" of firearms, no matter how large, without obtaining a license and without doing the Brady background checks on buyers.[50] This new loophole has created a new class of "gun show cowboys" (like Timothy McVeigh) who go from gun show to gun show, always claiming to sell guns from their "personal collections." As we have seen, the Columbine killers exploited this loophole to obtain their guns. According to ATF, the effect of the loophole "has often been to frustrate the prosecution of unlicensed dealers masquerading as collectors or hobbyists but who are really trafficking firearms to felons or other prohibited persons."[51] As noted earlier, ATF's gun-trafficking investigations reveal gun shows to be the second largest source of guns trafficked to criminals (second only to corrupt dealers).[52]

FOPA, then, was a disaster for enforcement of the Gun Control Act and, to this day, handcuffs ATF. For this, we have the NRA to thank, the same NRA that said President Clinton had "blood on his hands" for failing to enforce federal gun laws. As I have noted, FOPA had one salutary provision: its opponents did succeed in adding a floor amendment banning manufacture and sale of new machine guns to civilians. This was the provision David Koresh and his followers violated when they converted their semiautomatic assault weapons into fully automatic rifles. As soon as FOPA passed, the NRA sought repeal of the machine gun freeze[53]—the one provision in FOPA that did not weaken enforcement of federal gun laws.

SUPPORT ENFORCEMENT, WEAKEN THE BRADY ACT

As we have seen, the NRA, without hint of embarrassment, sought to overturn the Brady Act in court and then accused the Clinton administration of malfeasance in failing to enforce that very statute. After failing to destroy the statute in court, the gun lobby has done everything in its power to weaken it.

If the subject is NRA hypocrisy on enforcement issues, the gun lobby's vehement opposition to the Brady Act is particularly instructive. The lesson of the Brady Act is this: *sometimes it is necessary to pass new laws in order to enforce existing laws.* Before Brady was enacted, it already was illegal for felons to buy guns at gun stores. As we have seen, though, that law was difficult to enforce because felons would simply lie about their criminal history and buy their guns. The Brady background check is, in the final analysis, an enforcement tool. It allows the government to enforce the preexisting law against felons buying guns from dealers. For this reason, the Brady Bill was supported by every national police organization. When he gave the Brady Bill a huge boost by announcing his support, former President Ronald Reagan aptly described it as a new "enforcement mechanism" that "can't help but stop thousands of illegal gun purchases."[54] If the NRA had prevailed, "lie and buy" would still be mocking the legal bar on gun sales to criminals.

Having failed to defeat the legislation in Congress, or have it over-turned in court, the NRA has resorted to weakening the Brady Act as an enforcement tool. This is another case where the NRA's paranoia about gun records trumps any pretended support for strong law enforcement. Under the Brady Act's National Instant Criminal Background Check System, once the background check is completed and no disqualifying record is found, "all records of the system relating to the person or the transfer" are destroyed.[55] This record destruction requirement itself was a concession to the gun lobby's friends in Congress who sought to vanquish any hint of gun registration from the Brady Act. (Of course, the provision was not enough to satisfy the NRA, which opposed the bill anyway.) The statute does not, however, specify *when* the background check records must be destroyed. When the Clinton administration quite reasonably adopted the FBI's recommendation that the records be preserved for six months to allow for proper audits of NICS, the NRA charged off to court, seeking an order that the records be destroyed immediately on completion of the background check, because anything less would be equivalent to registration.[56] The U.S. Court of Appeals for the District of Columbia rejected the NRA's argument and the Supreme Court denied review.[57]

Though not legally required to do so, on its own initiative, the Clinton Justice Department then shortened the record retention period from six months to ninety days.[58] This, of course, was not good enough for the gun lobby and its friends in the Bush Justice Department. Under Bush's first attorney general John Ashcroft, the Justice Department instead proposed that the background check records on allowed sales be destroyed *within twenty-four hours of the sale,* citing the need to protect "the privacy interests of law-abiding citizens."[59]

There is no question that the twenty-four-hour rule has helped to arm criminals. Before the new rule went into effect, the General Accounting Office did a study of its likely effect. During the first six months of the Clinton administration's ninety-day retention policy, there were 235 cases in which prohibited gun buyers erroneously cleared the NICS background checks and were allowed to buy guns.[60] Because the records of these erroneous "approvals" had been retained, the FBI was able to discover the errors and retrieve the firearms. According to the GAO, *had the twenty-four-hour record destruction rule been in effect during the period examined, 97 percent of the prohibited buyers would have evaded detection and retained their guns.*[61] Chances are, some of those people would have committed violent crimes with their guns.

The Justice Department's inspector general also found that the twenty-four-hour rule would make it more difficult for the FBI to detect fraud by corrupt dealers seeking to cover up their sales to criminals.[62] Dealers could provide the FBI with a different name than that of the actual buyer to get NICS approval and then complete the sale to the actual prohibited buyer. Destroying the records within twenty-four hours, said the inspector general, would make such a scheme nearly impossible to detect.

The NRA's concern for the rights of "law-abiding citizens" has even extended to suspected terrorists. In 2005 the renamed Government Accountability Office (GAO) published a report revealing that numerous suspected terrorists had purchased firearms from licensed dealers in 2004. Federal law does not preclude known terrorists from buying firearms unless they already have been convicted of a felony or fall into another category of prohibited gun buyers. The GAO found that from February to June 2004, thirty-five persons whose names appeared on terrorist watch list records had cleared the background checks and bought firearms.[63] Following the GAO report, the NRA opposed proposals to strengthen the Brady Act to prevent known and suspected terrorists from buying firearms. Wayne LaPierre explained, "Every citizen is entitled to Constitutional freedoms."[64]

A FALSE CHOICE

Putting aside the NRA's selectivity, inconsistency, and outright hypocrisy in arguing for stronger enforcement of federal gun laws, does its core argument make sense? Even if we could strengthen enforcement of existing federal gun laws, is that a good reason to oppose new federal gun laws?

Public opinion surveys suggest, at first glance, that the NRA has struck a chord with its call for stronger enforcement instead of new laws. According to a Gallup poll taken in October 2006, when faced with a choice between "enforcing current gun laws more strictly and not passing new laws" versus "passing new laws in addition to enforcing current laws more strictly," 53 percent of respondents preferred stronger enforcement and no new laws, while only 43 percent favored new laws in addition to stronger enforcement.[65]

These poll results likely reflect the NRA's skill in framing its message, rather than the public's actual belief that stronger enforcement is a sensible substitute for good laws. Notice that the NRA's theme is "we need to enforce the laws we have, not pass *new* laws." It seems very likely that the polling results would be quite different if the choice presented were stronger enforcement versus "stronger" or "stricter" laws, rather than "new" laws. The public is understandably less than enthusiastic about passing new gun laws for their own sake. The application of a different adjective suggesting that the new gun laws would bring about some desirable change (i.e., stronger laws or stricter laws) likely would yield a higher level of support for the enforcement plus laws alternative. This is especially likely given that the same Gallup survey showed that 56 percent of respondents favor stricter gun laws.[66]

Sure enough, when the National Opinion Research Center at the University of Chicago posed the same question using different language, it got a different result. To the question, "Which of the following options would be most effective in reducing gun violence?" 54 percent of those surveyed said "passing *stricter* gun control laws and strict enforcement of both the current and new laws," while only 33 percent preferred only "strict enforcement of the current gun laws."[67] The NRA apparently figured out as well that Americans don't support new laws as much as they support strict laws. It is a further tribute to the NRA's capacity to frame the gun debate that its formulation of the enforcement versus new laws issue made its way into a Gallup poll, thus contributing to the illusion that the American people think enforcement of current laws is all we need to combat gun violence.

Giving the NRA credit for its inspired use of effective messaging, however, does not make its argument valid. The fatal fallacy in the NRA's claim is that it poses a false choice (i.e., between strong enforcement of current laws and the enactment of new laws). The NRA has never been able to answer the question, "If enacting new gun laws would save lives, why can't we have strong enforcement of current laws *and* enact new laws as needed?" It may well make sense for the Feds to prosecute more Brady Act cases and felon-in-possession cases and to seek longer sentences for those gun crimes. Even if this is so, why is it a reason to oppose stronger gun laws?

Let's take a specific example. We have seen that gun trafficking into the illegal market is regularly fed by dealers who make sales of multiple handguns to straw purchasers for gun traffickers. By prohibiting multiple sales, state one-gun-a-month laws can disrupt gun trafficking; a federal law would be even more effective. Assuming, for the sake of argument, that U.S. attorneys could prosecute more felon-in-possession cases than are now being brought, is this a sufficient reason to oppose the enactment of a federal law banning multiple handgun sales? Whether or not the Feds are currently prosecuting the maximum possible number of felon-in-possession cases has nothing to do with the wisdom of a curb on multiple sales. Indeed, our experience with state one-gun-a-month laws suggests that, by disrupting gun trafficking into the illegal market, those laws will prevent felons from acquiring guns in the first place.

It would be one thing if the failure to prosecute more felon-in-possession cases meant that a new federal curb on multiple sales would necessarily suffer from insufficient enforcement. But there is no reason to believe this would be true; indeed, a federal one-gun-a-month limitation would regulate the conduct of licensed gun dealers who, as a group, presumably would be far more law abiding than the convicted felons who are the target of the felon-in-possession statute.

Of course, a new federal law barring multiple sales must be supported by a sufficient threat of enforcement actions against dealers who do violate the law. But there is no logical reason why sufficient enforcement resources could not be directed toward dealer compliance with a new federal ban on multiple sales, while at the same time aggressively prosecuting felons caught in possession of guns. To the extent that the new law prevented felons from gaining access to guns in the illegal market, fewer enforcement resources would need to be directed at felon-in-possession cases.

The NRA's argument really amounts to the proposition that the solution to criminal gun violence is to increase federal prosecution and punishment of criminal offenders *instead of* enacting federal laws to prevent access to guns by criminals in the first place. What if our nation had applied this logic to the issue of airline security? Many years ago airliners were plagued by frequent hijackings. From 1968 to 1972 there were 364 hijackings worldwide.[68] One solution could have been to simply impose harsher punishments on hijackers of American airplanes. An alternative was not only to punish hijackers severely but also to require the airlines to do security checks on passengers to prevent them from bringing weapons aboard airplanes. The

NRA's logic would have supported a policy of increasing penalties *instead of* implementing new preventive policies. Our nation followed a different course. In 1973 the Federal Aviation Administration issued an emergency rule making inspection of carry-on baggage and scanning of all passengers by airlines mandatory. In 1974 Congress required the same in new legislation.[69] As a result, the number of American airplane hijackings has been sharply reduced. To the extent our preventive policies have failed (as in the 9/11 disaster), our response has been to tighten them, not abandon them in favor of a "punishment only" response.

When the NRA insists on greater enforcement of existing laws instead of enacting new laws, it also raises the question, How much more enforcement is enough? Regardless of the number of prosecutions, more could be brought. Regardless of the level of punishment, it could always be increased (within constitutional limitations, of course). For the NRA, however, it is quite clear that *no degree of enforcement or punishment is enough to justify considering new gun laws.* In response to a group of mayors calling for enactment of new "common sense gun legislation" to stem the flow of guns to criminals, Wayne LaPierre was quoted as saying, "You can have press conferences all day. Until you provide 100 percent enforcement of the existing laws, [criminals are] going to laugh at you, and . . . go about their business."[70] What, I wonder, is "100 percent enforcement"? Does it mean that we shouldn't consider enacting new federal gun laws unless every felon with a gun is caught and put in a federal prison? The NRA is clearly playing games here.[71]

Thus, the premise of the NRA's argument—that our nation must choose between strong enforcement and stronger laws—is simply wrong. The choice is a phony one. We should strongly enforce current laws but not ignore the need for new laws that also make us safer. Indeed, sometimes new laws are necessary to strengthen the enforcement of existing laws. I mentioned earlier that the Brady Law is a prime example of such a law. It was needed to enhance enforcement of gun control as it existed before Brady (i.e., the law against gun dealers selling guns to felons and other prohibited purchasers). The NRA opposes these enforcement-enhancing new laws, *even if they help us enforce the law against those who have actually used guns in violent crime.* For example, the NRA opposes new laws promoting technology that helps to catch perpetrators after their crimes have been committed.

As explained earlier, among available weapons that criminals could use in their activities, guns have many advantages. They also have one, very big, disadvantage. They leave evidence behind at crime scenes, namely bullets and cartridges. Unfortunately for criminals, every firearm leaves unique, reproducible markings on each bullet and cartridge case it fires. These markings are often referred to as "ballistic fingerprints." By comparing the markings on bullets and cartridges left at various crime scenes, trained forensic examiners can determine whether the same gun was used to commit multiple crimes.

In the D.C.-area sniper case in the fall of 2002, police used ballistic identification analysis to establish that the multiple sniper shootings had been committed with the same gun. This kind of analysis can be done quickly using the federal computerized database of digital images of cartridge cases and bullets recovered in criminal investigations, known as the National Integrated Ballistic Information Network (NIBIN). The NIBIN system shortens and simplifies the ballistic identification process for participating police agencies. Once the snipers had been arrested and their rifle taken into police custody, investigators also could test-fire the rifle and compare the ballistic fingerprints left by the rifle with those on the bullets at the crime scene. By doing so, they were able to connect the snipers' gun with those bullets and cartridges.

However, although police investigators could determine that the same gun had been used in multiple sniper attacks, the authorities had no way to determine which particular gun had been used *before* the sniper suspects had been arrested. Why? Because there is no database of ballistic fingerprints of guns sold, only of some guns associated with crime. If gun manufacturers were required to test-fire every gun before it was shipped into commerce and transmit the digital images of the cartridge and bullets to a central federal database, law enforcement would have a powerful new investigative tool. Based on a spent cartridge at a crime scene, police could determine the serial number of the gun used in a shooting and then trace the gun to the person who bought it from a licensed dealer. In states with gun registration, police could extend the trace to subsequent buyers. Crimes with guns would be solved faster, criminals apprehended faster, and other crimes prevented. Indeed, such a ballistics database could actually deter some criminals from selecting guns as their weapons of choice, precisely because they would leave such a strong evidentiary trail. As we have seen, reducing the use of guns in crime reduces the lethality of crime.

Also promising is an even newer technology known as microstamping. This involves the use of lasers to make microscopic engravings on the firing pin or breech face of a gun that, when the gun is fired, are then transferred to the discharged cartridge. These microscopic characters can identify the make, model, and serial number of the firearm. This would permit the gun to be traced based on the spent cartridges left at a crime scene, but without the need for a database of ballistic fingerprints of all guns sold. Legislation has been passed in California and proposed in several other states to require manufacturers to microstamp every new semiautomatic handgun to be sold in the state. Obviously, a federal law imposing such a requirement would be far superior to any state law.

The gun lobby constantly assures us it is in favor of severe punishment of gun criminals. Since it is difficult to punish criminals without catching them first, surely the NRA would support ballistic fingerprinting and microstamping as crime-fighting tools, right? Wrong. The NRA calls ballistic fingerprinting a "scheme" for "national gun registration"[72] and decries microstamping as "ammunition registration."[73] Of course, neither system need involve the registration of gun owners or gun sales. Under both systems, only gun owners associated with guns used in crime would be revealed to the authorities, in the same way that their identities are revealed to the authorities by crime gun tracing as it's currently done. The advantage of these new systems is that a crime gun trace can be done without police having custody of the gun used in the crime. The NRA's knee-jerk objection to these new technologies reveals, once again, that the gun lobby is not really interested in punishing criminals. It opposes new gun laws, even if they could help to put gun criminals behind bars.

The NRA's slogan supporting "enforcement of existing laws" instead of "new laws" is the gun lobby at its cynical worst. A product of pollsters and focus groups, carefully constructed by the right-wing messaging gurus to attack the Clinton administration, it should be admired for its success in helping to fend off additional gun control initiatives during the Clinton years. Its long-term impact is questionable, for several reasons. First, the message has the wrong messengers. The NRA does not really believe in enforcing the laws we have; it actually despises most of those laws. Hypocrisy can remain hidden only for so long. Second, most people can understand that enforcing current law is a sufficient policy against gun violence only if current law is sufficient for the task. Where strong enforcement is difficult precisely because the law is so weak, the case for new laws is made. Finally, there is no reason why our national policy toward gun violence should be forced into an artificial choice between strong enforcement and strong laws. Ultimately, the message manipulation of the gun lobby will likely yield to the conclusion required by common sense: we need strong laws *and* strong enforcement of those laws.

6.

"IS BUDWEISER RESPONSIBLE FOR DRUNK DRIVERS?"

THIS RHETORICAL QUESTION invokes a simple, and appealing, analogy that helped to give the NRA and the gun industry one of their most important legislative victories of the last decade. The analogy was used to oppose liability lawsuits against the gun industry and to argue in favor of federal legislation, signed into law by President Bush in 2005, to protect the industry from those lawsuits. When more than two dozen urban municipalities filed suit against major gun manufacturers in the late 1990s, seeking to recover some of the crushing public cost of gun violence, the industry responded by arguing that just as the beer industry should not be legally responsible for drunk driving, gun manufacturers should not be legally responsible for the misuse of guns. "You can't sue the manufacturer of a firearm, any more than you can sue Budweiser when someone gets involved in a drunk-driving accident," explained attorney Larry Keane of the National Shooting Sports Foundation.[1]

Makes sense, doesn't it? The victim of gun violence should pursue legal remedies against the person who pulled the trigger, so the argument goes, not against the manufacturer of the gun. To impose liability on the manufacturer is to shift responsibility from the party who inflicted the harm to another party who had nothing to do with the harm.

The argument would be sound if the only asserted basis for the industry's legal responsibility was that its products are used in crime. No accepted legal doctrine would support the idea that a gun's use by a criminal is a sufficient reason to hold the manufacturer or seller of a gun legally accountable for the crime. Legal liability of the gun industry on that ground really would be like holding Budweiser liable simply because a consumer became drunk and caused an accident.

The problem with the Budweiser analogy is that the lawsuits attacked by the gun lobby have not been based on the simplistic and indefensible idea that the gun industry should be legally responsible simply because some people misuse guns to cause harm. The analogy is yet another example of the gun lobby constructing an elaborate straw man and knocking it down. Yet this straw man framed the national debate over the legal liability of the gun industry. Taking advantage of years of spending by corporate America to demonize plaintiffs' trial lawyers under the banner of tort reform, it was not difficult to sell the idea that lawsuits against the gun industry were the trial lawyers' latest outrage, after they were finished suing McDonald's for selling coffee that is too hot.

A Gallup Poll in July 1999 asked a national sample of adults, "Would you favor or oppose allowing local governments to sue gun manufacturers in order to recover the costs incurred because of gun violence in their areas?" Sixty-one percent were opposed.[2] The question, however, said nothing about the rationale for such lawsuits.

During my career as a lawyer representing gun violence victims, I have been involved in most of the leading lawsuits against the gun industry. But if I were asked by a pollster whether gun manufacturers should be sued simply because people commit violent acts with guns, I would certainly answer "no."

There are, however, powerful arguments supporting the legal responsibility of gun manufacturers and sellers for much of the gun violence that plagues our nation. Gun manufacturers and sellers have made choices in the way guns are designed and sold that increase the risk of injury and death. When that risk becomes reality, those responsible should be held accountable in our courts.

AREN'T GUNS SUPPOSED TO BE UNSAFE?

Consider this tragic scenario, versions of which are repeated over and over again in gun-owning households across America. Two bored and curious teenage boys are at home, looking for something to do. One of the boys, wanting to impress the other, remembers his father's semiautomatic pistol stored unsecured, with loaded ammunition magazines, in his parents' bedroom. He's been told time and again never to touch the gun without a parent being present, but he retrieves it anyway. He takes the loaded magazine out, thinking he has unloaded the gun. What he doesn't know, and what the gun's design conceals from him, is that there is a round remaining in the firing chamber. Wanting to demonstrate his prowess with a real gun, he playfully points the gun at his friend and pulls the trigger. In an instant, two young lives are shattered. One suffers death or serious injury; the other a lifetime of guilt and shame.

In chapter 2, I discussed various laws that could prevent such a tragedy. A child access prevention law could have deterred the parent from leaving a loaded pistol accessible to the teenagers. If guns were regulated as other consumer products are, the government could have required the pistol to have additional safety features, such as a load indicator that could have alerted the teen that the gun was still loaded, or a magazine disconnect safety that would have prevented the pistol from firing after the magazine had been removed, or a personalization system that would have allowed only the parent to fire the gun.

Leaving aside, for a moment, the issue of what laws could prevent such shootings, there is the separate question of how our legal system should allocate responsibility when one occurs. We have a civil justice system that functions to award damages to innocent persons injured by the wrongdoing of others. When it's working as it should, the system compensates injured persons and deters similar wrongdoing by others. In the teen shooting scenario who, if anyone, should be required to pay damages to the victim or his family?

There is certainly enough blame to spread around. The boy who pulled the trigger was certainly irresponsible in ignoring his parent's instructions, along with every rule of safe gun handling. But liability need not be confined to a single party, even if that party were more responsible for the injury than anyone else. It is commonplace for our legal system to attach responsibility to multiple parties whose irresponsibility may have contributed to a single injury. We don't want to let a negligent party off the hook simply because others also were negligent in causing the injury. Therefore, in addition to the teen shooter, the adult gun owner arguably should be accountable for failing to take proper precautions to prevent access to the gun by his underage son. For example, a Louisiana court held that a gun owner could be liable for a shooting by a nine-year-old, even though the gun had been stored on a high shelf in a closet and the child had been instructed not to go into the closet. The court found that possession of a loaded gun carried with it a duty of "extraordinary care" that was not met by a "simple warning . . . that the pistol was off-limits and the placing of the pistol on a closet shelf."[3]

But, in our teen shooting scenario, what about the manufacturer of the gun? Is there any basis to hold the manufacturer legally responsible for the shooting? After all, the manufacturer didn't pull the trigger and had long before parted with possession or control of the gun. Nor was the gun defective in the ordinary sense of the word. The gun, unfortunately, operated exactly as it was designed to operate. The shooter pulled the trigger. The gun fired.

A strong case can be made, though, that the shooting could have been prevented had the manufacturer chosen to incorporate feasible, low-cost safety mechanisms in the gun. A magazine disconnect safety, for example, would cost the gun maker less than $.30 to install and would block discharge of a round if the magazine were out of the gun. Some pistols have them; most do not. Moreover, gun manufacturers know that this kind of accident happens *over and over again*. They know it happens, and they know that a feasible, low-cost design change could save young lives. Given these facts, why should the manufacturer of the gun in our teen-shooting scenario escape all responsibility?

The concept of "defect" in product liability law is far broader than the ordinary meaning of "defect" as a malfunction of the product. The Ford Motor Company was held liable because the placement of the fuel tank in its Pinto model caused fires in rear-end collisions. Even though the fuel tank's placement did not cause the car to malfunction, the car's design was defective because it created an unreasonable risk that passengers would be incinerated following a collision.

A product also can be defective in design because it lacks feasible safety mechanisms, even if it is perfectly manufactured and operates exactly as intended. Product liability law requires manufacturers of dangerous products to assume that consumers will make mistakes in using their products. For example, the Ohio Supreme Court held that the manufacturer of a disposable lighter could be liable for failing to child-proof its products to prevent children from using them. The court wrote, "[A] product may be found defective in design . . . where the manufacturer fails to incorporate feasible safety features to prevent harm caused by foreseeable human error."[4]

Manufacturers can be liable even though human errors contributed to the injury—the error of the child in misusing the lighter to start a fire and the error of the adult in leaving the lighter accessible to the child. The key to liability is whether the manufacturer could have foreseen the errors in the use of its product. In the disposable lighter case, the Ohio Supreme Court cited statistics showing that 5,800 residential fires, 170 deaths, and almost 1,200 injuries occur each year from children under five playing with lighters. "Lighters are commonly used and kept around the home," the Court wrote, "and it is reasonably foreseeable that children would have access to them and attempt to use them."[5]

Substitute guns for lighters and the statement is just as true. Because it is foreseeable to gun manufacturers that gun owners will leave guns accessible to minors and that minors will misuse them, they should also be held to a duty to design their products to prevent such misuse. As we have seen, thousands of kids die or are injured in gun accidents every year. Even though major gun manufacturers typically include warnings urging gun owners to store their guns unloaded, locked, and with gun and ammunition inaccessible to children, studies show millions of gun owners disregard those warnings. One 1994 survey found that 20 percent of all gun-owning households—and 30 percent of handgun-owning households—had a loaded, unlocked gun in the home.[6] An estimated 2.6 million children live in homes where at least one gun is stored either unlocked and loaded or unlocked with the ammunition in the same location as the gun.[7] In one study of eighty-eight California children under the age of fifteen who were unintentionally shot by other children or by themselves, "the most common case history was of children playing with a gun that had been stored loaded, unlocked, and out of view; the shooting often occurred in the room where the gun was stored."[8]

Gun makers should not need to read academic surveys to know kids have access to guns in the home and can use them to kill and injure other kids. The constant and depressing drumbeat of headlines reporting the individual tragedies establishes the foreseeability of these accidents. The Ohio Supreme Court, the same court that recognized the potential liability of manufacturers of disposable lighters for fires caused by children, four years later found that gun makers could be similarly liable for failing "to incorporate feasible safety features to prevent foreseeable injuries."[9] As a result, the court reversed a lower court ruling that had dismissed Cincinnati's case against the gun industry.

Other courts have found that gun manufacturers can be held liable for failing to design their products with feasible safety devices to prevent accidental shootings, especially those involving teens with access to guns. In one New Jersey case,[10] a police officer left his house one morning, leaving behind his fully loaded Glock semiautomatic in its holster, completely unsecured. Tyrone Hurst, the fifteen-year-old son of the officer's girlfriend, found the gun and showed it to his teenage friend as they prepared to walk to school together. Tyrone removed the magazine from the pistol and put in on the kitchen table. Thinking it was unloaded, his friend picked up the pistol, pointed it at Tyrone, and pulled the trigger, hitting him in the head. In finding that Glock could be liable (in addition to the police officer and Tyrone's friend), the court noted the testimony of experts that patents for magazine disconnect safeties had been granted as far back as 1910 because of the well-recognized danger of accidental firings after removal of the magazine from the gun.[11] Lest there be any doubt about the foreseeability of such accidents, the court quoted from an NRA magazine in 1957, noting "accidents caused by people thinking they have unloaded the gun when they have merely removed the magazine and left a cartridge in the chamber."[12]

Even in "gun friendly" states, courts have recognized the legal liability of gun makers for failing to build safety into their products. For example, in a 2001 ruling[13] the New Mexico Court of Appeals decided that Bryco Arms, a notorious manufacturer of cheap, low-quality, but highly concealable "Saturday Night Special" handguns, could be liable for failing to install magazine disconnect safeties in its guns.

Like so many others, the New Mexico case involved teenage boys fooling around with a handgun they thought they had unloaded by removing the magazine. Recognizing a gun manufacturer's "duty to consider risks of injury created by foreseeable misuse" of its products,[14] the court allowed the teenaged victim, who had survived being shot in the face by his friend, to proceed with his lawsuit against Bryco.

Incredibly, Bryco officials testified in the case that in making and selling the J-22 handgun involved in the shooting, they "did not consider additional safety devices for the J-22; that no product analyses were conducted on the J-22; that no one reviews Bryco products to see if they can be made safer; and that Bryco did not investigate what other manufacturers were doing to make their firearms safer."[15] Can you imagine an auto manufacturer that did not review its products "to see if they can be made safer"? Product liability lawsuits eventually drove Bryco into well-deserved bankruptcy, but many thousands of its handguns remain in circulation.

The gun industry concocts a host of arguments to avoid legal responsibility for failing to make its products safer.

First, the industry argues that guns are different from other products because their entire purpose is to be dangerous; indeed, consumers buy them because they are dangerous. This is an entirely legitimate distinction that, as I have argued, justifies a degree and kind of regulation—for example, criminal background checks on gun buyers—that we would not impose on other potentially dangerous products. It is a distinction, however, that furnishes no excuse for gun makers to design products that are unnecessarily unsafe. Although guns are designed to be lethal, presumably neither the manufacturer nor the consumer intends that they be used to accidentally kill or injure anyone. To the extent that guns can be designed to reduce the risk of accidental discharge, but still serve their lethal purpose, gun makers should be legally accountable if they make different design choices that expose gun consumers and the public to unnecessary risks. As the New Mexico Court of Appeals cogently argued, "The fact that handguns are meant to fire projectiles which can cause great harm is to our view all the more reason to allow the tort system to assess whether the product is reasonably designed to prevent or help avoid unintended—albeit careless— firings such as occurred here."[16]

Second, gun makers go to elaborate lengths to imagine shooting scenarios in which safety devices will impede the use of the gun. "What if you're in a firefight with a criminal," they argue, "and the magazine drops out of your pistol? With a magazine disconnect safety, you can't fire the round left in the chamber." Product liability law, however, requires courts to assess both the risks and benefits of alternative product designs versus current design.[17] Most safety features on products are not risk free. There are cases in which seat belts and air bags have caused injury or death, instead of preventing them. The issue is whether the risks of the safety feature are outweighed by the benefits. It is difficult to believe that magazine disconnect safeties, load indicators, and internal locks would cost nearly as many lives as they would save.

Third, the industry argues that gun makers should not be liable for the negligent acts of others. Here the industry's favorite tactic is to blame its customers. If a gun owner is stupid enough to leave a gun accessible to a child and to fail to keep the child away from the gun, the industry asserts, the gun owner, not the manufacturer, should be legally responsible. As we have seen, though, it is well established in the law that manufacturers are held to a duty to design their products to reduce the risk of injury from product misuse that is reasonably foreseeable.

Most auto accidents involve some kind of driver negligence, often involving illegal conduct such as speeding or running stop signs. Yet we don't insulate carmakers from liability because their customers make mistakes, often egregious ones. Indeed, in one case, Ford was held liable when the tread on its tires separated when one of its Mercury Cougar cars was being driven over a hundred miles per hour. A federal appeals court held that Ford had a duty to warn of the danger of tread separation at high speeds since, given that power and potential speed were part of the car's allure, particularly to youthful drivers, "It was not simply foreseeable, but was to be readily expected, that the Cougar would, on occasion, be driven in excess of the 85 mile per hour proven maximum safe operating speed of its Goodyear tires."[18]

Imposing liability on gun makers for injuries involving the tragic mistakes of gun owners does not "make the manufacturer liable for the negligence of others." The gun manufacturer is not liable for the gun owner's conduct, but for the manufacturer's own unreasonable choices. The manufacturer can install a magazine disconnect safety, or a load indicator, or an internal lock, or it can omit those features.

The gun industry's effort to shift all responsibility for tragic accidents to gun owners is supremely hypocritical because the industry's marketing of its products—particularly handguns—actually has encouraged its customers to engage in dangerous conduct. In court, the industry decries gun owners who leave loaded handguns in the nightstand and claims it had no way of anticipating such reckless behavior by its customers. But for years, this same industry tried to sell more handguns by exploiting the fear of being defenseless against a violent home intruder—precisely the fear that leads gun owners to store loaded guns unlocked in the nightstand.

In one notorious ad by Colt Firearms, which appeared in the southeast regional edition of *Ladies Home Journal*, a mother was seen tucking her young daughter into bed at night, a darkened window in the background. The headline read "Self-protection is more than your right . . . it's your responsibility." The ad recommended the purchase of a Colt semiautomatic pistol "for protecting yourself and your loved ones" and compared a firearm to a home fire extinguisher, stating, "It may be better to have it and not need it, than to need it and not have it." The message to young mothers? Danger lurks in the night outside your home; if you care about protecting your child's safety, buying a gun is practically a moral obligation; and failing to have a gun may expose your child to great harm. Of course, the ad failed to disclose that, according to the best available scientific evidence, bringing a gun into the home would expose a young family to far more danger than would deciding against having a gun.

Indeed, in 1996, seventy-five public health researchers and other medical professionals wrote to the Federal Trade Commission urging it to find such ads "deceptive" in suggesting that guns make families safer. Apart from the deceptiveness of the message conveyed, there is surely no doubt that consumers convinced by such fear-based advertising are more likely to store their guns at the ready for immediate self-defensive use, loaded and unlocked.

Another fear-mongering ad by Beretta went even further by actually depicting irresponsible gun storage. The ad showed a Beretta .380 semiautomatic pistol and a bullet for the gun sitting unsecured on what appeared to be a nightstand table. Next to the gun were a photo of a woman with two young children and an alarm clock showing the time as 11:26 p.m. The headline read, "Tip the odds in your favor." The text addressed those who are "considering a handgun for personal protection." Here the message was plainly addressed to single mothers: the night holds great danger for you and your children, and you need every advantage to repel a home invader. Incredibly, a pistol was shown unsecured on a nightstand next to its equally unsecured ammunition, in a home with two young kids, thus depicting a consumer who had disregarded the warnings in Beretta's own product manuals and every sensible rule of safe gun storage. It was as if General Motors had run an ad showing one of its cars with the driver and young children unsecured by seat belts, after warning in its owner manual that seat belts should always be buckled. Yet Beretta has argued in product liability lawsuits that it should escape all liability for accidental shootings caused by parents who leave guns accessible to children.

Finally, the industry argues that those who want to require safety features on guns should take their case to legislative bodies, not courts. If this argument justifies exempting gun makers from legal liability, then it should justify a similar exemption from makers of other dangerous products. Yet the courts did not dismiss the liability lawsuits against Ford on the ground that the only remedy for victims of exploding Pintos was to seek greater safety regulation of autos from Congress. With other industries, it is recognized that the incentives for safer products originate from two sources: regulatory bodies created by legislatures, as well as the threat of damages awarded by courts. Thus, cars are subject to both the regulatory requirements of the National Highway Traffic Safety Administration and the civil liability system.[19] Other consumer products are subject to safety standards and recalls under the Consumer Product Safety Act, but they are certainly not exempt from product liability lawsuits.[20]

For products other than guns, the regulatory system and the civil liability system work in tandem to create incentives for safer products. Again, the gun industry's argument amounts to pleading for special, favored treatment for makers and sellers of the most dangerous consumer product of all. Does that make sense?

For any product, not just guns, safety standards set by legislators and regulators are no substitute for accountability in court for selling unsafe products. When a legislature gives a regulatory body the power to set safety

FIGURE 6.1
COLT FIREARMS AD

standards, those standards operate only prospectively. If working properly, they make products safer, but they compensate no victims who have been injured by the manufacture and sale of unsafe products in the first place. Nor do safety standards hold companies accountable for their decision to sell unsafe products; they require them only to change those products. If product manufacturers and sellers are exempt from civil liability for unsafe products, they have to fear only that some day a regulatory agency will order them to change their products. They will nevertheless be able to retain the profits from the past sale of unsafe products with no accountability for the damage those products caused. Obviously the threat of civil damages to injured persons is a powerful incentive to make safer products. The prospect of future safety standards set by a regulatory body, although important, is a far weaker incentive.

The most powerful case for liability lawsuits against the gun industry comes from an unlikely source: a columnist for *Guns and Ammo* magazine. Some years ago, Tom Gresham, no friend of gun control, speculated that gun makers would be installing built-in gun locks "on more and more guns in the future." Indeed, he predicted that "in 10 years, no firearm will be made without one." Gresham asked a very good question: "Why are gun companies doing this when it's not yet required?" Here was his answer:

> Plunk your rear down in the witness chair. "Now, sir," says opposing counsel, "your company knew about these simple, inexpensive, effective locks, but you didn't include them? They cost how much, only a dollar or two each?"
>
> You can imagine the rest. To paraphrase a common line, "It's the liability, stupid."[21]

Virtually every major gun maker now sells at least some models with internal locks, even though no federal law or regulation requires them.

FIGURE 6.2
BERETTA U.S.A. AD

*Model 86, .380 ACP,
8-round magazine, double action.*

Tip the odds in your favor.

Introducing the Beretta Model 86, the only .380 automatic pistol with a tip-up barrel for easy and rapid loading. It allows for safe storage with an empty chamber, but simple, one-step loading in an emergency. Plus you'll get 8+1 firepower and all the safety, reliability and functional features traditionally found in Beretta medium frame pistols. If you're considering a handgun for personal protection, here's one that offers it all. See the Model 86 at your nearest Beretta dealer, or contact Beretta U.S.A. Corp., 17601 Beretta Drive, Accokeek, MD 20607. (301) 283-2191. **Beretta U.S.A.**

By making guns safer, the threat of civil liability likely has saved countless young lives that would have been lost in accidental shootings and suicides.

Of course, it is particularly disingenuous for the gun industry to argue that product safety should be a matter for legislatures and regulators, rather than courts since, as we have seen, *the gun industry is already exempt from federal product safety regulation.*[22] Having achieved an exemption from safety regulation that applies to other consumer products, the gun industry insists that it deserves an exemption from the civil liability system as well. This is beyond chutzpah, but with the NRA at your back, the gun industry has shown that anything is possible. Gun makers must be the envy of every other industry.

BLAME THE CRIMINALS, NOT THE GUN INDUSTRY

Setting aside the issue of unsafe guns, the gun industry has argued that it at least deserves protection from lawsuits seeking to blame it for the use of guns in crime. How could the company that made the gun, or sold the gun, be legally responsible when the gun is used in a criminal act? At least a gun's design is the product of a gun maker's decisions. How could the decisions of a gun maker or seller have anything to do with the harm inflicted by criminals using guns?

In fact, gun manufacturers and sellers repeatedly make irresponsible business decisions that increase the risk of criminal gun violence. And well-established legal principles support their liability to the victims of those decisions. Consider, for example, one of the worst mass shootings in American history and the supplier of the gun used in the shooting:

Gian Luigi Ferri was a gunman with a grudge. A failed businessman, he blamed his misfortunes on lawyers, particularly those at the prestigious law firm that once represented him, San Francisco's now-defunct Pettit & Martin. On July 1, 1993, he stepped onto an elevator at the sleek high-rise office building at 101 California Street in San Francisco's financial district. He was toting a briefcase containing enough firepower for a small army. He pushed the button to take him to the Pettit & Martin offices on the thirty-fourth floor and then proceeded to quickly and efficiently unpack the briefcase and prepare for his mission—to kill as many lawyers as possible.[23] By the time he stepped out of the elevator, he had two TEC DC-9 assault pistols equipped with high-capacity ammunition magazines containing from forty to fifty rounds of 9mm ammunition strapped across his chest, along with a .45-caliber handgun.

He quickly came upon a conference room where a deposition was being conducted. Raking it with gunfire through its curtained windows and then entering the room and continuing to fire, Ferri killed lawyer Jack Berman and witness Jody Sposato, while wounding court reporter Deana Eaves and lawyer Sharon O'Roke. Mr. Berman and Ms. Sposato were shot five or six times each. Ferri calmly walked out of the conference room and proceeded down a hallway, methodically shooting down anyone who he thought looked like a lawyer. In a matter of minutes, on three floors of the building, Ferri killed eight people and wounded six others. With the firepower of the TEC DC-9s allowing him to fire scores of rounds without pausing to reload, Ferri was able to, in the words of a police investigator, "walk through the building as if invulnerable." On the thirty-third floor, Ferri found John Scully, a young lawyer, and his wife, Michelle, hiding in the corner of John's office. John covered Michelle with his body, suffering several fatal wounds as he saved the life of his young bride. On the thirty-second floor, where Ferri mistakenly entered the offices of Trust Company of the West, he spray-fired Mike Merrill's office, killing him with four shots; shot Victoria Smith five times in her office (she survived); and shot Shirley Mooser four times and Deborah Fogel nine times, both fatally. Finally, retreating to a stairwell as the police approached, Ferri committed suicide.

In planning his deadly mission, Ferri chose, as his primary weapon, the TEC DC-9, a gun especially well adapted to a military-style assault on multiple targets. In a lawsuit brought by some of the 101 California victims and their families against Navegar, Inc., the gun's manufacturer, police experts described the TEC DC-9 gun as a "military-patterned weapon" of the type "typically issued to specialized forces such as security personnel, special operations forces, or border guards." The gun's standard thirty-two-round ammunition magazine could be emptied in seconds, and the gun could be equipped with even larger capacity magazines, as Ferri's was. This was firepower of the kind "associated with military or police, not civilian shooting requirements," as one expert testified.

The DC-9 had other unusual features, all designed to enhance its ability to engage in rapid-fire, close-quarter shooting at human targets. It had a barrel shroud to allow the shooter to grasp the barrel of the gun while protecting the hand from the extreme heat generated by the rapid fire of a large number of rounds. The barrel also was threaded, allowing the attachment of silencers, which are restricted under federal law because of their obvious interest to the criminal element. A police firearms expert testified that the TEC DC-9 was designed especially for spray-fire from the hip and was "completely useless for hunting," with "no legitimate sporting use." Government crime gun statistics revealed that, among assault weapons, the TEC DC-9 was the most favored weapon of the most dangerous criminals.

As the Bureau of Alcohol, Tobacco and Firearms said about assault weapons like the TEC DC-9, "You will not find these guns in a duck blind or at the Olympics. They are mass-produced mayhem."

Navegar's executives were acutely aware of the mayhem and seemed to revel in it. Michael Solodovnick, the company's marketing director, when asked about reports of TEC DC-9's popularity among criminals, told the *New York Times* that he was "kind of flattered" by such talk. "Hey, it's talked about, it's read about, the media write about it," he added. "That generates more sales for me. It might sound cold and cruel, but I'm sales oriented." Referring to the use of an AK-47-type assault rifle to murder schoolchildren in Stockton, California, Mike "Solo," as he was nicknamed, commented, "whenever anything negative has happened, sales have gone tremendously high."

Navegar's own advertising made it clear that the company did not have sportsmen in mind as its "target market." Its ads, in magazines such as *Soldier of Fortune*, *SWAT*, and *Combat Handguns*, referred to the gun as an "assault-type" pistol. It published brochures boasting of the gun's "excellent resistance to fingerprints." In a sworn deposition, Solo acknowledged that this representation could be interpreted to mean "fingerprints would not be left on this weapon," a feature uniquely interesting to those intending to use the gun in a criminal act. During his tenure as Navegar's marketing director, Solo was indicted for conspiracy to violate federal gun laws by distributing manuals and videotapes on how to illegally convert semiautomatic assault weapons to fully automatic fire.

When confronted with these facts about Navegar's TEC DC-9 and the company's conduct in marketing it, the California Court of Appeal ruled, in September 1999, that the victims of the 101 California Street massacre had a valid legal claim against Navegar for negligence in the design and sale of the gun. The court acknowledged that because "the risk of harm from the criminal misuse of firearms is always present" in a society in which the presence of firearms is widespread, a gun maker may not be found negligent merely because it manufactures and sells guns. However, the court found that gun makers have a "duty to use due care not to increase the risk beyond that inherent in the presence of firearms in our society."[24] The court ruled the evidence sufficient to allow the victims to go to trial, not because Navegar had acted illegally, but rather because "the manner in which Navegar manufactured and marketed the TEC DC-9 and made it available to the general public created risks above and beyond those citizens may reasonably be expected to bear."[25]

As with cases involving unintentional shootings, the "foreseeability" of harm is key to legal liability for those whose negligence contributed to a criminal act. As the court made clear in the *Navegar* case, a negligent actor can be liable even where the injury was inflicted by the *criminal* act of another, if the criminal act was the foreseeable result of the negligence. For example, courts have held that the owner of a vehicle who left the keys in the ignition in a high-crime area may be liable for injuries inflicted by a thief who recklessly caused an accident.[26] The court wrote in the *Navegar* case, "Here, the likelihood that a third person would make use of the TEC DC-9 in the kind of criminal rampage Ferri perpetrated is *precisely* the hazard that would support a determination that Navegar's conduct was negligent [emphasis in original]. . . . It is immaterial whether the hazardous conduct . . . is negligent or criminal."[27] In the *Navegar* case, it borders on the silly to suggest that a company that advertised its gun as an "assault-type pistol" with "excellent resistance to fingerprints" had no reason to foresee that its gun would be used in a criminal assault. To return to the alcohol analogy, Navegar's conduct was akin to Budweiser brewing a beer with three times the alcohol content of other beers and advertising it as "sure to get you drunker, faster."

The Court of Appeal ruling in the *Navegar* case was later reversed by the California Supreme Court, but not because the victims' legal claim lacked merit under general principles of liability law.[28] Rather, the State Supreme Court held that, regardless of its validity under those principles, a statute passed by the California legislature in 1982 to limit the liability of the gun industry barred the case. Because Justice Kathryn Mickle Werdegar, the dissenting judge, found the 1982 statute inapplicable, she was the only California Supreme Court Justice to address the validity of the claims under general legal principles. She found that the victims should have been allowed to go to trial. "The evidence . . . in this case demonstrated that Navegar's management not only should have known, but actually did know, that the technical and aesthetic characteristics of the TEC-9/DC9, together with its price, the manner of its promotion, and Navegar's instructions for its use, attracted criminal and mentally ill segments of the civilian gun market, foreseeably leading to the kind of mayhem that has produced this lawsuit."[29] Lest you imagine Justice Werdegar to be a jurist of the knee-jerk liberal activist persuasion, it is worth noting that she is the appointee of a Republican governor.

The *Navegar* case, then, furnishes a powerful response to the idea that gun manufacturers and sellers should never be liable for injuries inflicted by their products. Indeed, the public outcry in response to the California

Supreme Court's ruling for Navegar led the California legislature to repeal the 1982 liability-limiting statute on which the court had relied.

But, it may be argued, Navegar's conduct certainly was not typical of the gun industry. It manufactured an extreme product and promoted it in an extreme manner. Should makers and sellers of conventional firearms, marketed in conventional ways, be legally responsible when their guns are used in crime?

Internal industry documents uncovered in other liability cases, along with the testimony of industry insiders, show that "conventional" gun makers and sellers also increase the risk of gun violence by violating the duty of using due care in their business activities. Although their negligence may seem less sensational than Navegar's, it is arguably even more damaging to public health and safety.

A FEW BAD APPLES

We have seen that massive numbers of guns move rapidly from licensed gun dealers into the illegal market. In the words of the former chief of ATF's Crime Gun Analysis Branch, Joseph J. Vince Jr., "the most important single source of firearms for the illegal market is still illegal traffickers who are acquiring firearms from retail outlets."[30] We know that gun traffickers buy large numbers of guns from gun shops, often using straw buyers. As we have seen, because of this close connection between licensed dealers and the criminal market, strong regulation of licensed dealers can help dry up the supply of illegal guns. But this connection between gun dealers and illegal guns also raises another issue: To what extent should gun dealers be held legally accountable for criminal gun violence?

Crime gun trace data reveals an astonishing fact: *almost 60 percent of crime guns originate with only 1 percent of licensed gun dealers.*[31] This strongly suggests that the conduct of a relatively small number of gun dealers is feeding the supply of illegal guns. Especially when you consider that, *in a typical year, 85 percent of gun dealers sell no guns traced to crime.*[32]

Take Trader's Sports of San Leandro, California, outside Oakland. In 2005 alone, 447 crime guns were traced to Trader Sports, making it the second largest supplier of crime guns of any retailer in the country.[33] Trader Sports supplied 46 percent of the crime guns recovered in Oakland;[34] in 2005 law enforcement recovered crime guns sold by Trader's at an average rate of more than one every day.[35]

The gun industry typically claims that a large number of crime gun traces doesn't necessarily suggest a dealer is "doing anything wrong" but may simply be owing to the dealer's large sales volume. According to the industry, if a dealer sells many guns, more of its guns will be used in crime than will smaller-volume dealers'.

The theory is nice, but it doesn't reflect reality. In the case of Trader's Sports, for example, the shop's crime gun traces during the period 2003–2005 amounted to approximately 12 percent of its sales volume, a startling average of one of every eight guns sold later used in a crime or taken from a criminal.[36] During the same period, two other large-volume California dealers had crime gun traces constituting only 4 percent and 1 percent of their sales, respectively.[37] An internal study by the ATF reported the results of intensive government inspections of the 1 percent of dealers across the nation that had ten or more crime gun traces in 1999. Although these high-trace dealers accounted for more than 50 percent of crime guns in 1999, they accounted for less than 20 percent of guns sold in that year. The ATF report concluded, "sales volume alone does not account for the disproportionately large number of traces associated with these firearms dealers."[38] A later study of California gun dealers also found that a dealer's sales volume could not account for differences in the number of handguns traced to crime.[39]

What are these "high-risk" gun dealers doing that makes them such a dependable source of guns for traffickers?

First, far too many gun dealers are willing to facilitate straw purchases for gun traffickers because they don't think they'll be caught. In chapter 2 I related the case of two New Jersey police officers who were grievously wounded with a gun sold by a West Virginia dealer to an obvious straw buyer for an out-of-state gun trafficker. Chicago, Illinois, Gary, Indiana, and Wayne County, Michigan, filed suit against local gun dealers after conducting videotaped sting operations in which undercover officers posed as straw purchasing teams. In Chicago, undercover officers were able to purchase hundreds of firearms from suburban dealers even though the person picking out the weapons and paying for them was not the person filling out the federal paperwork in violation of federal law. Officers even went so far as to indicate they wanted their guns to settle scores or engage in other illegal activity but were not turned away.[40] Wayne County, Michigan, conducted similar stings of ten suburban dealers, and nine of them were willing to make an obvious straw sale. During one transaction, after being informed that the gun buyer had a felony record, a store clerk at the Sports Authority told the undercover officer posing as a straw buyer, "When the manager comes over to check this, it's your gun. You're not purchasing it for him. This is called a straw purchase. It's highly illegal. I don't know why . . . it's just . . . They consider it highly illegal." After openly acknowledging its illegality, the clerk nevertheless completed the sale and handed a gun and two boxes of ammunition to the officer posing as a convicted felon.[41] In 2006 New York City used undercover investigators to conduct similar stings on dealers in five states that accounted for large numbers of New York crime guns. Twenty-seven dealers were videotaped completing obvious straw sales.[42]

Second, even if straw buyers are not involved, dealers often sell large quantities of guns to single buyers who they suspect will sell the guns into the underground market. In chapter 1 I recounted the serial racial shootings committed by white supremacist Benjamin Nathaniel Smith. Since Smith was under a domestic violence restraining order, a background check had blocked him from buying a gun from a licensed dealer.[43] Instead, he turned to the classified section in the Peoria, Illinois, newspaper, which featured ads placed by a gun trafficker named Donald Fiessinger.[44] A licensed dealer, Old Prairie Trading Post of Pekin, Illinois, in turn, supplied Fiessinger. Fiessinger routinely purchased the same make and model of Bryco handguns from Old Prairie and resold them for a substantial profit. Over a two-year period, the dealer sold Fiessinger seventy-two Bryco handguns. The sales were staggered in an obvious effort to avoid triggering the federal reporting requirement for sales of two or more handguns in a five-day period. During a six-month stretch in 1998, Fiessinger received one gun from Old Prairie every Monday for twenty-five consecutive weeks.[45]

Or take the case of Sauers Trading, a licensed dealer in South Williamsport, Pennsylvania, that sold eleven guns to drug addicted gun trafficker Perry Bruce. All of them were cheap, easily concealable handguns with the exception of one assault pistol, a TEC DC-9.[46] Bruce used his welfare card for identification and gave his occupation as "unemployed," yet he paid for his guns with thousands of dollars in cash.[47] On at least one occasion, a Sauers sales clerk waited until all other customers had left the store before selling to Bruce.[48] Bruce testified that when he bought guns from Sauers, he often was high on drugs.[49] He also testified that Sauers "had to know what I was doing."[50] One of the guns Sauers sold to Bruce was used to shoot and kill seven-year-old Nafis Jefferson on the street in South Philadelphia.[51]

Should these dealers be liable in damages for the harm inflicted in these shootings? Certainly when their conduct is illegal—for example, knowingly engaging in straw sales—they should be liable, just as a tavern should be liable for knowingly selling alcohol to a minor. But gun dealers can also engage in very dangerous conduct that violates no laws, or at least exposes them to little danger of prosecution, because our gun laws are so weak and because the gun lobby has succeeded in making them so difficult to enforce. As we have seen, under federal law a dealer can legally sell a hundred assault weapons to a single buyer, even though there is little doubt that those guns will end up in the underground market. However, as we saw with the *Navegar* case, a defendant's conduct can be entirely legal, yet still be so irresponsible and create such a foreseeable risk of harm that it can be the basis for civil liability to its victims.

For example, in a landmark ruling in 1997, the Florida Supreme Court unanimously held that K-Mart could be liable for the sale of a rifle to Thomas Knapp, who had consumed a fifth of whiskey and a case of beer before he left a local bar to travel to K-Mart to buy a gun.[52] Although there was no direct evidence that the clerk knew he was drunk, Knapp required help with filling out the required paperwork because his handwriting was so illegible. Shortly after the purchase, Knapp returned to the bar, waited until his estranged girlfriend, Deborah Kitchen, left the bar, followed her car, forced it off the road, and shot her in the neck. The wound rendered her a permanent quadriplegic. While recognizing that K-Mart violated no statute in selling a gun to an obviously intoxicated buyer, the court nevertheless upheld a jury's award of damages to Deborah Kitchen. It was not enough, said the Florida Supreme Court, for K-Mart to act legally; rather, because firearms are "dangerous instrumentalities," the "highest degree of care is necessary . . . to avoid injuries to others."[53]

Other courts have likewise held that gun dealers can be liable for a wide range of negligent conduct, even though they violated no law, including selling to a buyer showing signs of mental illness,[54] failing to take reasonable precautions to guard against theft of firearms,[55] and failing to institute sufficient controls to account for the firearms taken into inventory.[56]

Given the general principle that gun dealers owe the "highest degree of care" to avoid injury, a strong case can be made for civil liability for dealer conduct that funnels guns into the criminal market, even if the conduct is not illegal or cannot be proved to violate a statute. Dealers like Old Prairie or Sauers Trading, who have every reason to believe they are supplying gun traffickers, create a foreseeable risk of harm at least as great as the K-Mart clerk who sold to an intoxicated Thomas Knapp. Such dealers should be held accountable, not because their guns were used in violent crimes but because their own irresponsible conduct enabled those guns to be used in violent crimes.

SEE NO EVIL, HEAR NO EVIL, SPEAK NO EVIL

But, the industry will argue, even if it may be appropriate to hold a few gun dealers accountable for selling guns to traffickers, why should gun manufacturers be liable? The manufacturers did not sell guns to straw buyers or gun traffickers. Nor were they even aware of these transactions. Returning to our alcohol analogy, the industry will argue that even if a tavern can be liable for selling beer to a minor, or for continuing to supply a customer long after he has become intoxicated, surely Budweiser cannot be liable for the tavern's irresponsibility.

This sounds like a reasonable position, until we imagine a different set of facts about Budweiser. What if Budweiser knew that almost 60 percent of drunk drivers were served by about 1 percent of the nation's taverns? What if Budweiser had the means to know the identities of those taverns and thus the means to know whether those taverns were serving Budweiser? What if the government actually offered to give Budweiser the information by which it could identify that 1 percent of taverns? What if Budweiser had made a conscious decision to remain ignorant of the identities of those taverns and, indeed, had refused the government's offer for help? What if Budweiser could enforce a code of conduct on those taverns to prevent irresponsible sales of beer and had refused to do so, even after being urged to take action by people within the beer industry and by the government? If these facts were true, then Budweiser's conduct could be more accurately compared to the conduct of gun makers. The dirty little secret of the gun industry is that manufacturers have maintained a conscious policy of "hear no evil, see no evil, speak no evil" when it comes to the stark reality of corrupt gun dealers.

How is it that gun makers can know so much about which gun dealers are funneling the most guns into the criminal market? The story starts with crime gun tracing.

As we have seen, ATF has, for many years, traced guns recovered by law enforcement authorities in connection with criminal investigations. A trace involves using the serial number of the recovered gun to document the sales history of the gun down to the first retail buyer from a licensed dealer. A crime gun trace always begins with the manufacturer, whose name, after all, appears on the gun itself. The manufacturer then discloses to ATF the identity of the distributor, who discloses the dealer, who discloses the first purchaser. Each ATF trace request, therefore, notifies the manufacturer that one of its guns has been associated with a crime.[57]

There is, of course, no doubt that the manufacturer could find out, from its own distributors, the identity of the dealer that sold each of those crime guns. Every gun manufacturer is capable of collecting information from its own distributors and dealers about how many of its dealers' guns have been traced to crime. It also could find out how many of those guns were traced a short time after they were sold, an indicator of gun trafficking. In short, each manufacturer could know, if it wanted to, whether its guns were being sold by the small minority of dealers who are the primary source of the crime gun problem. But no gun manufacturer wants to know. The manufacturers prefer to be willfully ignorant. It makes it easier for them to avoid all responsibility for the problem, while they profit from each dealer sale to a straw purchaser or a gun trafficker.

Incredibly, gun makers even refused such information when the government offered to give it to them. In February 2000 ATF offered to provide gun manufacturers and importers with a list, by serial number, of their guns that had been traced as crime guns during the previous year.[58] ATF made this offer of data to "enable the manufacturers and importers to police the distribution of the firearms they sell." ATF reiterated this offer in correspondence with specific manufacturers. For example, Special Agent Forrest Webb wrote to gun maker Taurus suggesting that it should use tracing data to determine whether "there is an unusually high number of Taurus firearms being traced to certain Federal firearms licensees" and advising that in such a case Taurus "look at [the licensees'] business practices more carefully."[59] This obviously was ATF's modest effort to enlist manufacturers such as Taurus to help the bureau combat trafficking from licensed dealers. In response, Taurus did nothing. Likewise, gun maker Sturm, Ruger responded to ATF's offer of data with a letter making it clear that the company wanted no part of the tracing information, adding that it would rather rely on ATF itself to address problems with Ruger's dealers funneling guns to crime.[60] The industry also has cheerfully supported the efforts of the gun lobby's friends in Congress to attach restrictions on ATF spending legislation that prohibit the bureau from sharing crime gun trace data, giving the manufacturers a ready-made excuse for not using trace data to identify problem dealers.

The manufacturers' willful ignorance of ATF crime gun trace data is only part of a broader strategy of turning a blind eye to any suggestion that they are knowingly doing business through reckless and corrupt gun dealers. For years, people within the industry itself often have warned the manufacturers about the "bad apple" dealer problem.

Until he passed away in 1996, Bill Bridgewater was a gun dealer in a small town in North Carolina and a passionate believer in gun rights. He was also a sharp thorn in the side of the gun industry. As the head of the leading gun dealer trade association, Bridgewater was angry that responsible dealers were forced to compete with the dealers who would rather cut corners and violate the law. It became difficult for the manufacturers to pretend they knew nothing of the bad dealer problem when Bridgewater insisted on reminding them of it. In his newsletter to the industry, Bridgewater pulled no punches: "No U.S. made firearm ever leaves the plant marked 'For delivery to Felon—To be used only in criminal activities'! Yet for us to pretend that none of our firearms achieves that status or that the flow of firearms into the hands of criminals is not our concern requires a level of stupidity that can seldom be achieved without major brain surgery."[61] Bridgewater scoffed at the manufacturers and distributors who disavowed all responsibility because they sold only through dealers licensed under federal law:

> If we don't separate ourselves from those who do divert firearms into the black market, we will be shut down in their name.
>
> These "licensees" who engage in the black market are perceived as no different than you and me by the general public, and certainly by law enforcement and the media. That is our fault for sitting quietly and saying nothing, knowing full well that there are felons hidden among us. You may continue to help shield these folks who operate this firearms black market among us and you will surely go down the drain with them whenever the public gets tired of every snot-nosed 13-year-old poking a gun in its face and demands draconian action.[62]

Bridgewater posed the issue to the gun industry in stark terms. "It is really your choice—do something about the felons among you who disguise themselves as legitimate businesses or die with them because their excesses are intolerable to our society."[63] Less than a year after he wrote those words, he was pressured to step down from the board of a trade association that included the major manufacturers and distributors, all of which had received his newsletter.[64]

Bridgewater was not alone among gun dealers in pleading with his industry to take action. Robert Lockett owned and operated the Second Amendment Gun Shop in Overland Park, Kansas. A columnist for *Shooting Sports Retailer* magazine, Lockett filed a column in 1999 calling on manufacturers and distributors to "wake-up" and control their distribution systems by requiring that dealers "adhere to some strict guidelines." Like Bridgewater, Lockett could not abide the manufacturers' "ignorance is bliss" posture toward corrupt dealers. He wrote in his column, "I've been told INNUMERABLE times by various manufacturers that they 'have no control' over their channels of distribution. . . . IF YOU DO NOT KNOW WHERE AND HOW YOUR PRODUCTS ARE ULTIMATELY BEING SOLD—YOU

SHOULD HAVE KNOWN OR ANTICIPATED THAT THEY WOULD BE ILLEGALY SOLD AND SUBSEQUENTLY MISUSED. Let's just get down and dirty. We manufacture, distribute, and retail items of deadly force."[65]The column sparked controversy even before it was published. A draft circulated within the top ranks of the industry, and the *Wall Street Journal* ran a story on the draft version and its implications.[66] When the column finally appeared in *Shooting Sports Retailer*, Lockett's text had been significantly changed. Whereas Lockett's version had addressed "Mr. Manufacturer," the edited version now addressed "Mr. Firearms Businessman" in a transparent effort to shift blame away from the manufacturers.[67]

Just as Bill Bridgewater had, Lockett discovered that the gun industry does not respond kindly to criticism from within its ranks. After his column appeared (even in its edited form), several distributors retaliated by refusing to supply his gun shop. The publisher of *Shooting Sports Retailer* told Lockett that gun manufacturer Glock pulled its advertising from the magazine because of the column.[68] The magazine never printed another Bob Lockett column.[69]

The explosive testimony of whistleblower Robert Ricker shows that the industry received the message dealers like Bridgewater and Lockett were sending—and decided to do nothing about it. In many ways, Ricker was the consummate industry insider. For eighteen years he worked tirelessly for the gun lobby, starting as a lawyer at the NRA and eventually rising to lead a large industry trade association. Ricker participated in formulating and advocating gun industry policy on every important issue—from the Brady Bill to child safety locks to lawsuits, among others. He was, and I say this from my personal experience as his erstwhile debate opponent, one of the most effective spokespeople for the pro-gun cause. Soft-spoken in manner, Ricker had the special ability to sound reasonable in advocating patently unreasonable positions.

I always had the feeling that Ricker's heart was not really in it. It turns out I was right. In May 2001, as I sat at the counsels' table in the courtroom of the California Supreme Court in San Francisco, preparing to argue the 101 California lawsuit against Navegar, I noticed Ricker sitting in the gallery. After the argument, as I was stuffing my notes back in my briefcase, I was taken aback when Ricker walked up to me. After a warm handshake, he said, "Dennis, I'm not in the gun industry anymore. We should talk." I could barely contain myself. A week later I returned to San Francisco to meet with him. He had a lot to say.

In a sworn affidavit submitted in support of the lawsuits against the industry filed by California cities,[70] Ricker confirmed what industry executives still try to deny: that the "firearm industry . . . has long known" of "the diversion of firearms from legal channels of commerce to the illegal black market," in which "firearms pass quickly from licensed dealers to juveniles and criminals . . . by corrupt dealers or distributors who go to great lengths to avoid detection by law enforcement authorities." "Leaders in the industry," said Ricker, "have long known that greater industry action to prevent illegal transactions is possible and would curb the supply of firearms to the illegal market." Nevertheless, industry leaders "have consistently resisted taking constructive voluntary action to prevent firearms from ending up in the illegal gun market and have sought to silence others within the industry who have advocated reform." Ricker reported on regular meetings of industry lawyers in which some discussed whether the industry should take greater voluntary action to curb illegal guns. "The prevailing view," he reported, "was that if the industry took action voluntarily it would be an admission of responsibility for the problem." Eventually, the lawyer meetings were ended because, in the words of one industry lawyer, the open discussion of such issues was becoming too "dangerous." As Ricker described it, the industry adopted a "see no evil, hear no evil, speak no evil approach" that encourages "a culture of evasion of firearms laws."

Internal industry documents uncovered in litigation confirm the industry's knowledge of the corrupt dealer problem. But whenever an industry official suggested the need for action to address it, the idea was quickly squelched. The industry's leading trade association, the National Shooting Sports Foundation (NSSF), was a graveyard for reform ideas. For example, a memo from NSSF official Doug Painter in 1993 reported on a random sampling of dealers by ATF showing that an astonishing 34 percent had committed federal firearms violations. Painter suggested a "proactive industry strategy" to address the serious "potential for illegal firearms transactions through ostensibly 'legal' FFL channels."[71] He proposed in the memo that the industry act "as an important step in better regulating the distribution of its products and as a means to minimizing the possibility of illegal transactions through unscrupulous FFL holders." Without even reviewing the ATF report, NSSF's executive director Robert Delfay rejected Painter's idea, instructing him to file the memo "for future reference," because the chair of NSSF's board, Arlen Chaney, was "not keen on doing anything right now." Having learned his lesson not to rock the boat, Painter eventually rose through the ranks to become NSSF's executive director.

The industry's public position is to insist that, even if it could identify the problem dealers, the manufacturers can do nothing about them. Manufacturers have no control over the conduct of retail dealers, the argument goes. Indeed, they generally sell their products to distributors, who in turn sell to retail dealers. Once guns leave their loading docks, they cannot control who sells them or who buys them, or so they claim.

The gun makers, however, seem to be powerless to deal with problem dealers only when the problem involves diversion of guns to criminals. When it comes to protecting the bottom line, manufacturers are able to find multiple ways of making sure dealers adhere to company policies.

My favorite example is Beretta. Gun makers like Beretta who sell through distributors typically have written contracts with their distributors imposing a variety of requirements designed to ensure the effective promotion of the manufacturer's products. Beretta was apparently concerned that its American retailers were selling Beretta guns outside the United States in competition with its foreign sales representatives. It therefore inserted a provision in its standard distributor agreement requiring the distributor to actively discourage dealers from selling its products overseas. The agreement makes it clear that any such foreign sales that "our distributors know or should have known are occurring," constitute violations of the agreement that could be grounds for termination of the distributor.[72]

Litigation against the industry revealed a letter Beretta had written to one of its distributors explaining the indicators that should put a distributor on notice that a dealer likely was engaged in unauthorized international sales. These included "the size of the order, past history of the particular dealer, the size and nature of the order relative to normal buying practices of the dealer, et cetera."[73] According to Donald Campbell, Beretta's national sales manager, Beretta was trying to "control the distribution process."[74]

As vigilant as Beretta was in preventing diversion of its guns to foreign markets, it has shown no such determination to prevent diversion of its guns to the illegal market. Beretta imposed no requirements on its distributors to monitor the number of crime guns a dealer sold, the number of suspect multiple sales it had made, or whether it had been cited by ATF for legal violations. Campbell testified that he never thought it was part of his job to try to curb the flow of guns into the illegal market, he never tried to think about ways to prevent it, and he knew of no measures Beretta instituted to prevent it during his entire tenure with the company.[75] See no evil. Hear no evil. Speak no evil. And do nothing.

This industry attitude showed contempt for the pleas of federal law enforcement authorities who repeatedly urged the industry to take action. ATF wrote that its "enforcement efforts would benefit if the firearms industry takes affirmative steps to track weapons and encourage proper operation of Federal Firearms Licensees to ensure compliance with all applicable laws."[76] The Justice Department urged gun manufacturers to "self-police" their distribution systems, urging them to "develop a code of conduct for dealers and distributors, requiring them to implement inventory, store security, policy and record keeping measures to keep guns out of the wrong hands."[77]

The gun industry's plea of powerlessness requires, of course, that the industry march in lockstep. Once one company shows action is possible to curb corrupt dealers, then the argument collapses for all of them.

During the 1990s Smith & Wesson repeatedly threatened to spoil the party for the entire industry. It implemented a code of ethics for its stocking dealers and informed them it might terminate sales to those who did not agree to refrain from making sales to straw purchasers.[78] It was the only gun maker to instruct its distributors to terminate sales to Chicago-area dealers who had been indicted for having made sales to undercover police officers posing as straw buyers for criminals.[79]

Then, on St. Patrick's Day 2000, the company committed an unforgivable sin. It entered into an agreement with many of the cities that had filed suit against the industry and with the Clinton administration (that had threatened a lawsuit). In that agreement, Smith & Wesson committed itself to imposing a far-reaching code of conduct on its distributors and dealers to help prevent sales into the illegal market.[80] In order to be authorized to sell Smith & Wesson products, a dealer had to implement safe sales practices that went far beyond the minimum legal requirements. The dealer had to

- Refrain from selling any gun until the Brady background check was completed (thus solving the "default proceed" problem).
- Refuse to sell at a gun show unless every seller at the show, including unlicensed sellers, conducts background checks on all sales (thus closing the "gun show loophole").
- Have its employees attend annual training and pass an exam on how to recognize the signs of a suspicious sale and on how to promote safe handling of guns.
- Sell guns only to persons who have passed a certified firearms safety course or exam.
- Implement specific security measures to prevent gun theft.
- Maintain an electronic record of every time one of its guns was traced to crime and submit those records to Smith & Wesson on a monthly basis.

Smith & Wesson CEO Ed Schultz said, in announcing the agreement, "A decision to enter this agreement, we realized, would not be popular with everyone. But we believe . . . it is the right thing to do."[81]

The agreement was a grave threat to the rest of the industry. It amounted to an admission by a major gun manufacturer that it was in a position to require its dealers to engage in safer sales practices, in the same way it would require them to effectively promote its products. This was a direct challenge to the industry's longtime strategy of avoiding responsibility for dealer misconduct by pretending there was nothing manufacturers could do to curb it. Hard-liners in the industry also knew that if one or two other manufacturers entered into similar agreements, it could fundamentally change the way guns are sold for many years to come.

The NRA and its allies in the industry were not about to let that happen. The NRA denounced the company as a foreign-owned business (its corporate parent was a British company) that had "run up the white flag of surrender" to the Clinton administration. The NRA's rage, and the inevitable calls for a boycott of Smith & Wesson products, was enough to terrify the other companies into submission. Industry hard-liners, in turn, went into overdrive to make sure no one else agreed to the Smith & Wesson reforms. NRA loyalist Robert Delfay, head of the industry's leading trade association, issued a statement that he was "deeply disturbed" that Smith & Wesson allowed the Clinton administration to "manipulate the company in this manner," but added, "We are confident that no other major manufacturers will desert."[82]

Andrew Cuomo, then-secretary of housing and urban development, who had played a key role in negotiating the deal with Ed Schultz, said, "It seems like the industry is doing everything it can to make an example out of Smith & Wesson."[83] Connecticut attorney general Richard Blumenthal, who had actively supported the agreement, described Smith & Wesson as "under absolutely unprecedented pressure, both financial and personal within the gun industry, with threats that are almost violent in nature, and I have heard the fear that it could be put out of business."[84] It almost was. Major distributors stopped selling the company's products. Its sales slowed to a trickle. Ed Schultz left the company. The agreement was never implemented. An example had been made.

At the same time the NRA and the industry were vilifying Smith & Wesson, Delfay's trade association commissioned a nationwide poll to find out public attitudes about the settlement. The survey found that 79 percent of those polled favored the settlement, with only 15 percent opposed. Even a majority of NRA members supported the agreement.[85] For obvious reasons, the survey was never released to the public; it was uncovered in pretrial discovery in the municipal lawsuits against the industry. What could be more damning than a survey, commissioned by the industry itself, showing how far the industry was out of step with the American people?

As inexcusable as the industry's conduct has been, is it the basis for legal liability? In other contexts, courts have held manufacturers of dangerous products legally accountable for using irresponsible intermediaries to distribute and sell their products. These courts recognize that since manufacturers choose how to distribute their products and who to do business with, they cannot hide from responsibility by having other companies and individuals do their dirty work. (Gun makers aren't legally required to use independent distributors and dealers at all and certainly aren't required to use the 1 percent of dealers who sell most of the crime guns.) For example, courts have held that a waste disposal company can be liable for using irresponsible companies to dispose of toxic waste,[86] a bulk manufacturer of paint thinner can be liable for danger to children when it did nothing to prevent retailers from packaging the product in used milk containers,[87] and a chemical company can be liable for selling chemicals to a company making illegal and dangerous fireworks.[88] In none of these cases was the manufacturer able to avoid liability simply because it did not directly engage in the wrongful conduct, but instead used others to do so.

Appeals courts in Ohio,[89] New Jersey,[90] and Indiana[91] have held that gun makers may be liable for distributing their products through irresponsible dealers, while showing willful blindness to their conduct. In a case brought by the NAACP in which the industry's conduct was scrutinized in a lengthy trial, a federal judge in New York issued a searing indictment of the industry, finding that its irresponsible distribution of guns so substantially contributes to the illegal gun market as to constitute a public nuisance.[92] Judge Jack Weinstein found that "careless practices and lack of appropriate precautions on the part of some retailers lead to the diversion of a large number of handguns from the legal primary market into a substantial illegal secondary market." "The flow of guns into criminal hands in New York," he wrote, "would substantially decrease if manufacturers and distributors insisted that retail dealers who sell their guns be responsible." Instead, "members of the industry continue to fail to take many obvious easily implemented steps" that "would substantially reduce the stream of illegally possessed handguns flowing into New York."

Judge Weinstein also found evidence of the gun industry's motive in continuing to sell guns through irresponsible dealers: a huge percentage of the industry's production serves the illegal market, generating significant profits. A study introduced into evidence showed that 18 percent of handguns sold in the year 1990 were in the hands of violent criminals or used in violent crimes by the year 2000. Every gun sold to a straw buyer or a gun trafficker adds to the sales and profits of the dealer, the distributor and the manufacturer. No one in the supply chain has an incentive to curb those sales unless, that is, they are held liable for the damage they inflict on individuals and communities.

It should be obvious, then, that the lawsuits against the gun industry seek to hold manufacturers and sellers liable, not simply because guns are misused by dangerous people but because the industry's own irresponsible choices, in the design and distribution of its products, enable and facilitate that misuse. The industry knows its choices lead to death and injury, knows it could make different choices, and refuses to do so because it would hurt the bottom line. And the rest of us end up paying a terrible price.

Yet the gun industry has had striking success misrepresenting the legal claims against it and portraying itself as the victim of greedy trial lawyers and rabid gun haters bent on holding it responsible for every shooting by a gangbanger. In enacting the misnamed Protection of Lawful Commerce in Arms Act in 2005, Congress thought it was barring lawsuits that would be comparable to "holding Budweiser responsible for drunk drivers" because that's how the gun lobby's friends in Congress framed the issue. Here's how the lawsuits were characterized by one of the bill's key supporters, Senator Jeff Sessions (R-Alabama): "The anti-gun activists . . . want to blame . . . violent, illegal acts by criminals—on manufacturers of guns, *because they manufactured the gun, and they want to be able to sue the seller who sold the gun simply for selling them* [emphasis added]. This doesn't make sense."[93] No, it doesn't make sense, Senator Sessions. But, of course, that's not what the lawsuits against the industry tried to do.

The sponsors of the bill repeatedly assured their colleagues that the legislation would not protect companies who engaged in objectionable conduct. Senator Larry Craig (R-Idaho), the bill's primary Senate sponsor and an NRA board member, put the matter this way: "[This bill] does not protect members of the gun industry from every lawsuit or legal action that could be filed against them. It does not prevent them from being sued for their own misconduct. This bill only stops one extremely narrow category of lawsuits, lawsuits that attempt to force the gun industry to pay for the crimes of third parties over whom they have no control."[94]Senator Lindsay Graham (R-Florida), another supporter, explained that the legislation "doesn't relieve you of duties that the law imposes upon you to safely manufacture and to carefully sell," but Congress was "not going to extend it to a concept where you are responsible, *after you have done everything right,* for what somebody else may do who bought your product."[95] Senator Max Baucus (D-Montana) offered similar assurances: "This bill . . . will not shield the industry from its own wrongdoing or from its negligence."[96]

Of course, after the bill was enacted into law, these assurances by the gun industry's defenders in Congress did not deter the industry from immediately using the new statute to seek dismissal of the suits against it for engaging in negligence and wrongdoing. Whether the industry will be successful in avoiding all accountability remains to be answered by the courts. But this much we know: The gun lobby won in Congress by portraying gun makers as the victims of frivolous lawsuits that were never brought, while diverting attention from the reality of their own knowing, callous, and highly profitable system of ensuring a ready supply of guns to criminals—a system that functions efficiently to this day. We all know who the real victims are.

7.

"FROM MY COLD, DEAD HANDS . . . "

CHARLTON HESTON WAS nearing the end of his rousing speech to the 2000 NRA Convention in Charlotte, North Carolina, where he accepted a third term as the group's president. After decrying "the divisive forces that would take freedom away," with square-jawed resolve he hoisted in one hand, high above his head, a colonial-era musket, symbol of rebellion against the powerful to ensure American liberty. Then, in his booming baritone that was close to a lion's roar, Heston issued his trademark challenge to the faithful gathered to heed the call: "*From my cold, dead hands . . .* " The moment was electric, the audience ecstatic, the response deafening. Heston kept the musket aloft for several seconds, soaking in the adulation, basking in the shared blood oath everyone in the room had implicitly taken. His message: I am willing to die for my guns. Their response: So are we.

Heston's musket drew a direct, visible link between the fight against tyranny that gave birth to our nation and the NRA's fight against the perceived tyranny of gun control. Patriots then and patriots now. For the committed NRA activist, moreover, Heston was symbolically drawing a connection to the Founding Fathers that is real and eternal because they wrote it indelibly into the charter of our freedoms—the Bill of Rights.

The second of the first ten amendments to the Constitution speaks of "the right of the people to keep and bear Arms" and commands that this right "shall not be infringed." For the "gun rights" partisan, the Second Amendment is the trump card in the gun debate, the argument of last resort. The gun control advocate can talk about the dangers of guns, their toll on society, and the need to regulate them at least as much as other dangerous products such as cars. But these arguments invariably draw the response that guns aren't like other dangerous products because the right to possess guns is uniquely protected by the Constitution.

There has, however, always been a problem with the NRA's use of the Second Amendment. Its words don't quite fit the NRA's narrative. If its intent was to guarantee a right to possess guns for private purposes like self-defense and hunting, its words seem oddly chosen:

> A well regulated Militia, being necessary to the security of a free State, the right of the people to keep and bear Arms, shall not be infringed.

The gun rights community has always been somewhat vexed by the language about the "well regulated Militia" and its necessity "to the security of a free State." What are such words doing in a provision that guarantees the right to have guns to defend one's home and family? What is their function? Even the phrase "keep and bear Arms" seems strange. The Framers could have written something like, "The right of the people to possess and use guns shall not be infringed." Why didn't they?

The NRA's primary strategy for dealing with the troublesome language about the "well regulated Militia" has been to pretend it isn't there. For many years, the NRA headquarters building on Thomas Circle in Washington, D.C., featured a heavily edited version of the Second Amendment on its facade. The first thirteen words were omitted.

Until its recent decision in *District of Columbia v. Heller*, the Supreme Court had been unwilling to interpret the Second Amendment by ignoring half of its text. In fact, in *United States v. Miller*, the Supreme Court's only extensive discussion of the amendment prior to *Heller*, the Court assigned decisive importance to the militia language. In *Miller*, a unanimous Court held that the "obvious purpose" of the guarantee of the people's right to "keep and bear Arms" was "to assure the continuation and render possible the effectiveness" of state militia forces and that the amendment "must be interpreted and applied with that end in view."[1] Indeed, in *Miller*, the High Court upheld the defendants' indictment for transporting a sawed-off shotgun across state lines without complying with the National Firearms Act because there was no evidence that such a gun could have a "reasonable relationship to the preservation or efficiency of a well regulated militia," noting that it could not simply assume "that this weapon is any part of the ordinary military equipment or that its use could contribute to the common defense."[2] The *Miller* Court found no reason to even address the question of whether such a gun could have utility for self-defense or some other nonmilitia activity.

Prodigious historical research into the origins of the Second Amendment confirms that it was intended to address the distribution of military power in society, not the need to have guns for self-defense or other private purposes. The Anti-Federalists, who opposed the Constitution as written and sought the addition of a Bill of Rights, were deeply worried that the Constitution had given Congress the power to raise a standing army (i.e., a professional military force), which many feared would become a tool of federal tyranny, as well as excessive power over the state militias. The state militias were nonprofessional military forces composed of ordinary citizens and were regarded as a strong check on the power of a federal standing army.

Leading Anti-Federalists argued that the Constitution's grant of power to Congress to organize and arm the militia amounted to an exclusive power to do so, thus rendering the state militias vulnerable to federal hostility or neglect. For example, Anti-Federalist George Mason argued during the Virginia ratification debates that Congress's new power would allow Congress to destroy the militia by "rendering them useless—by disarming them. . . . Congress may neglect to provide for arming and disciplining the militia; and the state governments cannot do it, for Congress has an exclusive power to arm them."[3]

Historians tell us that the Second Amendment was an effort by the Federalist defenders of the Constitution to allay these concerns by making the keeping and bearing of arms in a state militia a "right of the people," not dependent on federal action.[4] The Second Amendment was passed as a "fail safe" provision, ensuring that the state militias would be armed, even if Congress abandoned them.

For decades after *Miller* the lower courts consistently held that the Second Amendment guarantees the people the right to be armed only in connection with service in an organized state militia. Since the state militia of the founding era—a system of compulsory military service imposed on much of the adult, male population—had long ago disappeared into the mists of time, the courts routinely upheld gun control laws of every conceivable variety against Second Amendment challenge. Indeed, the judicial consensus on the meaning of the amendment had grown so strong that, in 1991, former Chief Justice Warren Burger—a conservative jurist who also was a gun owner—accused the NRA of perpetrating a "fraud on the American public" by insisting that the right to be armed existed apart from service in an organized militia.[5]

A couple of years into my tenure at the Brady organization, I became acutely aware of the intense emotional attachment of pro-gun activists to the Second Amendment. I was contacted by a personable lawyer with a private firm in Tucson, Arizona, named Sandra Froman, who invited me to participate in a symposium on the Second Amendment at the University of Arizona law school. There was, however, a catch. The Second Amendment Foundation (SAF), well-known as an even more extreme opponent of gun laws than the NRA, was funding the symposium. The SAF sponsorship, of course, destroyed any hope of balance in the program. Sure enough, each panel of speakers was carefully constructed to ensure that I would be part of a distinct minority of speakers supporting the prevailing "militia purpose" view.

When I finally met Froman face to face, I asked her about her own view of the Second Amendment. She said she "leaned toward" the broader "private purpose" view. It turns out she leaned pretty far. Years later, Sandy Froman was elected president of the NRA.

The audience for the Arizona symposium was composed almost entirely of rabid opponents of gun control, including a number of activists who had achieved great prominence in the pro-gun community. The title of my talk was "The Right to Be Armed: A Constitutional Myth." I don't deny it; I wanted to be provocative. But I never anticipated the reaction I would receive. As I carefully reviewed the court rulings establishing that individuals with no connection to a militia have no constitutional right to own guns, I could feel the room temperature rise. The faces in the audience began to turn an unhealthy shade of crimson, and I found myself competing with the low drone of people muttering to themselves and each other.

It is one thing to argue to the committed believers that guns are more dangerous than other weapons or that reasonable steps can be taken to keep guns out of the wrong hands. It is quite another to tell them they have no Second Amendment rights. I had just made the point that if they want the right to own guns for self-defense, they should seek to amend the Constitution, when the muttering became shouting. "Liar! Liar!" a few of them shouted. It was pure rage, and it was directed at me. At first their anger was perversely energizing. It was exhilarating to force them to hear the truth, even if they would never recognize it as the truth. At the same time, it was sobering to realize that I was despised by so many who were so well armed.

Now, after the *Heller* decision, the "militia purpose" view of the Second Amendment seems far less likely to be as much a flashpoint for pro-gun activists. Indeed, as we have seen, the Supreme Court's recognition of an individual right to be armed for private purposes, by helping gun control advocates respond more effectively to the slippery slope argument, may eventually reframe the gun debate in ways that make it more difficult for the NRA to keep the passion of their activists aroused at a fever pitch. But as helpful as *Heller* may be in this regard, there is another side to the ledger. Won't the new right recognized in *Heller* pose a direct threat to the constitutionality of other gun laws? *Heller* surely poses some new legal risk to gun control laws. Will it turn out to be a risk that outweighs any benefit from flattening the slippery slope? And will *Heller* not simply strengthen the gun lobby theme that the government's power to regulate guns should be far more limited than its power to regulate other dangerous products because gun possession is a fundamental constitutional right?

Heller, in fact, is the new paradox of the gun control debate. In *Heller*, the conservative majority on the Supreme Court engaged in an unprincipled abuse of judicial power in the pursuit of an ideological objective. Not quite *Bush v. Gore*, but close. Yet its ruling may turn out to have little practical impact on existing gun control laws and may weaken the gun lobby's power to block sensible gun control proposals that will dominate the debate in the future. To understand how confounding the *Heller* paradox may turn out to be, we should begin by understanding how indefensible the decision is as a matter of constitutional law.

EDITING THE CONSTITUTION

We have seen that the NRA conforms the Second Amendment's text to its own constitutional preconceptions by simply pretending that its first thirteen words were never written. Justice Antonin Scalia's majority opinion in *Heller*, joined by Justices Clarence Thomas, Anthony Kennedy, Samuel Alito, and Chief Justice John Roberts, also obliterates half of the amendment but is somewhat more sophisticated in attempting to disguise its rewriting of the Constitution.

Justice Scalia is well-known for his insistence that the text of the Constitution—not the search for the "intent" of the Framers and not the contemporary circumstances in which the text is applied—is of primary importance in deciding constitutional questions. Yet the brand of "textualism" he uses to interpret the Second Amendment is inconsistent and manipulative, showing little respect for the words the Framers actually wrote and ratified.

The core of his textual argument is devoted to listing various eighteenth- and nineteenth-century uses of the phrases "keep arms" and "bear arms" to refer to a right to be armed unrelated to militias. For example, he cites a

1734 text providing, "Yet a Person might keep Arms in his House, or on his Estate, on the Account of Hunting, Navigation, Travelling, and on the Score of Selling them in the way of Trade or Commerce, or such Arms as accrued to him by way of Inheritance."[6] In this instance, the use of "keep Arms" does appear to refer to the possession of arms for private purposes unrelated to militias. But how do we know this? Only because the context in which the phrase appears suggests that it refers to nonmilitia activities.

To take another of Scalia's examples, he cites various state constitutional provisions (all enacted after the Second Amendment) that guarantee "every citizen a right to bear arms in defence of himself and the State."[7] We know "bear arms" includes a nonmilitia right in those provisions only because of the context in which the phrase appears, particularly the phrase "defence of himself," suggesting private self-defense, not community defense as part of an organized militia. Scalia's own examples demonstrate that *context is critical to meaning*. As he wrote on another occasion, "In textual interpretation, context is everything."[8]

When it comes to the Second Amendment, however, Scalia interprets the phrase "keep and bear Arms" by ripping the phrase out of context, that is, by artificially separating the phrase from the words that precede it about ensuring "a well regulated Militia . . . necessary to the security of a free State" and determining its meaning without reference to the militia language.[9] (As we will see, Scalia addresses the militia language only *after* he has determined the meaning of the right independent of that language.) The issue is not, however, whether the phrases "keep Arms" and "bear Arms" could have nonmilitia meanings in other contexts. The issue is the meaning of the phrase "keep and bear Arms" *as it is used in the context of a provision of the Constitution declaring the importance of a "well regulated Militia" to "the security of a free State."*

Justice Scalia's opinion also notably insists on interpreting the phrase "keep and bear Arms" by first slicing and dicing it into the phrases "keep Arms" and "bear Arms" before presenting multiple examples of the use of each phrase, in isolation from the other, in nonmilitia contexts. Only in passing does the opinion note the Massachusetts Declaration of Rights of 1780, in which the two phrases appear joined together as "the right to keep and to bear arms," much as they appear in the Second Amendment. It is worth quoting the Massachusetts provision in its entirety, which Scalia does not do:

> The people have a right to keep and to bear arms for the common defense. And as, in time of peace, armies are dangerous to liberty, they

ought not to be maintained without the consent of the legislature; and the military power shall always be held in an exact subordination to the civil authority, and be governed by it.

Can there be any doubt that, in this provision, context establishes that the phrase "right to keep and to bear arms" refers entirely to military matters and has nothing whatever to do with private self-defense?[10] The provision guarantees "a right to keep and to bear arms *for the common defense*," and is followed by an articulation of the dangers of standing armies and the need for civilian control of the military. The militia language of the Second Amendment functions in the same way to elucidate the meaning of a similar phrase as referring to military matters.

Incredibly, though, the Scalia majority opinion in *Heller* concludes that in the Massachusetts provision, the right is not confined to militia service, but rather "secured an individual right to bear arms for defensive purposes."[11] Can there be any clearer indication that Justice Scalia and those joining him in the majority would find that the right to "keep and bear Arms" has a nonmilitia meaning *in every possible context* and, therefore, *regardless of context?* What became of Scalia's conviction that in interpreting constitutional text, "context is everything"? When it comes to the Second Amendment, context apparently is nothing. The imperative to discover a right to be armed for self-defense is everything.

Justice Scalia's majority opinion disguises its unprincipled use of context through the sleight of hand of referring to the militia language as merely "prefatory" as opposed to the other "operative" language of the amendment. Here he claims that the text of the Second Amendment itself indicates that the prefatory militia language does not have operative effect, comparing the language to "whereas" clauses in legislation and to the preamble to the Constitution itself.[12]

It is true that statutory language often is preceded by a series of "whereas" clauses discussing the problem the legislation is designed to address and stating its purpose, but having no independently enforceable effect as law. But the analogy of these "whereas" clauses to the militia language of the Second Amendment is clearly invalid. The portion of the Constitution analogous to statutory "whereas" clauses is the Constitution's own preamble, which, in language that speaks to the ages, sets out the broad values that "We the people" sought to pursue in establishing the new government— "to insure domestic Tranquility," and "to secure the Blessings of Liberty to ourselves and our Posterity"—but is not independently enforceable as law. But the first thirteen words of the Second Amendment are only less operative than the remainder of its text because five justices of the Supreme Court have now decreed it to be so.

Indeed, in his own writings, Justice Scalia has distinguished the Constitution's famous preamble from the remainder of the document, writing that the preamble sets forth only the "the aspirations of those who adopted it," while the "operative provisions of the document, on the other hand, *including the Bill of Rights*, abound in concrete and specific dispositions [emphasis added]."[13] Yet in *Heller*, when the goal is to create, by all means necessary, a new right unrelated to the militia, the amendment's first thirteen words become the only portion of the Bill of Rights that is not operative. Justice Scalia's textualism apparently allows him to select the words of the Constitution that are operative, at least when it becomes necessary to support his predetermined conclusion about what the Constitution means. And let there be no doubt that, at least as to Justice Scalia himself, the *Heller* conclusion was predetermined. Over a decade before *Heller*, Scalia had written that the Second Amendment concerned a "right of self-defense" that was "absolutely fundamental."[14]

In deciding that some words of the Second Amendment are not operative, the *Heller* majority also violated what the Supreme Court itself has called "the first principle of constitutional interpretation."[15] This principle—applied first in *Marbury v. Madison*—holds that the Constitution must be interpreted such that "real effect should be given to all the words its uses"[16] and that interpretations rendering some of its words "mere surplusage" must be avoided.[17] This principle is based on the profound respect accorded the constitutional text by the courts. As the Supreme Court phrased it long ago, "Every word appears to have been weighed with the utmost deliberation, and its full force and effect to have been fully understood. No word in the instrument, therefore, can be rejected as superfluous."[18] Well, at least until *Heller*. The phrase "mere surplusage" nicely describes the militia language under the *Heller* majority's reading of the Second Amendment. The majority held that the Second Amendment guarantees a right to possess guns in the home for self-defense. Under the majority's theory, it would have that meaning even if its first thirteen words were entirely deleted. Long before the *Heller* decision, Justice Scalia had written that "textualism is no ironclad protection against the judge who wishes to impose his will."[19] What better proof of this statement can be offered than his own majority opinion in *Heller*?

Justice Scalia's tortured path thus "elevates above all other interests the right of responsible citizens to use arms in defense of hearth and home,"[20] in a text in which this interest is entirely hidden and in which the "security of a free State," not the security of "hearth and home" is the only expressed purpose of the guarantee.[21] This is ideology talking. It certainly is not constitutional interpretation.

DON'T KNOW MUCH ABOUT HISTORY

The *Heller* majority's arrogation of the power to edit the constitutional text is particularly galling in the case of the Second Amendment because the history of the amendment's drafting and consideration by the First Congress demonstrates how important the Framers regarded the now-meaningless militia language. Indeed, the changes made in the amendment's text by its ratifiers in the First Congress were made to the very language that the *Heller* majority now has cast aside. Consider the text of the Amendment as originally drafted by James Madison and presented to the First Congress:

> The right of the people to keep and bear arms shall not be infringed; a well armed, and well regulated militia being the best security of a free country; but no person religiously scrupulous of bearing arms, shall be compelled to render military service in person.[22]

The First Congress made the following changes to the text before ratifying it: (1) the reference to "well armed" in the description of the militia was deleted, (2) the description of the militia as "being the best security of a free country" was changed to "necessary to the security of a free State," (3) the language barring compelled military service of those "religiously scrupulous of bearing arms" was dropped, and (4) the position of the militia language in the amendment was changed to make it *more* prominent. Other changes proved to be only temporary. For example, at one point in the process the words "composed of the body of the people" were inserted to describe the militia, but the phrase was deleted from the final version.[23]

The change in the order of the clauses to begin the text with the militia language is particularly interesting because, without that change, Justice Scalia could not treat the militia language as merely prefatory, and therefore not operative. Under Madison's original version, there was nothing prefatory about the militia language; it certainly did not function as a preface or prologue. Is it plausible that the First Congress sought to diminish the importance of the militia language by having it precede the guarantee of the right? Hardly. Scalia does not discuss the issue because, as noted below, his methodology dismisses the importance of all such legislative history.

I will leave it to others to debate the significance of each of these changes in the amendment's text. My point is only that they at least reflect the serious attention given by the Framers to the entire text of the Second Amendment, particularly the militia language. Why would the Framers have so actively edited these words if they, as does Justice Scalia, regarded them as merely "aspirational" (and thus analogous to the Constitution's preamble), having no effect whatever on the amendment's meaning? Justice Scalia is well-known for his view that constitutional interpretation should be governed by the "original meaning of the text, not what the original draftsmen intended."[24] Thus, he places little importance on the "legislative history" of the Constitution, including its drafting history and the statements made by those involved in writing and ratifying the Constitution. The *Heller* opinion is a strong example of how his disdain for legislative history leads him to distort the "original meaning" of the text.

One aspect of the legislative history deserves special attention: the conscientious objection clause that appeared in Madison's draft but was deleted by the First Congress. The clause provided that "no person religiously scrupulous of bearing arms, shall be compelled to render military service in person." The appearance of the provision in Madison's original version provides yet more context establishing that the right to "keep and bear Arms" had to do exclusively with military service.

First, the provision should end all doubt as to the meaning of the phrase "bear Arms" in the amendment. Unless one subscribes to the absurdity that "bear arms" and "bearing arms" had different meanings within Madison's original proposal, the conscientious objection clause establishes forcefully that "bear Arms" in the Second Amendment refers to rendering military service. Justice Scalia responds by arguing that, since Quakers opposed not just military service, but the use of arms for any reason, the clause should be read to mean that "those opposed to carrying weapons for potential violent confrontation" would not be compelled to render military service in which such carrying of weapons would be required.[25] For Scalia, therefore, the conscientious objection clause is compatible with the view that "bear Arms" in the amendment means to "carry Arms." Of course, under Scalia's account, it would make far more sense for the conscientious objection clause to refer to persons "religiously scrupulous of *keeping* Arms," rather than "*bearing* Arms," unless we are to believe that a Quaker's religious objection is not to having arms, but rather to physically carrying them.

In any event, Justice John Paul Stevens's dissent destroys Scalia's speculation by quoting a similar conscientious objection clause from the constitutional amendments proposed by Virginia's ratifying convention, in which Madison was an important participant. Two of the Virginia proposals had a transparently obvious influence on the text of the Second Amendment:

> 17th, That the people have a right to keep and bear arms; that a well regulated Militia composed of the body of the people trained to arms is the proper, natural and safe defence of a free State. That standing armies are dangerous to liberty, and therefore ought to be avoided, as far as the circumstances and protection of the Community will admit; and that in all cases the military should be under strict subordination to and be governed by the civil power.

> 19th. That any person religiously scrupulous of bearing arms ought to be exempted, *upon payment of an equivalent to employ another to bear arms in his stead.*[26]

Two points are important here. For one thing the seventeenth proposal clearly uses the phrase "right to keep and bear arms" in an entirely military context. For another thing, the nineteenth proposal, by specifying that conscientious objectors must, in effect, pay a fee to avoid military service, unequivocally uses "bear arms" to mean compelled military service, not the voluntary carrying of arms for self-defense. The notion that Madison was using "bearing arms" to have an entirely different meaning in his Second Amendment conscientious objector language is completely implausible.

Even if Scalia's account of "bearing Arms" in the conscientious objector language were correct, the appearance of the clause in Madison's initial proposal would still be inexplicable under the *Heller* majority's view of the Second Amendment. Under that view, the original meaning of the amendment was to guarantee individuals the right to *choose* to have a gun for private purposes or, presumably, to choose not to have a gun. If this was the meaning, why would it have ever occurred to Madison to include a clause allowing conscientious objection to compelled military service? Indeed, under this meaning, the internal logic of Madison's proposal would collapse. Madison's inclusion of a conscientious objector clause is comprehensible only if the right to "keep and bear Arms" in its text refers to the right to be armed in connection with service in the militia—service, which, as we will see below, was compulsory, not a matter of choice. As Justice Stevens observed in dissent, "the State simply does not compel its citizens to carry arms for the purpose of private 'confrontation,' [citation omitted] or for self-defense."[27]

Justice Scalia's opinion cautions against reliance on text that was deleted from the Second Amendment,[28] but the legislative history, by illuminating why the provision was deleted, also undercuts Scalia's argument. The core objection to the clause was that it would be used to weaken the militia. Representative Elbridge Gerry argued, for example, that the clause would enable the government to "declare who are those religiously scrupulous, and prevent them from bearing arms." Gerry continued, "What, sir, is the use of the militia? It is to prevent the establishment of a standing army, the bane of liberty."[29] It is certainly reasonable to assume that the clause was deleted because of this anticipated effect on the militia. There is certainly no evidence that it was deleted because it was unnecessary, indeed nonsensical, in a provision having only to do with guaranteeing individuals the freedom to possess guns for private, nonmilitia use.

The *Heller* majority has no credible explanation for why the Framers included language about the importance of the militia in a constitutional amendment intended to guarantee the right of individuals to possess guns for self-defense. The majority also has no explanation for the Framers' failure to adopt an alternative version, based on other proposals made at the time, that clearly would have guaranteed an individual right for private, nonmilitia purposes.

We have seen that Madison's original proposal bore a striking resemblance to the militia-based proposed amendment of the Virginia ratification convention. Justice Stevens's dissenting opinion cites proposals originating in other states that guaranteed the right to be armed, with no reference to the militia.[30] For example, the New Hampshire proposal read, "Congress shall never disarm any Citizen unless such as are or have been in Actual Rebellion." Another proposal, rejected by the Pennsylvania ratifying convention, read, "That the people have a right to bear arms for the defense of themselves and their own State, or the United States, or for the purpose of killing game; and no law shall be passed for disarming the people or any of them unless for crimes committed, or real danger of public injury from individuals." As in the Virginia proposal, this language was then followed by expressions of the dangers of standing armies and the need for civilian control of the military. But the reference to "killing game" and the far-reaching prohibition on disarming law-abiding citizens, indicates that the "right to bear arms" in the defeated Pennsylvania proposal was not confined to militia service. No such language appeared in the Virginia proposal and nothing like it appears in the Second Amendment.

Justice Stevens's dissent points to another proposal, which failed to muster a majority in the Massachusetts ratification convention and read,

"That the said Constitution never be construed to authorize Congress to . . . prevent the people of the United States, who are peaceable citizens, from keeping their own arms." (It is instructive to compare this broad language, defeated in the Massachusetts Convention, with the narrower "common defense" language, cited earlier, which already was part of the Massachusetts State Constitution.) These broader formulations of the right to be armed presumably were known by Madison and the First Congress.

If the *Heller* majority's reading of the Second Amendment is right, then Madison and the First Congress sought to guarantee a nonmilitia right by choosing language emphasizing the importance of a "well regulated Militia," while avoiding other available formulations making no reference to the militia at all. Unlikely, to say the least.

In place of the well-established principle that the Constitution must be interpreted to give each word meaning and effect, Justice Scalia's opinion substitutes a new principle—for which he cites no support in prior Supreme Court cases—that the only requirement is that there be a "logical connection" between words and phrases in the Constitution.[31] Having determined, without reference to the militia language, that the Second Amendment guarantees a right to have arms for self-defense, Scalia then finds that the only remaining task is to ensure that this right "is consistent with the announced purpose" expressed in the militia clause. He finds this consistency by asserting that the right to be armed for self-defense "furthers the purpose of an effective militia no less than (indeed, more than) the dissent's interpretation."[32]

Scalia's claimed "logical connection" is based on a gross misunderstanding of the nature of the "well regulated Militia" and how it was armed. In the Founding Era, the militia was not, as Justice Scalia seems to presume,[33] simply an unorganized "pool" of "able-bodied men" from which the Congress had the power to organize an effective fighting force. By its very nature, a militia existed only to the extent that it was organized. Indeed, the definition of "militia" in Noah Webster's famous dictionary—cited by Scalia himself[34]—undercuts the concept of an "unorganized militia": "The militia of a country are the able bodied men organized into companies, regiments and brigades . . . and required by law to attend military exercises on certain days only, but at other times left to pursue their usual occupations."

Justice Scalia is correct in observing that the militia existed prior to the Constitution, but he is wrong in asserting that it preexisted the Constitution as an unorganized collection of individuals. The state militias existing at the time of the Constitution were creatures of state statutory law. As discussed in Justice Stevens's dissent, these preexisting state militia statutes imposed extensive requirements on those enrolled in the militia. Of greatest significance for Second Amendment purposes was the common requirement that militiamen "keep arms" in their homes for use when called to militia duty. Stevens quotes the Virginia militia law requiring militiamen to "constantly keep the aforesaid arms, accoutrements, and ammunition, ready to be produced whenever called for by his commanding officer."[35] In fact, one year after the Constitution was ratified, Congress enacted the Second Militia Act of 1792 requiring that each militiaman "within six months" after enrollment in the new federally organized militia, "provide himself with a good musket or firelock."[36] (This statute was responsive to the Anti-Federalist fear that animated the push for the Second Amendment, namely that Congress would fail to exercise its new power to arm the militia.) Thus, not only was the militia inherently organized, but the arming of the militia was a matter of government command, not simply reliance on the individual choices of militiamen to acquire guns, or not to acquire them.

Justice Scalia describes the militia at the time of ratification as "the body of all citizens capable of military service, who would bring the sorts of lawful weapons that they possessed at home to militia duty."[37] He fails to mention that these militiamen were *required by law* to keep militia weapons at home. As Justice Stevens comments, "'keep and bear arms' thus perfectly describes the responsibilities of a framing-era militia member."[38]

Once the militia is properly understood as a government-organized system of compulsory armed service, it becomes plain that there is no "logical connection" between the militia and a guaranteed right to possess guns for purposes unrelated to militia service. Nor is there any logic to the inclusion of language about the importance of the militia in a provision guaranteeing the right to possess guns "in defense of hearth and home."

A principled approach to interpreting the Second Amendment—that is, one not determined, by hook or by crook, to arrive at a predetermined conclusion—would surely look to the amendment's text as an integrated whole, reading each word in context and giving each a functional meaning. Instead, the *Heller* majority's "slice and dice" approach—surgically removing the second half from its connection to the first half, then carving up the phrase "keep and bear Arms"—gives the amendment a meaning that would have been foreign to those who ratified it. In showing the folly of the Court's approach, I cannot improve on Justice Stevens's analogy to the parable of the six blind men and the elephant. He applied the parable to what he called "the Court's atomistic, word-by-word approach": "In the parable, each blind man approaches a single elephant; touching a different part of the elephant's body in isolation, each concludes that he has learned its true nature. One touches the animal's leg, and concludes that the elephant is like a tree; another touches the trunk and decides that the elephant is like a snake; and so on. Each of them, of course, has fundamentally failed to grasp the nature of the creature."[39] In approaching the meaning of the words and phrases of the Second Amendment in isolation from one another, the *Heller* majority, too, failed to grasp the nature of the amendment as a whole.

It is not surprising that the *Heller* majority opinion has been the subject of scathing scholarly attack for its "results-oriented" approach. Indeed, some of the sharpest criticism has come from conservative legal theorists with a long history of opposition to judicial activism.[40] In an extraordinary article disclosing his own family's gun violence tragedy some years ago, Pepperdine University law professor Douglas Kmiec, who once shared an office with Samuel Alito in the Reagan Justice Department, praised Justice Scalia's career of "reminding his fellow judges how important it is not to read their own personal experiences or desires into the law." But Kmiec found that principle dishonored in Scalia's *Heller* opinion. "From their high bench on that morning," he wrote, "it would not be the democratic choice that mattered, but theirs. Constitutional text, history, and precedent all set aside."[41]

Judge Richard Posner of the U.S. Court of Appeals for the Seventh Circuit, who is also a law professor at the University of Chicago and undoubtedly the leading conservative legal thinker of our time, found the *Heller* decision to be "evidence that the Supreme Court, in deciding constitutional cases, exercises a freewheeling discretion strongly flavored with ideology."[42] Commenting on the sheer length of Scalia's majority opinion (almost twenty thousand words), Posner found it "evidence of the ability of well-staffed courts to produce snow jobs." Unkind words, but well deserved.

A third broadside has come from Judge J. Harvie Wilkinson III of the U.S. Court of Appeals in Richmond, who was on the "short list" for the Supreme Court throughout the George W. Bush administration (and was, incidentally, my Constitutional Law professor at the University of Virginia Law School long before he was appointed to the bench). Judge Wilkinson is somewhat more charitable than Kmiec and Posner to the evidence presented by the *Heller* majority supporting the "personal rights" view of the Second Amendment. Nevertheless, he sees *Heller* as improper "judicial lawmaking" in defiance of conservative legal principles counseling restraint and deference to the judgments of popularly elected legislatures.[43] "In fact, *Heller* encourages Americans to do what conservative jurists warned for years they should not do: bypass the ballot and seek to press their political agenda in the courts," he writes.[44] Wilkinson especially singles out Justice

Scalia for committing the same sins of judicial activism in *Heller* that Scalia has spent a career denouncing in *Roe v. Wade*.[45]

IS *HELLER* A LETHAL WEAPON AGAINST GUN CONTROL?

For those involved in the gun control debate, there is an odd "good news, bad news" quality to the *Heller* opinion. (What part is good news and what part is bad, of course, depends on your point of view.) For the gun lobby, the good news is that there is now a right to have guns in the home that is entirely divorced from militia service. However, the bad news (and it seems likely to be very bad news indeed) is that *Heller* contains some extraordinary language suggesting that a wide range of gun control laws do not violate this new right. "Like most rights, the right secured by the Second Amendment is not unlimited," wrote the *Heller* majority. According to the Court, "the right was not a right to keep and carry any weapon whatsoever in any manner whatsoever and for whatever purpose."[46]

It is highly unusual for a court, in interpreting the Constitution, to comment on the constitutionality of laws not before it, particularly when it is not citing prior court rulings on the issue. The *Heller* majority, however, went out of its way to offer the assurance that "nothing in our opinion should be taken to cast doubt" on a wide range of gun control laws, which the Court said remain "presumptively lawful" under the Court's ruling.[47] These include

- laws imposing "conditions and qualifications" on the commercial sale of arms (a category broad enough to include background checks, waiting periods, licensing, registration, safety training, limits on large-volume sales, etc.);
- prohibitions on gun possession by felons and the mentally ill;
- prohibitions on carrying concealed weapons;
- laws forbidding firearms in "sensitive places" such as schools and government buildings; and
- bans on "dangerous and unusual weapons" (which could include machine guns and assault weapons).

As if this list were not enough to make the NRA squirm, the Court added that these "presumptively lawful regulatory measures" are given "only as examples" and that the list "does not purport to be exhaustive."[48]

Later in the opinion, the Court stated that its analysis also does not "suggest the invalidity of laws regulating the storage of firearms to prevent accidents,"[49] which presumably would include laws against leaving loaded guns accessible to kids. It is equally significant that the Court, in commenting on the many cases in which gun laws have been upheld against Second Amendment challenge under the "militia purpose" view, cautioned that "it should not be thought that the cases decided by these judges would necessarily have come out differently under a proper interpretation of the right."[50]

Why did the *Heller* majority so gratuitously suggest that its historic ruling recognizing a constitutional right to be armed for self-defense may have little practical impact on gun control laws? It is not unreasonable to speculate that much of this reassuring language was inserted as the price of getting four other justices to join Scalia's opinion. Intuitively, it seems unlikely that such language originated with Justice Scalia (one of Dick Cheney's hunting buddies and an obvious gun enthusiast), rather than being a concession by him to other justices.

It also is unclear how the majority derived its categories of "presumptively lawful" gun control measures. Although the majority seems to attach great importance to whether the gun restrictions at issue are "longstanding," the opinion leaves unclear how longstanding they must be. It also is unclear whether a specific restriction (such as a waiting period) must be longstanding, or whether the specific restriction must be part of a category of restrictions (e.g., "laws imposing conditions and qualifications on the sale of arms") that is longstanding.

However the language came about, and recognizing its uncertain scope, the commentary on other gun control laws in *Heller* is nonetheless significant. It is likely to be interpreted by the lower federal courts as a sign that the Supreme Court has drawn a sharp distinction between laws that function to ban guns commonly possessed in the home for self-defense (like the D.C. law) and other laws that impose regulation on guns, even tight regulation, but yet allow individuals, not governments, to make the ultimate decision about gun ownership.

It also is significant that the *Heller* majority did not adopt a stringent legal standard for future judicial review of gun control laws, though the lawyers for Mr. Heller vigorously urged the Court to do so. The strict scrutiny test, urged by Mr. Heller and used in certain First Amendment cases, would require courts reviewing gun laws to determine whether the law being challenged is "narrowly tailored to achieve a compelling government interest."[51] Though the prevention of death and injury from gunfire would seem to qualify as a "compelling government interest," the requirement that the law be "narrowly tailored" would invite right-wing activist judges to decide that gun control laws they don't like are insufficiently narrow in their impact on gun rights. As Justice Breyer's separate dissenting opinion notes, the *Heller* majority implicitly rejected a strict scrutiny test.[52] Indeed, the majority adopted no test at all. Whereas strict scrutiny would have erected a strong presumption against the constitutionality of gun control laws, requiring narrow tailoring to overcome the presumption, the *Heller* majority described a lengthy list of gun control measures as "presumptively lawful." Good news for public safety.

Although the *Heller* majority makes some comparison of its new Second Amendment right to our First Amendment rights,[53] its surprising commentary on gun control laws, and failure to endorse strict scrutiny of those laws, suggest that at least some justices in the majority understand that the right to possess handguns in the home is dramatically different in nature from our First Amendment rights. As interpreted by *Heller*, the Second Amendment, unlike the First Amendment, guarantees a right to possess a lethal weapon. It should be obvious, but bears saying anyway, that the right to possess lethal weapons affects the public's interest in safety and security more directly than the right to express oneself about lethal weapons (or other topics, for that matter). Pro-gun advocates will continue to make crazy analogies to the First Amendment, like David Kopel of the libertarian Independence Institute who says, "Guns are like books or churches."[54] But it is hard to maintain that the *Heller* decision treats guns "like books or churches."

Since gun control advocates like myself have strongly advocated the narrow "militia purpose" view of the Second Amendment for many years, the gun lobby may well charge that this analysis of *Heller* is simply an effort by the losers in *Heller* to give a "silver lining" spin to the ruling. Indeed, it may be asked, if the rejection of the "militia purpose" view is so beneficial to gun control advocates, why did we resist it so forcefully? One answer, of course, is that only the militia view is defensible as a matter of constitutional law. But apart from the merits of the legal issue, it should be kept in mind that, before the actual ruling, there was considerable risk that a decision severing the right to be armed from its express militia purpose would provide the legal foundation for successful challenges to gun control laws generally, particularly if the Court had adopted a strict scrutiny standard or something like it. The opinion the Court issued, however, appears to have put important limits on the practical implications of its own ruling. This was hardly inevitable. Indeed, it likely was an unpleasant surprise to the gun lobby.

The *Heller* ruling already is prompting an avalanche of Second Amendment lawsuits and legal claims. Even before the ruling came down, Larry

Pratt of the radical Gun Owners of America was projecting "a kazillion court cases" and advising that if he were "a young man today, I'd be smart to go to law school and become a Second Amendment lawyer." "I'd be able to send my grandkids to college," he enthused.[55] The NRA's Wayne LaPierre called the ruling "the opening salvo," telling his members that the fight "is just beginning."[56] Within forty-eight hours after the *Heller* decision was handed down, the NRA and its allies had filed six lawsuits against local jurisdictions with handgun bans.[57] Within months of *Heller*, the NRA was talking about the need to "expand its reach."[58] *Heller* also has been enthusiastically embraced by criminal defense lawyers anxious to use it to challenge the gun laws under which their clients are being prosecuted. Indeed, the vast majority of legal claims based on *Heller* likely will arise in criminal cases. As of this writing, criminal defendants have used *Heller* to challenge prosecutions involving felons illegally in possession of guns, gun possession by domestic abusers, guns carried illegally on government property or in schools, and illegal possession of machine guns, though the outcome of these challenges has yet to be determined.

There is no question that there is greater uncertainty about the constitutionality of gun regulation after *Heller*. Moreover, future changes in the Supreme Court's composition may well affect the strength of the new right to be armed as a legal weapon against gun control laws. Based on the *Heller* decision alone, however, it seems likely that the vast majority of gun laws ultimately will survive the post-*Heller* attacks. When the constitutional dust settles, the legal significance of our newfound constitutional right to have handguns in the home may prove to be more symbol than substance.

THE SECOND AMENDMENT AS AN ARGUMENT AGAINST GUN CONTROL

We have seen that *Heller* may pose only a marginal threat to the future constitutionality of gun laws less restrictive than a broad gun ban. Although the legal risk to gun laws may be low, there is yet another possible impact of *Heller* to consider. *Heller* gives guns a protected constitutional status enjoyed by no other product. Doesn't that special status help the gun lobby to argue forcefully against analogies between guns and other dangerous products for which government regulation is commonplace and widely accepted?

We have noted that pro-gun advocates typically respond to the cars/guns analogy by noting that there is no constitutional right to have a car. Before *Heller* it was possible for gun control advocates to respond that there is no constitutional right to have a gun either. Not so after *Heller*. We have seen that, from a strictly legal standpoint, *Heller* does not seem to create a new presumption against gun control laws generally. But does it create a new presumption against gun control in the public's mind, placing a greater burden on gun control advocates to justify their proposals as sound policy?

Heller would appear to have this impact on the gun control debate only if support for gun control before *Heller* were dependent, to a substantial extent, on the public's belief that the Second Amendment does not guarantee a broad, nonmilitia right. We have seen, from public opinion polls, that supermajorities of the public have long supported a broad gun control agenda, the only exception being a ban on handguns. If this support were somehow premised on the public's conviction that the Constitution does not protect a right to gun ownership for private purposes, then *Heller*, by destroying that premise, could be expected to shake the foundation of the public's support for gun control.

But, in fact, public opinion surveys have long shown that the public believes that the Second Amendment is concerned with individual rights, not militias. A 1995 *U.S. News & World Report* poll reported that 75 percent of Americans believe that "the Constitution guarantees you the right to own a gun."[59] On the day *Heller* was argued in the Supreme Court, the *Washington Post* released a nationwide poll showing that 72 percent of those surveyed believe the Second Amendment "guarantees the right of individuals to own guns," while only 20 percent said it guarantees "only the right of the states to maintain militias."[60] While one could quarrel with the wording of these poll questions, they do suggest that the "militia purpose" view—long dominant in the courts—did not seriously penetrate the public's consciousness in the modern era. This is hardly surprising, given the strangeness, to modern ears, of the phrase "well regulated Militia."

This means that a large majority of Americans has long believed, and continues to believe, *simultaneously* in a broad gun control agenda and in a broad interpretation of the Second Amendment. For the general public, the *Heller* ruling is consistent with what it had long understood to be true: the Second Amendment guarantees a right to have guns, but that right is not absolute and is subject to sensible restrictions.

Given the public's longstanding view of how the Second Amendment affects gun control, *Heller* may actually weaken the argument that gun control proposals should be rejected because the Constitution guarantees a right to possess guns.

Before *Heller*, gun control advocates typically would respond to the Second Amendment argument in two ways. First, they would argue that the courts already had determined that the Second Amendment relates only to the militia and thus was no barrier to gun control laws. Although this argument was true, it did not conform to the public's beliefs about the amendment's meaning—beliefs that were difficult to alter given the constant din of gun lobby propaganda on the constitutional issue and the fact that courts don't issue press releases. Second, gun control advocates would assert that even if the Second Amendment were broader than militia service, no rights are absolute and the right to be armed surely should be subject to reasonable restrictions. This argument had substantial persuasive appeal before *Heller* because it was consistent with public attitudes. It has even greater appeal after *Heller*, given the *Heller* Court's reassuring language about the presumptive constitutionality of gun regulation. When pro-gun partisans trot out the Second Amendment—joyfully citing *Heller*—they will now be met with the response that the *Heller* opinion itself—written by one of most conservative and gun-loving justices in recent history—found no inconsistency between the Second Amendment and a host of gun regulations.

Barack Obama's message about guns during the 2008 campaign took full advantage of *Heller* in successfully overcoming the NRA's virulent opposition (and his own reference to "bitter" gun owners). Obama constantly emphasized his support for the Second Amendment—and, specifically, for the *Heller* interpretation—while not backing down from his record of support for reasonable gun laws.[61] His message was consistent with *Heller* and reflected the views of most Americans.

As we have seen, the public's support for gun control has never been premised on a belief that the Second Amendment guarantees only a militia-related right. The polling data suggests that, for most Americans, their views about gun control are not dependent on their beliefs about the Second Amendment; indeed, it is more true to say that most Americans adjust their views about the Second Amendment to accommodate them to their views about gun control. If they think gun control is sound public policy, they will conclude that it is not prohibited by the Constitution.

Putting the point another way, few Americans who believe that gun control laws save lives will nevertheless oppose them because they think they violate the Second Amendment. And because most Americans support strong gun control laws, they believe the Second Amendment is of secondary importance. For many years the Pew Research Center has asked Americans whether they think it is more important to "protect gun owners' rights" or "control gun ownership." In April 2008 58 percent of those surveyed said it was more important to "control gun ownership," while only 37 percent said it was more important to "protect gun owners' rights." The results were virtually identical in 1993, fifteen years before.[62]

The reality is that, of all the gun lobby's arguments, the constitutional argument has been the least effective in resisting gun control. For all its symbolic and emotional importance to the NRA, the gun lobby has never convinced the public that gun control violates our constitutional values. By both recognizing gun rights and, at the same time, confirming the public's long-held belief that gun regulation is entirely compatible with those rights, *Heller* is likely, over the long term, to further diminish the importance of the Second Amendment argument as a barrier to the enactment of strong gun laws.

So we return to the paradox of the *Heller* ruling. In *Heller* the "gun rights" advocates achieved vindication for their view of the meaning of the Second Amendment, though the Supreme Court had to abandon every pretense of devotion to neutral, principled constitutional interpretation to give them that victory. There is, however, good reason to believe that *Heller* may prove sharply disappointing to the gun lobby as a legal weapon against gun control laws short of a handgun ban, while weakening both the slippery slope argument, and the constitutional argument itself, as reasons to oppose gun regulation. Viewing *Heller* from the perch of the NRA's leadership, an old expression comes to mind: "Be careful what you wish for. It could come true."

EPILOGUE

FROM LETHAL LOGIC TO SENSIBLE SOLUTIONS

ON THE SNOWY MORNING of April 16, 2007, the bucolic, sprawling Blacksburg, Virginia, campus of Virginia Polytechnic Institute and State University—better known as Virginia Tech—became the scene of the bloodiest mass shooting in American history. A mentally disturbed student, senior Seung Hui Cho, murdered thirty-two and wounded seventeen students and faculty.[1] The horror began around 7:15 in the morning, when Cho entered West Ambler Johnson dormitory and fatally wounded student Emily Hilscher. Moments earlier, Emily had been dropped off at the dorm by her boyfriend, who was a student at Radford University, but who lived in Blacksburg. Why Cho singled out Emily Hilscher is still unknown.

Hearing noises from Emily's room, Ryan Clark, a resident adviser who lived next door, checked to see what was happening. He, too, was shot and killed. Cho was able to leave the building without being stopped. He did not claim his next victim until over two hours later, when he carried two handguns and almost four hundred rounds of ammunition packed in high-capacity magazines, into Norris Hall, a building of classrooms, and chained shut the pair of doors at each of the three main entrances to the building used by students. He walked into an Advanced Hydrology engineering class in room 206, shot and killed the instructor, and methodically fired on the students, killing nine and injuring two others. He crossed the hall and entered room 207, shot the professor teaching a German class, and then killed four students while wounding six others. He attacked two other classrooms, returning to most of the classrooms more than once to continue shooting.

It took Cho only about ten to twelve minutes to murder twenty-five students and five teachers in Norris Hall. Another seventeen were shot, but they survived. He fired at least 174 rounds from his two semiautomatic pistols. The police found seventeen empty ammunition magazines, each capable of holding ten to fifteen rounds. The rampage ended with Cho taking his own life as the police closed in.

As we remember the tragedy at Virginia Tech, I invite the reader to join me in a flight of imagination. Picture, for a moment, a world in which the lethal logic of the gun lobby does not dictate our nation's gun policies. Picture, rather, a world where reason and common sense have prevailed over ideology and bumper sticker slogans on the gun issue. Would the thirty-two innocent students and teachers slain at Virginia Tech still be alive? Could the seventeen others who were wounded have escaped the excruciating pain and lifelong trauma of those gunshots?

We know that no gun law would have cured Cho of the mental illness that fed his violence. But could a gun law have denied him the weapon that enabled him to become a mass murderer? The answer is yes. And the gun law that could have saved those lives was already on the books.

The Brady Act should have stopped Cho from buying his guns. Incredibly, Cho was able to walk into two gun shops, undergo the mandatory Brady background checks and, within minutes, walk out with the guns *even though he was legally prohibited from buying guns.* How did this happen? Because the record disqualifying Cho from buying guns was not in the database checked by the Virginia authorities.

In December 2005 Cho was found by a Virginia judge to be both mentally ill and a danger to himself. That court order disqualified him from future gun purchases by virtue of the provision of the 1968 Gun Control Act barring gun sales to persons "adjudicated as a mental defective." (The use of the term "mental defective" provides a glimpse into the unenlightened view of the mentally ill prevailing in the late '60s.) Federal regulations define the term "adjudicated as a mental defective" as a "determination by a court . . . or other lawful authority that a person, as a result of . . . mental illness . . . is a danger to himself or to others." Cho clearly was prohibited.[2]

The court order disqualifying Cho, however, never made it into the federal database checked by the Virginia State Police. Why? Because the Virginia authorities were entirely focused on reporting mental health records that they believed disqualified Virginia gun buyers under *Virginia* law but appeared to recognize no need to report mental health records that disqualified gun buyers under *federal* law. Because Cho was ordered by the Virginia court to undergo only outpatient treatment, the Virginia authorities apparently thought he was not disqualified under state law and thus his court order need not be reported.[3] But his disqualification under federal law cannot be disputed.

The failure of Virginia authorities to report Cho's disqualifying court order to the federal background check system turns out to be the tip of a gigantic and deadly iceberg. Ironically, Virginia, at the time of Cho's gun purchase, actually led the nation in reporting mental health records to the Brady system. Overall, the performance of the states in this regard has been nothing short of miserable. As of 2006 less than 10 percent of an estimated 2.6 million disqualifying mental health records had been transmitted to the federal database.[4] It's easy to dismiss this as a paperwork problem, until you realize that every one of those millions of missing records represents a person *who already has been found too dangerous to have a gun.* Yet each of them can walk into a gun shop tomorrow and, like Cho, walk out with a gun.

Although some committed gun control opponents might use Cho's crime as an illustration of the futility of gun laws ("When guns are outlawed, only outlaws will have guns"), such an argument would be transparently specious. The Virginia Tech shooting was not a failure of the Brady Act, but a failure of the Brady Act to be properly administered. More records of disqualified gun buyers need to be put into the Brady database, but the fact is that millions of other records are in the system and Brady background checks have blocked more than 1.5 million purchases by prohibited buyers.

Does the Virginia Tech shooting support the NRA's argument that we don't need new laws, we simply need to enforce existing laws? No, because the NRA's argument is that we should have strong enforcement as a *substitute* for strong laws. Following the NRA's logic, we should never have enacted the requirement of Brady background checks in the first place; we should have simply better enforced the laws against gun sales to felons and the dangerously mentally ill. The Virginia Tech case is compelling proof that we need strong laws *and* strong enforcement of those laws.[5]

In our imaginary world, where reason has triumphed over bumper sticker slogans, the importance of stopping gun sales to dangerous people would be so readily understood that the Brady background check system would be flush with names of prohibited buyers and Cho would have been turned away from the gun stores empty-handed. What then? Cho was the kind of gun buyer least likely to be able to find an alternative source of guns. He was not a member of a violent street gang, with ready access to black market gun sources. Indeed, he was an incommunicative loner, with no social network at all, much less a network that would lead him to a supplier of illegal guns. He could, of course, have searched the classified ads or the Internet for a legal private seller not required to do background checks, or perhaps have attended a local gun show where such private sellers abound. But in our imaginary world, background checks would be required on all gun purchases, not just those from licensed dealers. Even if Cho found a private seller, he would be stopped by a background check.

Although theft would have been another possible avenue for Cho to have acquired a gun, it does not seem to be a realistic alternative in his case. He would need to find a vulnerable gun owner and then execute a crime for which he was not caught, even though he likely had never committed a crime of any kind in his life. A gun theft is a far different matter than planning a shooting destined to end with his own death. And in our imaginary world, all guns would be required to have an internal lock or other personalization system to block use by unauthorized owners. And all gun owners would be legally obligated to store their guns locked. Thus, it is unlikely that Cho would be able to use a gun that he acquired by theft.

Can we say that Cho would definitely have been denied a gun in our imaginary world? Perhaps not. But we don't demand absolute certainty of success from other laws. In Cho's case, there is every reason to believe that he would have been denied a gun had the right laws been enacted and properly enforced. With no gun, it is still possible that he would have initiated a violent attack. But there is no way that thirty-two people would have died.

Still in our imaginary world, let's assume that somehow Cho was able to get his guns from a licensed dealer despite the legal barriers. Would his rampage still have occurred? Maybe not.

Remember that almost two and a half hours elapsed between Cho's murder of Emily Hilscher and Ryan Clark in the dormitory and his mass shooting of students and teachers in the classroom building. During that time, police were called to the dorm and began their investigation. They were on the scene by 7:30 a.m. They began interviewing students in the dorm and learned that Emily had been visiting her boyfriend. They also learned his name and that he owned a gun. The boyfriend immediately became a "person of interest" in the investigation. The police sent out an alert for his pickup truck and searched for it in the campus parking lots. At 9:30, just as Cho was preparing his assault on Norris Hall, the police stopped the boyfriend's pickup on the road. He passed a field test for gunpowder residue. They knew then that the boyfriend was a false lead.

For the first two hours after the dormitory shootings, the police were pursuing the reasonable, but incorrect, theory that they were dealing with a double murder that was most likely the result of a domestic argument and that the shooter was no longer on campus. The police initially reported the incident to university officials as a possible murder-suicide and then as a domestic dispute, and then they said that the suspect probably had left the campus. The police did not urge the administration to take further action to protect against additional violence.

In our imaginary world, how would this course of events have been altered?

First, in a world when the NRA's bumper sticker logic has been routed, federal law would require every semiautomatic pistol to be equipped with microstamping technology that imprints the serial number of the gun on each ejected shell casing. Those shell casings littered Emily Hilscher's dorm room after the shootings.

Second, in our imaginary world, the gun lobby's opposition to handgun registration would have been overcome, the restrictions in federal law on computerization of handgun records would have been repealed, and the police would be able to use a gun's serial number to access information about every legal seller and purchaser of the gun with the click of a computer mouse. Given this capability, it is reasonable to assume that police investigating reports of a shooting would have a laptop at the ready, with easy access to computerized gun records. Since reading serial numbers from ejected shell casings would have become standard operating procedure in any shooting investigation, the police also would be equipped with magnifying equipment for accomplishing that task. The police investigators in Emily's dorm room, therefore, would quickly trace the gun used in the shooting to find its last lawful owner. With microstamping, they would be able to trace the gun from the casings left behind, with no need for the gun itself.

What would the gun trace have revealed? That the last legal purchaser of the gun was Seung Hui Cho, not Emily Hilscher's boyfriend. Literally within minutes of their arrival on the scene, and hours before the Norris Hall massacre, investigators would have known Cho's name. A phone call to the Virginia Tech registrar's office would have established that Cho was a current student and indicated where he was living. It is hardly much of a stretch to think that Cho could have been stopped for questioning before he entered the classroom building with his arsenal. Cho returned to his dorm room after the first shootings, where he stayed until at least 7:25 and perhaps as late as 8:00. Thereafter, he was observed in several public places, including near the Virginia Tech Duck Pond and the off-campus post office in Blacksburg, where he mailed a now-infamous package to NBC News in New York, containing a CD with a group of about twenty videos of himself presenting his largely incoherent complaints against the world, as well as pictures of himself wielding weapons.

Even if Cho had not been apprehended, the immediate identification of Cho as the last owner of the gun used in the dorm shooting, ending suspicion of the off-campus boyfriend, likely would have changed the university's reaction to the event. As described by the Virginia Tech Review Panel appointed by Virginia Governor Tim Kaine, as a result of the premature assumption that the shooting was a single, violent event that had come to an end, with no danger of a gunman on the loose on campus, "the university body was not put on high alert by the actions of the university administration and was largely taken by surprise by the events that followed."[6] The panel continued, "Warning the students, faculty, and staff might have made a difference. Putting more people on guard could have resulted in quicker recognition of a problem or suspicious activity, quicker reporting to police, and quicker response of police. Nearly everyone at Virginia Tech is adult and capable of making decisions about potentially dangerous situations to safeguard themselves. So the earlier and clearer the warning, the more chance an individual had of surviving."[7]

In our imaginary world of strong, sound gun laws, once Cho fired those semiautomatic pistols, everything would have been different. Of course, no one can predict with certainty that the shootings at Norris Hall would not have occurred. But the Virginia Tech Review Panel concluded that "all things considered," if the university had canceled classes and announced it was closed after the first shooting, "the toll could have been reduced."[8] These actions would have been far more likely if Cho had been linked to the murder weapon shortly after the dormitory shootings. He may well have arrived at Norris Hall with his arsenal, only to find no one inside.

I don't deny the element of speculation in this analysis. It's impossible to be certain about how many lives would have been saved if Cho had found himself in our imaginary world. But can anyone seriously argue that the toll of death and injury would have been the same had Cho been confronted with the reality of strong, sensible gun laws? Can anyone seriously assert that our national toll of gun death and injury would be the same if the gun lobby's lethal logic were replaced by sensible solutions?

Innocent people died that day at Virginia Tech because our nation has allowed bumper sticker logic to replace reason and evidence in making gun policy. Innocent people die every day for the same reason. They die on inner city streets, in suburban shopping malls, in schools of every description. If the students attending their classes at Virginia Tech that snowy April day were not safe, then none of us is safe.

Ideas have consequences. The gun lobby's logic has lethal consequences. But it has those consequences only because the American people have yet to demand a different national discussion of guns and violence. They have yet to insist on more from their elected officials than rote repetition of empty slogans.

Ultimately, if we continue to allow bumper stickers to dictate gun policy to deadly effect, we have ourselves to blame. We know that guns do kill people, and they do it more effectively, and more often, than any other weapons. We know that the issue is not "outlawing" guns, but preventing them from falling into dangerous hands. We know that irrational fear of the "slippery slope" is an empty excuse for inaction. We know we already have an armed society that is anything but polite. We know that strong law enforcement is not a substitute for strong laws. We know that gun makers and sellers should be accountable not for the violence of others, but for their own conduct that aids and abets the violence of others. We know that the "cold, dead hands" that should concern us are those of the innocent victims of gun violence, not the fantasy of self-styled patriots who risk little in promoting their extreme and dangerous agenda.

Now we must act on what we know. There are lives to save.

NOTES

PROLOGUE

1. National Center for Injury Prevention and Control, "Rates of Homicide, Suicide, and Firearm-Related Death Among Children—26 Industrialized Countries," *Morbidity and Mortality Weekly Report* 46 (1997): 101.
2. Project Safe Neighborhoods, "Letter from the President," http://www. illinoiscrimestoppers.org/psn/images/letters/GWBush-FullSize.gif.
3. In the gun violence context, Handgun Control, Inc., first used this phrase in an award-winning poster contrasting the number of handgun murders in the United States with the number in other industrialized countries.
4. Robert J. Spitzer, *The Politics of Gun Control*, 3rd ed. (Washington, DC: CQ Press, 2004), 99.
5. *National Journal*, March 5, 2005, 645.
6. Harris Interactive, "The American Red Cross, AARP, the Nature Conservancy, and the U.S. Chamber of Commerce Are among the Most Trusted Beltway Groups," *Harris Poll #88*, December 13, 2006, http://www.harrisinteractive. com/harris_poll/printerfriend/index.asp?PID=715.
7. James Ridgeway, Daniel Schulman, and David Corn, "There's Something about Mary: Unmasking a Gun Lobby Mole," *Mother Jones*, July 30, 2008, http://www. motherjones.com/news/feature/2008/07/mary-mcfate-sapone-gun-lobby-nra-spy.html.
8. NBC News/Wall Street Journal poll by Peter Hart and Robert Teeter, Study 6038, November 8–10, 2003 (on file with author).
9. Tom W. Smith, *1998 National Gun Policy Survey of the National Opinion Research Center: Research Findings* (Chicago: National Opinion Research Center, 1999); Greenberg Quinlan Rosner Research and the Tarrance Group, *Americans Support Common Sense Measures to Cut Down on Illegal Guns* (Washington, DC, April 2008) (87 percent of those surveyed favor requiring everyone who sells guns at gun shows to do background checks on purchasers).
10. David Hemenway, *Private Guns, Public Health* (Ann Arbor: University of Michigan Press, 2004), 163.
11. Tom W. Smith, *Public Opinion on Gun Control* (Chicago: National Opinion Research Center, December 2003), 53.
12. Douglas S. Weil and David Hemenway, "I Am the NRA: An Analysis of a National Random Sample of Gun Owners," *Violence & Victims* 8 (1993): 353, 353–365, 377–385.
13. Spitzer, *The Politics of Gun Control*, 101.

14. Bill Clinton, *My Life* (New York: Knopf, 2004), 630.
15. Bob Cusack and Elizabeth Fulk, "The Last Nail in Gun Control," *The Hill*, February 20, 2005, http://www.thehill.com/thehill/export/TheHill/News/Frontpage/020305/gun.html.
16. James Bovard, "What's Happened to John McCain?" *America's 1st Freedom*, July 2001, 29.
17. John C. Sigler, "Obama-Biden a Clear and Present Danger," *America's 1st Freedom*, November 2008, 10.
18. National Rifle Association, *Gun Ban Barack Obama*, http://www.gunbanobama.com.
19. Spitzer, *The Politics of Gun Control*, 102.
20. Gary Langer, "Mental Health Measures Broadly Backed, but Culture Gets More Blame Than Guns," *ABCNews.com*, April 23, 2007, http://abcnews.go.com/Politics/print?id=3068449.
21. Joseph Dolman, "Mayor's Promise on Guns Is Noble," *Newsday*, February 15, 2006.
22. James Carville and Paul Begala, *Take It Back: Our Party, Our Country, Our Future* (New York: Simon & Schuster, 2006), 49–50.
23. Clinton, *My Life*, 733–734.
24. Carville and Begala, *Take It Back*, 50.
25. Ibid., 49.
26. Ibid.
27. Bureau of Alcohol, Tobacco and Firearms, *Following the Gun: Enforcing Federal Firearms Laws against Firearms Traffickers* (Washington, DC, June 2000), 13 (Table 3).
28. Department of Justice and Department of the Treasury, *Gun Shows: Brady Checks and Crime Gun Traces* (Washington, DC, January 1999), 7.
29. Associated Press, "Man Accused of Shipping Arms, Ammunition to Beirut," November 21, 2000.
30. Judy L. Thomas, "Gun Shows Caught amid Heated Crossfire," *Kansas City Star*, March 26, 2006.
31. Ben Barnes, *Barn Burning Barn Building: Tales of a Political Life, from LBJ to George W. Bush and Beyond* (Albany, TX: Bright Sky Press, 2006), 74.
32. Clinton, *My Life*, 558.
33. Ibid., 631.

CHAPTER 1: "GUNS DON'T KILL PEOPLE. PEOPLE KILL PEOPLE."

1. Quote from gun dealer Max Bosworth to KPVI NBC Newschannel 6, October 10, 2003, www.kpvi.com.
2. Tom Clancy, "Introduction," in Wayne LaPierre, *Guns, Crime and Freedom* (Washington, DC: Regnery Publishing, Inc., 1994), xiv.
3. Charlton Heston, testimony in Senate Committee on the Judiciary, *Whose Right to Keep and Bear Arms? The Second Amendment as a Source of Individual Rights: Hearing before the Subcommittee on the Constitution, Federalism and Property Rights of the Senate Committee on the Judiciary*, 105th Cong., 2nd sess., 1998, 33.
4. Kevin M. Cunningham, "When Gun Control Meets the Constitution," *St. John's Journal of Legal Commentary* 10 (1994): 59, 61.
5. Allen Beck and others, *Survey of Adult Inmates 1991*, NCJ-136949 (Washington, DC: Department of Justice, Bureau of Justice Statistics, 1993).
6. Department of Justice, Bureau of Justice Statistics, *Background Checks for Firearm Transfers, 2006* (Washington, DC, March 19, 2008), Table 1, http://www.ojp.usdoj.gov/bjs/pub/html/bcft/2006/table/bcft06st01.htm.

7. National Rifle Association, *Firearms Safety in America 2007*, October 19, 2007, http://www.nraila.org/Issues/FactSheets/Read.aspx?id=120&issue=009.

8. Spitzer, *The Politics of Gun Control*, 59.

9. Arthur L. Kellermann and others, "Injuries and Deaths Due to Firearms in the Home," *Journal of Trauma* 45 (1998): 263.

10. Arthur L. Kellermann and others, "Suicide in the Home in Relation to Gun Ownership," *New England Journal of Medicine* 327 (1992): 467.

11. David A. Brent and others, "Firearms and Adolescent Suicide: A Community Case-Control Study," *American Journal of Diseases of Children* 147 (1993): 1066.

12. Consumer Product Safety Commission, "CPSC Bans Lawn Darts," Document #5053, http://www.cpsc.gov/cpscpub/pubs/5053.html.

13. Data derived from National Center for Health Statistics Vital Statistics System, 1996–1998, United States, Unintentional Firearm Deaths and Rates per 100,000 in 1999–2000, United States, http://www.cdc.gov/ncipc/wisqars.

14. Elizabeth C. Powell and others, "Incidence and Circumstances of Nonfatal Firearm-Related Injuries among Children and Adolescents," *Archives of Pediatrics and Adolescent Medicine* 55 (December 2001): 1364–1368.

15. Consumer Product Safety Commission, News Release #79-007, February 5, 1979.

16. Consumer Product Safety Commission, News Release #79-031, June 29,1979.

17. Consumer Product Safety Commission, News Release #95-009, October 17, 1994.

18. Philip J. Cook, *Guns in America: Results of a Comprehensive National Survey on Firearms Ownership and Use* (Washington, DC: Police Foundation, 1996), 39.

19. Craig Perkins, *Weapon Use and Violent Crime*, NCJ-194820 (Washington, DC: Department of Justice, Bureau of Justice Statistics, September 2003).

20. Ibid.

21. Jane Leavy, *Sandy Koufax: A Lefty's Legacy* (New York: Harper Perennial, 2002), 162.

22. 18 U.S.C.§ 922(x)(1); 18 U.S.C.§ 922(b)(1).

23. Gary Kleck, *Targeting Guns: Firearms and Their Control* (Edison, NJ: Aldine Transaction, 1997), 221.

24. Henri E. Cauvin and Patricia Davis, "Sniper Suspect Lee Boyd Malvo Shot from Afar, He Says, but He Stalked from Up Close," *Washington Post*, November 22, 2003, B5.

25. Ibid.

26. Garen J. Wintemute, "Guns and Gun Violence," in *The Crime Drop in America*, ed. A. Blumstein and J. Wallman (New York: Cambridge University Press, 2000), 56–57.

27. Brendan G. Carr and others, "Outcomes Related to the Number of Anatomic Placement of Gunshot Wounds," *Journal of Trauma* 64 (2008): 197.

28. Stephen Halbrook, "Does the United States Need a National Database for Ballistic Fingerprints?" *Insight*, November 26, 2002.

29. Franklin E. Zimring, "Is Gun Control Likely to Reduce Violent Killings?" *University of Chicago Law Review* 35 (1968): 721, 728. See also Franklin Zimring and Gordon Hawkins, *Crime Is Not the Problem: Lethal Violence in America* (New York: Oxford University Press, 1997), 114.

30. Linda Saltzman and others, "Weapon Involvement and Injury Outcomes in Family and Intimate Assaults," *JAMA* 267 (June 10, 1992): 3043.

31. Philip J. Cook, "The Technology of Personal Violence," in *Crime and Justice, A Review of Research*, ed. Michael Tonry (Chicago: University of Chicago Press, 1991), 17.

32. Kleck, *Targeting Guns*, 216.

33. Zimring and Hawkins, *Crime Is Not the Problem*, 108.
34. Josefina Card, "Lethality of Suicidal Methods and Suicide Risk: 2 Distinct Concepts," *Omega Journal of Death & Dying* 5 (1974): 37.
35. These results concerning the lethality of various methods of suicide have been confirmed by later studies. See A. A. Elnour and J. Harrison, "The Lethality of Suicide Methods," *Injury Prevention* 14 (2008): 39; E. D. Shenassa, S. N. Catlin, and S. L. Buka, "Lethality of Firearms Relative to Other Suicide Methods: A Population Based Study," *Journal of Epidemiology & Community Health* 57 (2003): 120.
36. Zimring and Hawkins, *Crime Is Not the Problem*, 730–735.
37. Ibid., 732.
38. Ibid., 734.
39. A more recent study of more than two thousand violent and potentially violent events, as described by offenders, found no evidence to support the theory that highly motivated assailants, if deprived of guns, would simply choose another weapon and expend the extra effort required to carry out a lethal attack. Instead, the researchers found support for an instrumentality effect apart from differences in intent, as a result of the "technical properties" of guns and "because doing serious harm with a gun requires less strength and sustained effort on the part of an assailant." William Wells and Julie Horney, "Weapon Effects and Individual Intent to Do Harm: Influences on the Escalation of Violence," *Criminology* 40 (2002): 265, 291.
40. Zimring and Hawkins, *Crime Is Not the Problem*, 728.
41. Jeremy Olson, "Outside Metro Areas, Access to Guns Is Easy," *Omaha World-Herald*, May 16, 2005.
42. Ibid.
43. Ibid.
44. Zimring and Hawkins, *Crime Is Not the Problem*, 35–39.
45. Ibid., 109.
46. Ibid. (Reporting study by Ronald Clarke and Pat Mayhew, "The British Gas Suicide Story and Its Criminological Implications," in *Crime and Justice*, 107.
47. Hemenway, *Private Guns, Public Health*, 199, and studies cited therein.
48. "Molly Ivins on Gun Control," *Dallas Morning News*, February 1, 2007.
49. National Safety Council, *Odds of Death Due to Injury, United States, 2005* (Itasca, IL, n.d.), http://www.nsc.org/research/odds.aspx.
50. Kleck, *Targeting Guns*, 296.
51. Ibid.
52. Ibid.
53. Although there are, apparently, gun owners who would allow, and even encourage, very young children to fire machine guns under adult supervision. In October 2008, an eight-year-old child fatally wounded himself while firing a machine gun at the annual Machine Gun Shoot and Firearms Expo in Westfield, Massachusetts. Ads for the event said there was "no age limit or licenses required to shoot machine guns" and boasted that the entry fee would be waived for kids under sixteen. Although the ads made clear that "you will be accompanied to the firing line with a Certified Instructor," it assured prospective participants that "You Are in Control—Full Auto Rock & Roll." David Abel, "Boy's Death Spurs Hard Look at Laws for Guns, Children," *Boston Globe*, October 28, 2008. As a *Boston Herald* columnist wrote about the adults involved in this travesty, "You've got to be out of your mind." Margery Eagan,

"Letting an 8-year-old Play with a Machine Gun; Are You Crazy?" *BostonHerald. com*, October 28, 2008, http://www.bostonherald.com/news/columnists/view.bg?articleid=1128272.

54. "Questions for Ozzy Osbourne," *New York Times*, June 28, 1998, http://query.nytimes.com/gst/fullpage.html?res=9C00E4D6153CF93BA15755C0A96E958 260&sec=&spon=&partner=permalink&exprod=permalink.

55. Mark Obmascik and David Olinger, "Two Killers Rampaged as 6 Officers Awaited Aid," *Denver Post*, May 16, 2000.

56. Howard Kurtz, "Let the Blame Begin," *Washington Post*, April 26, 1999, C1.

57. Chuck Raasch, "Gingrich: Liberalism Led to Colo. Massacre," *USA Today*, May 13, 1999.

58. Fred Hiatt, "A Littleton Massacre Every Day," *Washington Post*, April 25, 1999.

59. Ibid.

60. Michael Janofsky, "Columbine Victims Were Killed Minutes into Siege at Colorado School, Report Reveals," *New York Times*, May 17, 2000.

61. Tom Kenworthy, "At Littleton, a Pattern of Multiple Gun Wounds," *Washington Post*, May 2, 1999.

62. Obmascik and Olinger, "Two Killers Rampaged."

63. Philip Cook and others, "Regulating Gun Markets," *Journal of Criminal Law & Criminology* 86 (1995).

64. Eric Harris, journal entry, December 3, 1998 (JC-001-026017), Columbine Documents, Jefferson County Sheriff's Office, http://www.thedenverchannel.com/download/2006/0706/0477579.pdf.

65. Lynn Bartels, "Gun Dealers Rejected Columbine Killers," *Rocky Mountain News*, January 27, 2000.

66. David Olinger, "Following the Guns," *Denver Post*, August 1, 1999.

67. Tom W. Smith, *1999 National Gun Policy Survey of the National Opinion Research Center: Research Findings* (Chicago: National Opinion Research Center, July 2000), 12.

68. Ibid., 12–13.

69. Ibid., 42 (Table 6).

70. Marttila Communications Group, *National Gun Control Survey* (Boston, July 11–14, 2003), 16.

71. Spitzer, *The Politics of Gun Control*, 133. The reaction of the U.S. Congress to the school shootings stands in marked contrast to the legislative reaction in other developed countries to mass shootings. The murder of sixteen schoolchildren and a teacher in Dunblane, Scotland, in March 1996 led to a nearly total prohibition of handguns, with a compulsory buy-back of handguns already legally owned. In April of that year, the Port Arthur massacre, in which a lone gunman killed thirty-five persons with a semiautomatic rifle, led Australia to prohibit certain categories of weapons with a buy-back of those weapons, along with new licensing, registration, safe storage and firearm training requirements. See Peter Reuter and Jenny Mouzos, "A Massive Buyback of Low-Risk Guns," in *Evaluating Gun Policy: Effects on Crime and Violence*, ed. Jens Ludwig and Philip J. Cook (New York: Oxford University Press, 2003), 121–156.

72. 145 Cong. Rec. H4582, June 17, 1999 (statement of Rep. Smith).

73. 145 Cong. Rec. H4581, June 17, 1999 (statement of Rep. Everett).

74. 145 Cong. Rec. H4582, June 17, 1999 (statement of Rep. Peterson).

75. 145 Cong. Rec. H4578, June 17, 1999 (statement of Rep. Rothman).

76. 145 Cong. Rec. H4605, June 17, 1999 (statement of Rep. McCarthy).

CHAPTER 2: "WHEN GUNS ARE OUTLAWED, ONLY OUTLAWS WILL HAVE GUNS."

1. "Excerpts: Charlie Gibson Interviews GOP Vice Presidential Candidate Sarah Palin," ABC News, September 12, 2008, http://abcnews.go.com/print?id=5789483.

2. This has been consistently true for years, with the exception of a Louis Harris poll in 1993 showing 52 percent of those polled supported a handgun possession ban. Spitzer, *The Politics of Gun Control*, 101; Hemenway, *Private Guns, Public Health*, 163.

3. For an interesting discussion of the use of red herring arguments in the gun control debate (and of the origin of the term "red herring") see Andrew Jay McClurg, "The Rhetoric of Gun Control," *American University Law Review* 42 (1992): 53.

4. Americans for Gun Safety Foundation, *No Questions Asked: Background Checks, Gun Shows, and Crime* (Washington, DC, April 2001), 10.

5. Garen J. Wintemute, "Gun Shows across a Multistate American Gun Market: Observational Evidence of the Effects of Regulatory Policies," *Injury Prevention* 13 (2007): 150, 153.

6. Richard Gardiner, director of state and local affairs, Institute for Legislative Action, National Rifle Association, quoted in Osha Gray Davidson, *Under Fire: The NRA and the Battle for Gun Control* (New York: H. Holt, 1993), 45.

7. The "change the subject" strategy often involves simply misrepresenting the gun control proposal at issue to make it appear to be equivalent to a gun ban. For example, any proposal to require guns to have specified safety mechanisms is labeled a "gun ban" by the NRA because it would "ban" any gun that doesn't have the mechanism. The issue, of course, is whether it is feasible to install the mechanism. If it is, then the choice of whether to sell the gun with the safety mechanism is the manufacturer's. The government has not "banned" the gun; the manufacturer has simply chosen not to make its guns safer. If a manufacturer decided to take its cars off the market rather than install seat belts and air bags to comply with government regulations, we would not say the government had "banned cars."

8. Marttila, *National Gun Control Survey*.

9. *District of Columbia v. Heller*, 128 S.Ct. 2783 (2008).

10. *United States v. Miller*, 307 U.S. 174 (1939).

11. *Heller*, 128 S.Ct. 2821.

12. Ibid., 2822.

13. Sandra Froman, "President's Column," *America's 1st Freedom*, December 2006, 10.

14. Daniel D. Polsby and Dennis Brennen, *Taking Aim at Gun Control* (Chicago: Heartland Institute, 1995), 9–10.

15. Although the NRA says it supports laws barring felons from possessing guns, it worked hard to defend a ridiculous federal program to use taxpayers' money to restore gun rights to felons who somehow were able to convince ATF that they can be trusted with a gun. See Michael Isikoff, "BATF Allows Some Felons to Own Guns," *Washington Post*, September 24, 1991. Congress shut the program down in 1992 by barring appropriated monies from being spent by ATF for this purpose. See Public Law 102-393 (October 6, 1992).

16. The scope of the federal ban on gun possession by persons convicted of domestic violence misdemeanors was the subject of a recent Supreme Court ruling. In *United States v. Hayes*, 2009 WL 436680 (Feb. 24, 2009), the Court ruled that the phrase "misdemeanor crime of domestic violence" in this provision refers not only to crimes in which a domestic relationship is an element of the

crime (e.g., "battery of a spouse"), but also applies more broadly to any violent misdemeanor involving persons in a domestic relationship.

17. Garen J. Wintemute and others, "Prior Misdemeanor Convictions as a Risk Factor for Later Violent and Firearm-Related Criminal Activity among Authorized Purchasers of Handguns," *JAMA* 341 (1998): 2083.

18. James D. Wright and Peter H. Rossi, *Armed and Considered Dangerous: A Survey of Felons and Their Firearms* (Piscataway, NJ: Aldine Transaction, 1986).

19. Bradley A. Buckles, foreword by the director, in *Following the Gun*, iii.

20. Mike Seate, "Gun Pros Say House Has Wrong Target," *Pittsburgh Tribune-Review*, September 12, 2006.

21. The incorrect assumption that criminals are both smart and rational appears to underlie the oversimplified view of the Brady Act by "rogue economist" Steven Levitt in his runaway bestseller, *Freakonomics*. Levitt and his coauthor Stephen Dubner observe that the Brady Act "may have seemed appealing to politicians, but to an economist it doesn't make much sense. Why? Because regulation of a legal market is bound to fail when a healthy black market exists for the same product. With guns so cheap and so easy to get, the standard criminal has no incentive to fill out a firearm application at his local gun shop and then wait a week. The Brady Act, accordingly, has proven to be practically impotent in lowering crime." Stephen D. Levitt and Stephen J. Dubner, *Freakonomics: A Rogue Economist Explores the Hidden Side of Everything* (New York: William Morrow, 2005), 132. This analysis features several problems. First, it does not recognize that, for guns, the legal market is the primary source for the illegal market. Second, it makes the classic economist's mistake of basing public policy conclusions on the assumption that everyone behaves rationally. The assumption of rationality is unjustified for the public at large; it is even more so for the criminally inclined. It may make no sense to an economist that a criminal would try to buy a gun at a gun dealer after Brady, but over 1.5 million of them have done so. Third, whatever effect the Brady Act has on the "standard criminal" (whatever that is), it may well have substantial public safety benefits if it interferes with access to guns by only a subset of the criminal population. Finally, the analysis seems to forget the first principle of economics as it would apply to criminals and guns; that is, raising the "price" (as measured in inconvenience, danger, etc.) for criminals to get guns should be expected to reduce the demand of criminals for guns. Needless to say, *Freakonomics* makes no attempt to explain why the dramatic decline in violent gun crime coincided almost exactly with the implementation of the Brady Act.

22. M. A. Wright and others, "Effectiveness of a Program to Deny Legal Handgun Purchase to Persons Believed to be at High Risk for Firearm Violence," *American Journal of Public Health* 89 (1999): 88.

23. Kleck, *Targeting Guns*, 377.

24. Department of Justice, Bureau of Justice Statistics, "Crimes Committed with Firearms, 1973–2006," in *Key Facts at a Glance* (Washington, DC, January 5, 2008), www.ojp.usdoj.gov/bjs/glance/tables/guncrimetab.htm.

25. Department of Justice, Bureau of Justice Statistics, *Criminal Victimization, 2004* (Washington, DC, September 2005), 10.

26. Bureau of Justice Statistics, "Crimes Committed with Firearms, 1973–2006."

27. Department of Justice, Bureau of Justice Statistics, *Homicide Victimization, 1950–2005* (Washington, DC, July 11, 2007), http://www.ojp.usdoj.gov/bjs/homicide/tables/totalstab.htm.

28. Department of Justice, Bureau of Justice Statistics, *Background Checks for Firearms Transfers, 2005*, Bureau of Justice Statistics Bulletin (Washington, DC, November 2006).

29. Douglas Weil and Rebecca Knox, "Effects of Limiting Handgun Purchases on Interstate Transfer of Firearms," *JAMA* 275 (June 12, 1996): 1759.

30. Because federal law requires gun dealers to obtain from purchasers proof of residence in the gun dealer's state, a gun trafficker from New York City could not walk into a Virginia gun store and buy a handgun. See 18 U.S.C. § 922(b)(3). She must recruit a Virginia resident to act as an intermediary or straw buyer.

31. Cook and others, "Regulating Gun Markets," 59, 72 n.56.

32. 18 U.S.C. § (g)(3)(A).

33. Weil and Knox, "Effects of Limiting Handgun Purchases," 1760.

34. Ibid.

35. Peter Baker, "Va. Gun Sale Law Curbs Traffic to North, Study Says," *Washington Post*, August 3, 1995, B11.

36. Lynn Waltz, "Brotherhood of the Gun Runners," *Virginian-Pilot*, September 8, 1996, A1.

37. Ibid.

38. Lynn Waltz, "Virginia Law Cuts Gun Pipeline to Capital's Criminals," *Virginian-Pilot*, September 8, 1996, A7.

39. Toby Coleman, "The Trading Game," *Charleston Daily Mail*, February 26, 2004, A11.

40. See Complaint, *Lemongello v. Will Company, Inc., et al.*, Civil Action No. 02-C-2952 (November 14, 2002), 6–7.

41. Kleck, *Targeting Guns*, 88.

42. Bureau of Alcohol, Tobacco and Firearms, Youth Crime Gun Interdiction Initiative, *Crime Gun Trace Analysis Reports: The Illegal Youth Firearms Market in 27 Communities* (Washington, DC, October 1998), 12.

43. Ibid.

44. ATF, *Crime Gun Trace Analysis Reports*, part II.

45. Ibid.

46. Brady Campaign to Prevent Gun Violence, "Statement of Sarah Brady on Inaccurate Comment by Howard Dean," press release, November 16, 2003.

47. Dean acknowledged the interstate flow of guns only in claiming that "the cross border issue has been resolved in the one case I know of where it became a big issue" because "Virginia now limits the availability of gun purchases because so many Virginia guns were turning up in New York City illegally." Apparently Governor Dean believed that Virginia was the only "source state" for trafficked guns and that since Virginia enacted its one-gun-a-month law, the interstate movement of guns across the country has ceased.

48. Hemenway, *Private Guns, Public Health*, 231.

49. ATF, *Crime Gun Trace Analysis Reports*, 8.

50. Joseph Tartaro, "When Is a Gunowner Database Not a Registry?" *Gun Week*, November 10, 2004, 15.

51. 18 U.S.C.§ 923(g)(6).

52. William J. Vizzard, *Shots in the Dark: The Policy, Politics, and Symbolism of Gun Control* (Lanham, MD: Rowman & Littlefield Publishers, Inc., 2000), 162.

53. California Attorney General, "Attorney General Lockyer Announces Arrest Warrants Issued for Two Los Angeles Men on Gun Possession and Trafficking Charges," press release, May 4, 2005.

54. Aaron Diamant, *I-Team: Trail of a Gun*, TMJ4 Milwaukee, February 15, 2007, http://www.todaystmj4.com/features/iteam/5808641.html.
55. D. W. Webster and others, "Relationship between Licensing, Registration, and Other Gun Sales Laws and the Source State of Crime Guns," *Injury Prevention* 7 (2001): 184–189.
56. Ibid.,189.
57. Jerry Seper, "Two Held in Mexico Weapons Ring," *Washington Times*, November 25, 2005.
58. Sergio Chapa, "Strict Mexican Gun Laws Creating Black Market for U.S. Weapons," *Brownsville Herald*, August 16, 2005.
59. Jens Ludwig and Philip Cook, "Homicide and Suicide Rates Associated with Implementation of the Brady Handgun Violence Prevention Act," 284 *JAMA* (2000): 585.
60. Douglas Weil, *Traffic Stop: How the Brady Act Disrupts Interstate Gun Trafficking* (Washington, DC: Center to Prevent Handgun Violence, 1997).
61. Philip Cook and Jens Ludwig, "The Effects of the Brady Act on Gun Violence," in *Guns, Crime, and Punishment in America*, ed. Bernard E. Harcourt (New York: New York University Press, 2003), 294 (reporting data in Philip J. Cook and Anthony Braga, "New Law Enforcement Uses for Comprehensive Firearms Trace Data," in ibid., 179). Cook and Ludwig point to the difficulty of showing that this dampening effect on interstate gun trafficking into Chicago reduced the availability of guns to dangerous people, although they note that in the first five years after Brady was enacted, there was little change in the fraction of Chicago homicides that involved firearms. Cook and Ludwig, in ibid., 294. This fact about Chicago homicides hardly seems strong evidence that Brady's impact in reducing interstate gun trafficking had no effect on homicides nationwide, particularly in light of the dramatic reduction in the use of guns in crime nationally, and the corresponding reduction in homicides, during the first ten years of the Brady law.
62. Ludwig and Cook, in ibid., 590.
63. Jens Ludwig and Philip Cook, "Impact of the Brady Act on Homicide and Suicide Rates (Letter)," *JAMA* 284 (2000): 2721.
64. See generally Spitzer, *The Politics of Gun Control*, 111.
65. The NRA has described the machine gun regulatory system as follows: "Under the NFA, persons wishing to purchase an automatic firearm had to be at least 21 years old, submit to an extensive criminal background check by the FBI, pay a $200 transfer tax, make formal application for such transfer by duplicate copies including photographs and fingerprints and have a local law enforcement official certify that they had no felony record and met the requirements for purchase. The applicant would have to wait three to six months between purchase and delivery of the machine gun." National Rifle Association, *Monitor* 13, no. 13 (August 15, 1986).
66. The bureau's name has since been changed to Bureau of Alcohol, Tobacco, Firearms, and Explosives. I will refer to it throughout as ATF.
67. Kleck, *Targeting Guns*, 109.
68. National Center for Policy Analysis, *Will Banning Assault Weapons Reduce Crime?* Brief Analysis No. 102 (Dallas, TX, February 7, 1994), http://www.ncpa.org/ba/ba102.html.
69. Kleck, *Targeting Guns*, 109.
70. Department of Justice, Bureau of Justice Statistics, *Guns Used in Crime* (Washington, DC, July 1995), 4.

71. Bureau of Alcohol, Tobacco and Firearms, Youth Crime Gun Interdiction Initiative, *Crime Gun Trace Reports: National Report* (Washington, DC, 2000), www.atf.gov/firearms/ycgii/2000/index.htm.
72. General Accounting Office, *Potential Effects of Next-Day Destruction of NICS Background Check Records* (Washington, DC, July 2002), 13 n.17.
73. Third Way, *Missing Records: Holes in Background Check System Allow Illegal Buyers to Get Guns* (Washington, DC, May 2007), 5.
74. General Accounting Office, *Firearms Purchased from Federal Firearms Licensees Using Bogus Identification* (Washington, DC, March 2001), 4.
75. NRA Institute for Legislative Action (on file with author).
76. Spitzer, *The Politics of Gun Control,* 111.
77. Brady Center to Prevent Gun Violence, based on data from the WISQARS system, Center for Disease Control, http://www.cdc.gov/ncipc/wisqars/.
78. Ibid.
79. Hemenway, *Private Guns, Public Health,* 36.
80. Ibid., 38.
81. Ibid., 39. Some research suggests that at least some of the correlation between gun ownership and suicide risk may be due to the fact that individuals with above average suicidal tendencies are more likely to own a gun and to live in areas with relatively many gun owners. See Mark Duggan, "Guns and Suicide," in *Evaluating Gun Policy,* 42–43. However, a more recent study has questioned this hypothesis, finding that higher rates of firearm ownership are associated with higher suicide rates, but finding no significant association between household firearm ownership and nonfirearm suicide. Matthew Miller and others, "Household Firearm Ownership and Rates of Suicide Across the 50 United States," *Journal of Trauma* 62 (2007): 1029. The authors find that the data support the hypothesis that "where ready access to household firearms is less likely, suicidal acts are, on average, less likely to prove lethal." Ibid., 1033. See also Susan B. Sorenson, "Mental Health and Firearms in Community-Based Surveys," *Evaluation Review* 32 (June 2008): 239, 252 (finding that suicide risk among gun owners [and those who reside with gun owners] is greater even though those who own a gun [or reside with someone who owns a gun] do not differ from non-gun owners in rates of general emotional and mental health, sadness and depression, functional mental health, or mental health seeking).
82. Brent and others, "Firearms and Adolescent Suicide," 1066.
83. Colin Loftin and others, "Effects of Restrictive Licensing of Handguns on Homicide and Suicide in the District of Columbia," *New England Journal of Medicine* 325 (1991): 1615–1620.
84. David Lester and Mary E. Murrell, "The Influence of Gun Control Laws on Suicidal Behavior," *American Journal of Psychiatry* 137 (January 1980): 121–122; Bijou Yang and David Lester, "The Effect of Gun Availability on Suicide Rates," *Atlantic Economic Review* 19 (1991): 74. See generally Hemenway, *Private Guns, Public Health,* 44.
85. Myron Boor and Jeffrey H. Bair, "Suicide Rates, Handgun Control Laws, and Sociodemographic Variables," *Psychological Reports* 66 (1990): 923.
86. David C. Grossman and others, "Gun Storage Practices and Risk of Youth Suicide and Unintentional Firearm Injuries," *JAMA* 293 (February 9, 2005): 707.
87. Daniel Webster and others, "Association Between Youth-Focused Firearm Laws and Youth Suicides," *JAMA* 292 (August 4, 2004): 594.
88. Garen Wintemute and others, "Mortality among Recent Purchasers of Handguns," *New England Journal of Medicine* 341 (1999): 1583.

89. General Accounting Office, *Gun Control: Implementation of the National Instant Criminal Background Check System* (Washington, DC, February 2000), 10.

90. David Hemenway, "Gun Accidents," in *Guns in American Society: An Encyclopedia of History, Politics, Culture, and the Law,* ed. Gregg Lee Carter (Santa Barbara, CA: ABC-CLIO, 2002), 1: 2.

91. Ibid.

92. Ibid., 3.

93. Daniel Webster and Marc Starnes, "Reexamining the Association Between Child Access Prevention Gun Laws and Unintentional Shootings Deaths of Children," *Pediatrics* 106 (December 2000): 1466, 1468.

94. Hemenway, *Private Guns, Public Health,* 28.

95. National Center for Injury Prevention and Control, "Rates of Homicide, Suicide, and Firearm-Related Death," 101, 102.

96. Hemenway, "Gun Accidents," 3.

97. National Rifle Association, *Firearms Safety in America 2007.*

98. Hemenway, "Gun Accidents," 3.

99. Tom W. Smith, *2001 National Gun Policy Survey of the National Opinion Research Center: Research Findings* (Chicago: National Opinion Research Center, December 2001). See also Renee Johnson and others, "Firearm Ownership and Storage Practices, U.S. Households, 1992–2002, A Systematic Review," *American Journal of Preventive Medicine* 27 (2004): 173, 181 (reviewing studies finding between 30 percent to 35 percent of U.S. households contain guns).

100. Grossman and others, "Gun Storage Practices and Risk of Youth Suicide."

101. Webster and Starnes, "Reexamining the Association Between Child Access Prevention Gun Laws and Unintentional Shootings Deaths of Children," 1467.

102. Ibid., 468.

103. See the excellent summary of the history of auto safety in Hemenway, *Private Guns, Public Health,* 10–19.

104. Jon S. Vernick and others, "Unintentional and Undetermined Firearm Related Deaths: A Preventable Death Analysis for Three Safety Devices," *Injury Prevention* 9 (2003): 307.

105. Ibid., 308.

106. Centers for Disease Control, NCHS Vital Statistics System, *United States, Firearms Deaths and Rates per 100,000* (Washington, DC, 2002).

107. Fox Butterfield, "Social Isolation, Guns and a 'Culture of Suicide,'" *New York Times,* February 13, 2005, 6.

108. Ibid.

109. Dorothy Samuels, "Congress 101: If You Want Success, Don't Mess with the Gun Lobby," *New York Times,* October 3, 2004.

110. Gary Kleck and Don B. Kates, *Armed: New Perspectives on Gun Control* (Amherst, NY: Prometheus Books, 2001), 21.

111. National Institute of Justice, *Felony Defendants in Large Urban Counties* (Washington, DC, 1998).

112. Philip J. Cook and others, "Criminal Records of Homicide Offenders," *JAMA* 294 (August 3, 2005): 598.

113. "'Who Were These Boys?' Pair Carried an Arsenal—and a Grudge, Witnesses Say," *South Florida Sun-Sentinel,* March 26, 1998, A1; John Kifner and others, "From Wild Talk and Friendship to Five Deaths in a Schoolyard," *New York Times,* March 29, 1998.

114. Anne Rochell, "Arkansas School Shooting Grandfather of Suspect Says Boys

Stole Guns, 'Everybody's Lives Are Ruined,'" *Atlanta Journal-Constitution*, March 25, 1998, A1.

115. Ron Scherer, "Gun-Control Laws Scrutinized after Empire State Shooting," *Christian Science Monitor*, February 27, 1997, 3.

116. Blaine Harden, "Shooter Bought Gun by Using New Florida ID; Palestinian Attacker at Empire State Building Gained Residency while Living in Motel," *Washington Post*, February 25, 1997, A1.

117. Clifford Krauss, "Rampage at the Empire State Building: The Weapon; Loophole Let Gun Buyer in Florida Evade Waiting Period for Foreigners," *New York Times*, February 25, 1997, B5.

118. Beth Reinhard, "Campus Killings Have Little Political Impact," *Miami Herald*, May 14, 2007 (quoting Giuliani's presidential website as stating, "Rudy understands that what works in New York doesn't necessarily work in Mississippi or Montana.").

119. See 62 Fed. Reg. 19442, *Residency Requirements for Persons Acquiring Firearms* (April 21, 1997); 27 C.F.R. §178.124(c)(3)(ii).

120. Oddly, ATF has never used its regulatory authority to make it harder for Americans, as opposed to aliens, to falsify their residences to purchase guns. A purchaser of a handgun must be a resident of the state in which he seeks to buy the gun. The examples are legion in which individuals have obtained driver's licenses, with phony in-state addresses, which they have then used to buy handguns. New Yorkers also have been victimized by this easily filled loophole. In December 1993, Colin Ferguson vented his rage against whites and what he called "Uncle Tom Negroes," when he opened fire with a Ruger P-89 semiautomatic pistol on the Long Island Railroad, killing six and wounding fifteen. As noted previously, among the victims were the husband and son of Representative Carolyn McCarthy (D-New York). Ferguson, a Brooklyn resident, bought the gun in California after obtaining a California driver's license by giving the address of a nine-room hotel in Long Beach, where he stayed for three weeks. See Joseph Treaster, "Death on the L.I.R.R.: The Weapon; 16 Days in California and a Fateful Purchase," *New York Times*, December 9, 1993, B10. In July 2003 Othniel Askey murdered New York City councilman James Davis with a handgun he had purchased in North Carolina by providing a driver's license with the address of an abandoned farmhouse. See Andy Geller, "Davis' Killer Got Gun through Fatal Flaws in System," *New York Post*, Online Edition, July 30, 2003.

CHAPTER 3: "BUT WHAT YOU REALLY WANT . . . "

1. LaPierre, *Guns, Crime and Freedom*, 48.
2. National Rifle Association, Institute for Legislative Affairs, *Firearms Registration: New York City's Lesson*, fact sheet, January 27, 2000, www.nraila.org/Issues/FactSheets/Read.aspx?ID=41.
3. National Rifle Association, Institute for Legislative Affairs, *One Gun A Month: Rationing a Constitutionally Protected Right*, fact sheet, March 9, 2000, www.nraila.org/Issues/FactSheets/Read.aspx?ID=140.
4. Warren Cassidy, quoted in Davidson, *Under Fire*, 44.
5. Charlton Heston, Opening Remarks to Members, NRA Annual Meeting—Charlotte, North Carolina, May 2000, http://www.nra.org/Speech.aspx?id=6044.
6. Charlton Heston, "Winning the Cultural War," Harvard Law School Forum, February 16, 1999, http://www.nraila.org/news/read/Speeches.aspx?ID=22.

7. National Rifle Association, Institute for Legislative Affairs, "NRA Applauds Congressional Leaders for Including Gun Ownership Rights in their 'American Values Agenda,'" press release, June 29, 2006 (on file with author).

8. Davidson, *Under Fire*, 44.

9. For example, Josh Sugarmann, the executive director of the Violence Policy Center, has written a book titled *Every Handgun Is Pointed at You: The Case for Banning Handguns* (New York: New Press, 2001).

10. Sarah Brady, *A Good Fight* (New York: Public Affairs, 2002), 104.

11. Richard Harris, "A Reporter at Large—Handguns," *New Yorker*, July 26, 1976, 57–58, quoted in Kleck and Kates, *Armed*, 138, 150.

12. Pete Shields, *Guns Don't Die—People Do* (Westminster, MD: Arbor House Publishing, 1981), 98.

13. Ibid.

14. Kleck and Kates, *Armed*, 138–139.

15. Sarah Brady, *New York Times*, August 15, 1993, quoted in ibid., 134.

16. Kleck and Kates, *Armed*, 161.

17. Josh Sugarmann, *NRA: Money, Firepower, Fear* (Washington, DC: National Press Books, 1992), 261.

18. Kleck and Kates, *Armed*, 134.

19. See Hemenway, *Private Guns, Public Health*, 193.

20. Kleck and Kates, *Armed*, 157.

21. See Kellerman and others, "Injuries and Deaths Due to Firearms in the Home," 263.

22. Department of Justice, Federal Bureau of Investigation, *Uniform Crime Reports*, Expanded Homicide Data Table 7 (Murder Victims, by Weapon, 2003–2007) (Washington, DC, September 2008), http://www.fbi.gov/ucr/cius2007/offenses/expanded_information/data/shrtable_07.html; and Expanded Homicide Data Table 14 (Justifiable Homicide by Weapon, Private Citizen, 2003–2007) (Washington, DC, September 2008), http://www.fbi.gov/ucr/cius2007/offenses/expanded_information/data/shrtable_14.html.

23. Kleck and Kates, *Armed*, 135.

24. Don Kates, Michael Krauss, Abigail Kohn, and Wendy Kaminer, "Straight Shooting on Gun Control: A Reason Debate," *ReasonOnline*, May 2005, http://www.reason.com/0505/fe.ak.straight.shtml.

25. This slippery slope fallacy is discussed outside the gun context in Eric Lode, "Slippery Slope Arguments and Legal Reasoning," *California Law Review* 87 (1999): 1469, 1499–1500. See also Frederick Schauer, "Slippery Slopes," *Harvard Law Review* 99 (1985): 361, 379. ("Such arguments illustrate the fallacy of assuming that the lack of an obvious stopping point along a continuum renders imprecise the point that is ultimately chosen.")

26. The version of the Brady Bill signed into law provided that, during the first five years the law was in effect, law enforcement would have five business days to complete the background checks. The five-day period was a recognition that time would be required to manually review criminal history records that had not been computerized in many states. The Brady Bill also authorized funds to assist the states in computerizing their criminal records. After this five-year "interim" period, the National Instant Criminal Background Check System (NICS) became operational, with the checks to be completed by federal authorities within three business days. As we have seen, the computerization of records under NICS is still inadequate, years after the system was established. If NICS had gone into effect in 1994, as the NRA proposed, it would have

been completely ineffective in blocking over-the-counter gun purchases by criminals.

27. See, e.g., Joseph E. Olson and David B. Kopel, "All the Way Down the Slippery Slope: Gun Prohibition in England and Some Lessons for Civil Liberties in America," *Hamline Law Review* 22 (1999): 399; Eugene Volokh, "The Mechanisms of the Slippery Slope," *Harvard Law Review* 116 (2003): 1026.

28. "The *post hoc* fallacy is said to occur when it is concluded that *A* causes *B* simply because one or more occurrences of *A* are correlated with one or more occurrences of *B*. The full Latin name for this traditional fallacy is *post hoc, ergo propter hoc*, meaning 'after this, therefore, because of this.'" Douglas N. Walton, *Informal Logic: A Handbook for Critical Argumentation* (New York: Oxford University Press, 1989), 213.

29. See, e.g., Olson and Kopel, "All the Way Down the Slippery Slope."

30. NRA-ILA, *Firearms Registration: New York City's Lesson.*

31. Ibid.

32. See *Allegheny County Sportsmen's League v. Edward G. Rendell*, 860 A.2d 10 (Pa. 2004).

33. See Webster and others, "Relationship between Licensing, Registration, and Other Gun Sales Laws and the Source State of Crime Guns," 186.

34. See 18 U.S.C. 922(o).

35. Volokh, "The Mechanisms of the Slippery Slope."

36. Smith, *2001 National Gun Policy Survey*, 6.

37. Olson and Kopel, "All the Way Down the Slippery Slope," 449.

38. Smith, *2001 NORC National Gun Policy Survey*, 33 (Table 10).

39. Transcript of *To the Point*, hosted by Warren Olney, Public Radio International (July 1, 2008), quoted at Paul Helmke, "NRA: Gun Licensing and Registration 'Tougher to Criticize' Now," *Brady Blog*, July 3, 2008, http://www.bradycampaign.org/blog/?s=michel.

40. *Heller*, 128 S.Ct. 2813, n.23.

41. See Adam Winkler, "The Reasonable Right to Bear Arms," *Stanford Law & Policy Review* 17 (2006): 599.

42. *Kalodimos v. Village of Morton Grove*, 470 N.E.2d 266 (Ill. 1984).

CHAPTER 4: "AN ARMED SOCIETY IS A POLITE SOCIETY."

1. LaPierre, *Guns, Crime and Freedom*, 23.

2. The Kennesaw law was enacted in 1982 to "send a message" in response to local gun bans in places like Morton Grove, Illinois. The ordinance included no penalties for its violation and was never enforced as a serious attempt to require private gun ownership. This did not prevent Kennesaw city officials from boasting of dramatic decreases in burglaries from 1981 to 1985, a claim of success that was echoed by pro-gun writers such as Don Kates and Gary Kleck. It turns out that this claimed decrease in burglaries was a statistical mirage, the result of an atypical spike in burglaries in the first six months of 1981, followed by a return to more typical levels in the years after. Scholars who compared burglaries in Kennesaw during a more meaningful time period (1976–1986) found that "burglaries were relatively stable through the entire period" with "no visible change following introduction of the ordinance." David McDowall and others, "Did Mandatory Firearm Ownership in Kennesaw Really Prevent Burglaries?" *Sociology and Sociological Research* 74 (October 1989): 48, 49.

3. Zimring and Hawkins, *Crime Is Not the Problem*, 37–39.

4. Hemenway, *Private Guns, Public Health*, 46.

5. Ibid., 197. Researchers have developed two reliable measures of general gun "availability" in a country—the percentage of households reporting ownership of guns and (revealingly) the percentage of suicides committed with guns. As Gary Kleck (also revealingly) points out, the two measures are almost perfectly correlated, meaning that the greater the percentage of households with firearms in a given country, the more likely it is that firearms will be the suicide method of choice. Kleck, *Targeting Guns*, 254. Apart from the obvious relevance of this fact for the issue of guns and suicide, for present purposes the point is that there appears little dispute among researchers as to relative gun availability across nations. Regardless of the measure, the United States has the greatest gun availability in the industrialized, high-income world.

6. We have seen, in chapter 1, that the greater the involvement of guns in crime, the more lethal crime becomes. Although it seems to be true that gun use in crime causes crime to be more lethal, this is not the same as arguing that higher rates of gun ownership cause higher rates of crime, violent crime, or homicide.

7. David Hemenway and Matthew Miller, "Firearm Availability and Homicide Rates Across 26 High-Income Countries," *Journal of Trauma* 49 (December 2000): 985, 987.

8. Don Kates, *Proposition H: Mythology Instead of Criminology* (Oakland, CA: Independent Institute, November 23, 2005), http://www.independent.org/newsroom/article.asp?id=1621.

9. Ibid.

10. LaPierre, *Guns, Crime and Freedom*, 170–171.

11. Ibid., 171.

12. See Hemenway, *Private Guns, Public Health*, 197; Hemenway and Miller, "Firearm Availability and Homicide Rates," 986.

13. Embassy of Switzerland, Canberra, Australia, Information Service 2004, "Swiss Gun Legislation" (on file with author). See also Wendy Cukier and Victor W. Sidel, *The Global Gun Epidemic: From Saturday Night Specials to AK-47s* (Westport, CT: Praeger Security International, 2006), 191.

14. LaPierre, *Guns, Crime and Freedom*, 171.

15. Embassy of Switzerland, Information Service 2004

16. Cukier and Sidel, *The Global Gun Epidemic*, 191.

17. LaPierre, *Guns, Crime and Freedom*, 174.

18. Ibid.

19. Hemenway, *Private Guns, Public Health*, 46, 200; Hemenway and Miller, "Firearm Availability and Homicide Rates," 986.

20. Walter Rodgers, "Strict Israeli Gun Control Laws Aim for Security Balance," *CNN.com*, September 17, 1999, http://www.cnn.com/WORLD/meast/9909/17/israel.gun.control/index.html.

21. Ibid.

22. Dan Williams, "Under the Gun," *Jerusalem Post*, November 17, 2000, B4.

23. Sandra Froman, "President's Column," *America's 1st Freedom*, December 2006, 10.

24. Matthew Miller and others, "Rates of Household Firearm Ownership and Homicide Across US Regions and States, 1988–1997," *American Journal of Public Health* 92 (December 2002): 1988, 1989. This study used the percentage of suicides committed with guns as a "proxy" for firearm ownership, which, as noted above, is a widely accepted technique for measuring relative firearm availability. A later study by the same Harvard team reached a similar

conclusion, using survey-based estimates of household firearm ownership. See Matthew Miller and others, "State-level Homicide Victimization Rates in the US in Relation to Survey Measures of Household Firearm Ownership, 2001–2003," *Social Science & Medicine* 64 (2006): 656.

25. Miller and others, "Rates of Household Firearm Ownership," 1990.
26. Ibid., 1990–1991.
27. Ibid., 1992. In a later study, however, the same Harvard team found significant reason to doubt the "reverse causation" possibility. Miller and others, "State-level Homicide Victimization Rates," 7. Using survey evidence to measure state firearms ownership levels, they found that higher rates of household firearm ownership were associated with significantly higher homicide victimization rates, but not with non-firearm homicides rates. They also found that rates of robbery and aggravated assault were not associated with household firearm prevalence. These findings militate against the possibility that high firearm prevalence was an effect of, not a cause of, high homicide rates. Another study by Philip Cook of Duke University and Jens Ludwig, now of the University of Chicago, using the percentage of suicides committed with a gun as a proxy for gun prevalence, also found a strong association between gun prevalence and high homicide rates, with no evidence of reverse causation. Philip J. Cook and Jens Ludwig, "The Social Costs of Gun Ownership," *Journal of Public Economics* 90 (2006): 379. Cook and Ludwig found that "gun prevalence is positively associated with overall homicide rates but not systematically related to assault or other types of crime. Together, these results suggest that an increase in gun prevalence causes an *intensification* of criminal violence [emphasis in original]—a shift toward greater lethality, and hence greater harm to the community." Ibid., 387.
28. Philip J. Cook and Jens Ludwig, "Guns and Burglary," in *Evaluating Gun Policy*, 74.
29. Ibid., 88.
30. Ibid., 98.
31. See Kleck, *Targeting Guns*, 183; David B. Kopel, "Lawyers, Guns, and Burglars," *Arizona Law Review* (Summer 2001): 345, 347.
32. Cook and Ludwig, "Guns and Burglary," 81.
33. Ibid.
34. Ibid., 104.
35. Kleck, *Targeting Guns*, 244.
36. Ibid.
37. Wright and Rossi, *Armed and Considered Dangerous*, 150.
38. David Hemenway and others, "Firearms and Community Feelings of Safety," *Journal of Criminal Law & Criminology* 86 (1995): 121, 124.
39. Ibid.
40. See photo available at www.gunguys.com/?p=1215.
41. See www.shotshow.com.
42. See, e.g., National Rifle Association, Institute For Legislative Action, *U.S. Conference of Mayors: Strong on Dislike of Guns, Weak on Facts*, fact sheet, October 6, 1999, www.nraila.org/Issues/FactSheets/Read.aspx?ID=40 ("Guns are used for self-protection approximately 2.5 million times annually [citing Kleck] . . . , up to five times the number of firearm-related violent crimes" [citing the FBI]).
43. Gary Kleck and Marc Gertz, "Armed Resistance to Crime: The Prevalence and Nature of Self-defense with a Gun," *Journal of Criminal Law & Criminology* 86 (1995): 150, 184, Table 2.

44. Hemenway, *Private Guns, Public Health*, 240.
45. David McDowall and Brian Wiersema, "The Incidence of Defensive Firearm Use by US Crime Victims, 1987 through 1990," *American Journal of Public Health* 84 (December 1994): 1982.
46. Ibid., 1984.
47. Hemenway, *Private Guns, Public Health*, 69.
48. McDowall and Wiersema, "The Incidence of Defensive Firearm Use," 1984.
49. Ibid.
50. Jacquielynn Floyd, "Under the Gun, She Was in Control," *Dallas Morning News*, November 10, 2005.
51. Ibid.
52. Cam Edwards, "Granny Deserves Self-defense," *Town Hall*, November 16, 2005, http://townhall.com/columnists/CamEdwards/2005/11/16/granny_deserves_self-defense.
53. Hemenway, *Private Guns, Public Health*, 239.
54. Kleck, *Targeting Guns*, 153.
55. Hemenway, *Private Guns, Public Health*, 241.
56. Ibid., 242.
57. Douglas Weil, "Gun Control Laws Can Reduce Crime," *The World & I*, February 1997, 300, 303.
58. Ibid.
59. Ibid.
60. Ibid.
61. Department of Justice, Federal Bureau of Investigation, *Uniform Crime Reports, Crime in the United States, 2007*, Expanded Homicide Data Table 14 (Justifiable Homicide by Weapon, Private Citizen, 2003–2007) (Washington, DC, September 2008), http://www.fbi.gov/ucr/cius2007/offenses/expanded_information/data/shrtable_14.html.
62. Kleck and Gertz, "Armed Resistance to Crime," 163.
63. David Hemenway and others, "Gun Use in the United States: Results from Two National Surveys," *Injury Prevention* 6 (2000): 263, 265.
64. Ibid., 266.
65. Ibid.
66. Gary Kleck, "Struggling Against 'Common Sense,' The Pluses and Minuses of Gun Control," *The World & I*, February 1997, 287, 295.
67. Bureau of Justice Statistics, *Criminal Victimization, 2004*, 10 (showing 1,054,820 incidents of non-fatal violent gun crime in 1993).
68. ABC News, *20/20*, transcript, December 30, 2005.
69. McDowell and Wiersema, "The Incidence of Defensive Firearm Use," 1984.
70. David Hemenway and Deborah Azrael, "The Relative Frequency of Offensive and Defensive Gun Uses: Results from a National Survey," *Violence and Victims* 15 (2000): 257, 269.
71. I owe this insight to Doug Weil, my former colleague at the Brady Center.
72. Arthur L. Kellermann and others, "Weapon Involvement in Home Invasion Crimes," *JAMA* 273 (June 14, 1995): 1759, 1761.
73. Ibid.
74. Kellermann and others, "Injuries and Deaths Due to Firearms in the Home," 263, 265.
75. Arthur L. Kellermann and Donald T. Reay, "Protection or Peril? An Analysis of Firearm-Related Deaths in the Home," *New England Journal of Medicine* 314 (June 12, 1986): 1557, 1558.

76. Deborah Azrael and David Hemenway, "'In the Safety of Your Own Home': Results from a National Survey on Gun Use at Home," *Social Science & Medicine* 50 (2000): 285, 289.
77. Arthur L. Kellermann and others, "Gun Ownership as a Risk Factor for Homicide in the Home," *New England Journal of Medicine* 329 (October 7, 1993): 1084.
78. Kleck, *Targeting Guns*, 244.
79. James E. Bailey and others, "Risk Factors for Violent Death of Women in the Home," *Archives of International Medicine* 157 (April 14, 1997): 777.
80. Peter Cummings and others, "The Association between the Purchase of a Handgun and Homicide or Suicide," *American Journal of Public Health* 87 (June 1997): 974.
81. Douglas J. Wiebe, "Homicide and Suicide Risks Associated with Firearms in the Home: A National Case-Control Study," *Annals of Emergency Medicine* 41 (June 2003): 771, 778.
82. "Accidental Gunshot Hurts 2 at Restaurant," *Indianapolis Star-News*, November 11, 1997, A1.
83. "APHA Members Turn Personal Trauma into Professional Opportunity," *Nation's Health*, December 1997.
84. Gary J. Gemme, Worcester, Massachusetts, police chief, quoted in Scott Croteau, "Police Chiefs Blast Healey on Gun Permits," *Worcester Telegram & Gazette*, October 19, 2006.
85. Mason-Dixon poll conducted May 6–8, 1995, cited in Marcus Nieto, *Concealed Handgun Laws and Public Safety*, California Research Bureau, California State Library, November 1997, 18 (on file with author).
86. Mason-Dixon poll conducted January 13–15, 1995, cited in ibid.
87. David McHugh, "Bill Would Let More Carry Guns," *Detroit Free Press*, November 23, 1994.
88. Paul Sloca, "State Senator Leaves Cuba to Cast Critical Vote on Guns," Associated Press, September 12, 2003, http://medialab.semissourian.com/story/print/119491.html.
89. Pauline Vu, "Lawmakers Go AWOL when Military Calls," *Stateline.org*, November 1, 2006, http://www.stateline.org/live/printable/story?contentId=153573.
90. Hemenway, *Private Guns, Public Health*, 98.
91. Ibid., 99.
92. Ibid., 98.
93. Scott Gutierrez, "Alleged Folklife Shooter Had Mental Health History and Gun Permit," *Seattle Post-Intelligencer*, May 27, 2008.
94. Daniel Yee, "Ga. Town Reeling from Hospital Slayings," Associated Press, March 27, 2008.
95. Walter Pacheco, "Deputies: Drivers Fired Guns; Two Daughters Were in Vehicle of One Suspect," *Orlando Sentinel*, February 21, 2008.
96. Mike Tobin, "Hough Known for Bursts of Anger," *Cleveland Plain Dealer*, July 7, 2007.
97. "Charges Approved for Concealed Gun Licensee; Man Faces Manslaughter Count in School Shooting," *Tulsa World*, February 12, 1997, A1.
98. "Pistols Aplenty: State's Requirements for Handgun Licensing Are Easy to Meet," *Pittsburgh Post-Gazette*, September 10, 1997, A1.
99. "Black Oak Man Is Killed Following Argument at Café," *Jonesboro Sun*, February 25, 1999.

100. Associated Press, "Mother 'Played by the Rules,' and She and Daughter Died," December 21, 1998.
101. "Police Link Grudge to Doctor's Slaying; Handyman with Disability Arrested in Surgeon's Death," *Sun Sentinel of Fort Lauderdale*, January 19, 1999, A1.
102. "Suspect No Stranger to Guns, Explosives," *Hartford Courant*, September 4, 1998.
103. "Once Inside He Immediately Started Firing," *Seattle Times*, July 29, 2006.
104. Adam Liptak, "15 States Expand Right to Shoot in Self-Defense," *New York Times*, August 7, 2006.
105. Henry Pierson Curti, "OPD Thefts Put Rifles on Street, Spur New Policy," *Orlando Sentinel*, January 30, 2007.
106. William C. Rempel and Richard A. Serrano, "Felons Get Concealed Gun Licenses under Bush's 'Tough' Gun Law," *Los Angeles Times*, October 3, 2000, A1.
107. Megan O'Matz and John Maines, "License to Carry: A Sun-Sentinel Investigation," *South Florida Sun-Sentinel*, January 28, 2007–February 15, 2007.
108. John R. Lott Jr. and David B. Mustard, "Crime, Deterrence, and Right-to-Carry Concealed Handguns," *Journal of Legal Studies* 26 (January 1997): 1.
109. The scholarly response to Lott is concisely summarized in Hemenway, *Private Guns, Public Health*, 101.
110. Daniel Webster and others, "Flawed Gun Policy Research Could Endanger Public Safety," *American Journal of Public Health* 87 (June 1997): 918, 920.
111. Ibid., 920.
112. It appears that Lott was able to discern an impact on the robbery rate only by being inconsistent in his methodology. Correcting Lott's error eliminates any downward effect of "shall issue" laws on robbery rates. See John J. Donohue, "The Impact of Concealed-Carry Laws," in *Evaluating Gun Policy*.
113. Lott and Mustard, "Crime, Deterrence, and Right-to-Carry Concealed Handguns," 24.
114. Weil, "Gun Control Laws Can Reduce Crime," 303.
115. Jens Ludwig, "Concealed-Gun-Carrying Laws and Violent Crime: Evidence from State Panel Data," *International Review of Law & Economics* 18 (1998): 239.
116. Dan A. Black and Daniel S. Nagin, "Do Right-to-Carry Laws Deter Violent Crimes?" *Journal of Legal Studies* 27 (January 1998): 209, 214.
117. Ibid.
118. Ibid.
119. Hemenway, *Private Guns, Public Health*, 244.
120. Ibid.
121. Ibid.; and Ludwig, "Concealed Gun-Carrying Laws," 241–242.
122. Kleck, *Targeting Guns*, 372.
123. Center to Prevent Handgun Violence, *Concealed Truth: Concealed Weapons Laws and Trends in Violent Crime in the United States* (Washington, DC, 1999).
124. Ibid., 2.
125. Donahue, "The Impact of Concealed-Carry Laws," 289–290.
126. Letter from Chris W. Cox, Chief Lobbyist for the NRA, to the editor, *New York Times*, September 10, 2006, 11.
127. National Rifle Association, *Right to Carry—2006*, fact sheet, May 6, 2008, http://www.nraila.org/Issues/FactSheets/Read.aspx?id=18.
128. Data compiled by Brady Center to Prevent Gun Violence from U.S. Bureau of the Census, *Statistical Abstract of the United States* (Washington, DC, 1987–2005) and from Department of Justice, Federal Bureau of Investigation, *Uniform Crime Reports* (Washington, DC, 1987–2005).

129. Tomislav V. Kovandzic and Thomas B. Marvell, "Right-to-Carry Concealed Handguns and Violent Crime: Crime Control through Gun Decontrol," *Criminology and Public Policy* 2 (2003): 363, 382.

130. Jon Wiener, "Gun Research 'Freak'-out," *Los Angeles Times*, May 31, 2006. Lott's suit was dismissed. *Lott v. Levitt*, 2009 WL 322148 (7th Cir. 2009).

131. See e.g., John R. Lott Jr., "The Real Lesson of the School Shootings," *Wall Street Journal*, March 27, 1998; John R. Lott Jr., "Letting Teachers Pack Guns Will Make America's Schools Safer," *Los Angeles Times*, July 17, 2003.

132. Wayne LaPierre, speech to NRA Annual Meeting, Denver, Colorado, May 1, 1999, http://www.nrawinningteam.com/meeting99/waynsp1.html.

133. Jacob Sullum and Michael W. Lynch, "Cold Comfort: An Interview with John R. Lott," *Reason*, January 2000, www.reason.com/0001/fe.js.cold.shtml.

134. Ibid.

135. Quotations from Mary Rosh are taken from blogger Tim Lambert's website, http://timlambert.org/2003/01/maryrosh/.

136. See Julian Sanchez, "The Mystery of Mary Rosh," *ReasonOnline*, May 2003, http://www.reason.com/0305/co.js.the.shtml.

137. Apparently Lott has claimed that his sixteen-year-old son posted Mary Rosh's rave book review. See Timothy Noah, "The Bellesiles of the Right? Another Firearms Scholar Whose Dog Ate His Data," *Slate*, February 3, 2003, http://slate.msn.com/toolbar.aspx?action=print&id=2078084. He must have been a pretty precocious teenager. As noted above, the book review contained a number of sophisticated statements, noting, for instance, that "Lott examined 54,000 observations and the previous largest study looked at 170 observations."

138. John R. Lott Jr., letter to editor, *Science* 300 (June 6, 2003): 1505.

139. Donald Kennedy, response to John Lott, *Science* 300 (June 6, 2003): 1505.

140. John R. Lott Jr., *More Guns, Less Crime: Understanding Crime and Gun-Control Laws* (Chicago: University of Chicago Press, 1998), 3.

141. John R. Lott Jr., "Childproof Gun Locks: Bound to Misfire," *Wall Street Journal*, July 16, 1997, A22.

142. John R. Lott Jr., "Gun-Lock Proposal Bound to Misfire," *Chicago Tribune*, August 6, 1998.

143. Otis Dudley Duncan, "Gun Use Surveys: In Numbers We Trust?" *Criminologist* 25 (January/February 2000): 1.

144. Ibid.

145. "John R. Lott, Jr.'s Reply to Otis Duncan's Recent Article in The Criminologist," *Criminologist* 25 (September/October 2000): 1.

146. Ibid.

147. John R. Lott Jr., *More Guns, Less Crime: Understanding Crime and Gun-Control Laws*, 2nd ed. (Chicago: University of Chicago Press, 2000), 3.

148. The exchange between Lindgren and Lott is described by historian Jon Wiener in his excellent book on fraud in academia titled *Historians in Trouble*, which devotes an entire chapter to John Lott. See Jon Wiener, *Historians in Trouble: Plagiarism, Fraud, and Politics in the Ivory Tower* (New York: New Press, 2005), 136–147.

149. Quoted in Wiener, *Historians in Trouble*, 138.

150. See Noah, "The Bellesiles of the Right?"

151. Following the controversy over the origin of Lott's 98 percent figure, Lott apparently actually did conduct a survey in 2002 that arrived at an estimate that mere brandishing occurs 95 percent of the time. This survey also has

been attacked for its failure to adhere to accepted academic standards. See David McDowall, "John R. Lott, Jr.'s Defensive Gun Brandishing Estimates," *Public Opinion Quarterly* 69 (Summer 2005): 246, 249. Professor McDowall notes that other survey estimates of mere brandishing range from around 70 to 80 percent of defensive gun uses. Ibid., 256.

152. Michelle Malkin, "The Other Lott Controversy," *WorldNetDaily*, February 5, 2003, http://www.worldnetdaily.com/news/article.asp?ARTICLE_ID=30873.
153. Donald Kennedy, "Research Fraud and Public Policy," *Science* 300 (April 18, 2003): 393.

CHAPTER 5: "WE DON'T NEED NEW GUN LAWS. WE NEED TO ENFORCE THE LAWS WE HAVE."

1. 151 Cong. Rec. S9389 (daily ed. July 29, 2005) (statement of Sen. George Allen).
2. O'Matz and Maines, "Investigation Reveals Criminal Pasts of Those Toting Guns."
3. Rep. John Dingell (D-Michigan), quoted in LaPierre, *Guns, Crime and Freedom*, 178.
4. "'Cult Had Illegal Arms,' Expert Says," *New York Times*, January 15, 1994.
5. LaPierre, *Guns, Crime and Freedom*, 191.
6. Ibid.
7. Ibid.
8. "Time for Congress to Rein in BATF," *American Rifleman*, April 1995, 39.
9. Ibid.
10. Wayne LaPierre, "Standing Guard," *American Rifleman*, January–February 1995, 7.
11. Wayne LaPierre, "Standing Guard," *American Rifleman*, April 1995, 7.
12. Peter H. Stone, "NRA Under New Fire for Rhetoric on Assault Weapons Ban, U.S. Authorities," *Baltimore Sun*, May 7, 1995, F6.
13. Guy Gugliotta, "NRA, Backers Have Focused Ire on ATF," *Washington Post*, April 26, 1995, A16.
14. Stone, "NRA Under New Fire."
15. Wayne LaPierre, NRA Fundraising Letter, April 13, 1995. See Fox Butterfield, "Long Before Bombing, Gun Lobby Was Lashing Out at Federal Agents," *New York Times*, May 8, 1995, A17.
16. Lou Michael and Dan Herbeck, *American Terrorist: Timothy McVeigh and the Oklahoma City Bombing* (New York: Harper, 2001), 228.
17. Paul Stephens, "'Detached' Letter from McVeigh," *USA Today*, May 3, 1995, A2.
18. Michael and Herbeck, *American Terrorist*, 120.
19. Ibid., 137.
20. For a more extensive discussion of the "insurrectionist theory" of the Second Amendment, see Dennis A. Henigan, "Arms, Anarchy and the Second Amendment," *Valparaiso University Law Review* 26 (1991): 107. See also, Carl T. Bogus, "The Hidden History of the Second Amendment," *UC Davis Law Review* 31 (1998): 309, 386–405; and Garry Wills, *A Necessary Evil: A History of American Distrust of Government* (New York: Simon & Schuster 1999), 189–223.
21. Thomas M. Moncure Jr., "The Second Amendment Ain't About Hunting," *Howard Law Journal* 34 (1991): 589.
22. Seth Mydans, "California Gun Control Law Runs into Rebellion," *New York Times*, December 24, 1990.
23. "Bush Quits NRA after Assailing 'Slander' against Federal Agents," *Atlanta Journal-Constitution*, May 11, 1995, B1.

24. Wayne LaPierre, "Standing Guard," *American Rifleman*, May 1997, 10.
25. Ibid.
26. Ibid.
27. "Line Up and Shut Up. Face Forward. Stay in Line. Last Name First," *American Rifleman*, January 1994, 32.
28. Brief *Amicus Curiae* of the National Rifle Association of America in Support of Petitioners, *Printz v. United States* (Nos. 95-1478, 95-1503). The Supreme Court ultimately struck down only the provision in the Brady Act requiring local police to do background checks, as a violation of the Tenth Amendment to the Constitution. *Printz v. United States*, 521 U.S. 898 (1997). However, it rejected the NRA's plea that the entire law be struck down, finding the mandatory background check provision severable from the rest of the statute. The Supreme Court's ruling kept in place the five-day period during which law enforcement authorities could *voluntarily* perform background checks on gun purchasers. Local police were, of course, quite willing to do so. The core of the Brady Act thus remained in effect despite the NRA-supported lawsuits, and Brady background checks had, at last count, stopped over 1.5 million prohibited purchasers from buying guns from licensed dealers.
29. Department of Justice, *Gun Violence Reduction: National Integrated Firearms Violence Reduction Strategy* (January 12, 2000), 5.
30. See generally Steven Raphael and Jens Ludwig, "Prison Sentence Enhancements: The Case of Project Exile," in *Evaluating Gun Policy*, 251, 253–254.
31. National Rifle Association, "Targeting Criminals, Not Gun Owners," August 17, 2006, www.nraila.org//Issues/Articles/Read.aspx?ID=202.
32. National Rifle Association, *Prosecution Is Prevention*, www.nraila.org/media/misc/prevention/aspx.
33. Raphael and Ludwig, "Prison Sentence Enhancement," 257. These researchers found, however, that the significant drop in the Richmond homicide rate in 1998, widely attributed to Project Exile, was largely a continuation of a downward trend which began before Project Exile, interrupted by a large homicide increase in 1997, Exile's first year of operation. They concluded, "The impressive declines in gun homicide rates in Richmond around the time of Project Exile can be almost entirely explained by the fact that the city had unusually large increases in gun homicides through the mid-1990s, and the cities with larger-than-average increases in gun homicide rates subsequently experience unusually large declines." Ibid., 275.
34. "Where Richmond Ranks: Our Place in the Nation According to Recent Research," *Richmond Times-Dispatch*, June 18, 2006, E6.
35. *America's 1st Freedom*, February 2001, 29.
36. Ibid.
37. Americans for Gun Safety Foundation, *The Enforcement Gap: Federal Strategy Neglects Sources of Crime Guns* (Washington, DC, October 2004), 26.
38. Department of Justice, Office of the Inspector General, *Review of the Bureau of Alcohol, Tobacco, Firearms and Explosives' Enforcement of Brady Act Violations Identified Through the National Instant Criminal Background Check System*, Executive Digest, Report Number I-2004-06 (Washington, DC, July 2004), viii.
39. *Bryan v. United States*, 524 U.S. 184, 190 (1998).
40. See, e.g., *United States v. One Assortment of 89 Firearms*, 465 U.S. 354, 355–356 (1984).
41. See generally, Brady Center to Prevent Gun Violence, *Death Valley: Profile of a Rogue Gun Dealer: Valley Gun* (Washington, DC: June 2006).
42. ATF, *Following the Gun*, 43.

43. Any other inspection can be conducted only with a search warrant. To obtain a warrant, ATF is in the catch-22 of being required to already have information that a dealer is violating record-keeping laws, when ATF generally can uncover those violations in the first place only by conducting an inspection.
44. Steven Higgins, statement in House Subcommittee on Crime and Criminal Justice, *Federal Firearms Licensing: Hearing before the Subcommittee on Crime and Criminal Justice of the House Committee on the Judiciary,* 103rd Cong., 1st. sess., 1993, 46.
45. Department of Justice, Office of the Inspector General, *Inspections of Firearms Dealers by the Bureau of Alcohol, Tobacco, Firearms and Explosives* (Washington, DC, 2004), 20.
46. See Pub.L. 95-429; 92 Stat. 1002 (October 10, 1978).
47. See 18 U.S.C. § 926(a).
48. Bureau of Alcohol, Tobacco and Firearms, *Gun Shows: Brady Checks and Crime Gun Traces* (Washington, DC, January 1999), 1.
49. Ibid., 8.
50. See 18 U.S.C.§ 921(a)(21)(C), (a)(22).
51. ATF, *Gun Shows,* 2.
52. ATF, *Following the Gun,* 13.
53. "Fight Begins to Repeal Machine Gun Ban," *American Rifleman,* August 1988.
54. Ronald Reagan, "Why I'm for the Brady Bill," *New York Times,* March 29, 1991, A23.
55. See 18 U.S.C. § 922 (t)(2)(C).
56. Petition for a Writ of Certiorari, *National Rifle Association et al. v. John Ashcroft* (United States Supreme Court), 13–15.
57. *National Rifle Association v. Reno,* 216 F.3d122 (D.C. Cir. 2000), *cert. denied,* 533 U.S. 928 (2001).
58. Department of Justice, *National Instant Criminal Background Check Regulation,* 66 Fed. Reg. 6471 (Jan. 22, 2001).
59. Department of Justice, *National Instant Criminal Background Check System,* 66 Fed. Reg. 35,567 (July 6, 2001).
60. GAO, *Potential Effects of Next-Day Destruction of NICS Background Check Records,* 4.
61. Ibid.
62. Office of the Inspector General, *Inspections of Firearms Dealers,* 53.
63. Government Accountability Office, *Gun Control and Terrorism, FBI Could Better Manage Firearm-Related Background Checks Involving Terrorist Watch List Records* (Washington, DC, January 2005), summary page.
64. ABC World News Tonight, March 8, 2005.
65. Frank Newport, Gallup News Service, October 20, 2006, http://www.galluppoll.com/content/default.aspx?ci=25090&pg=2.
66. Ibid.
67. Smith, *2001 National Gun Policy Survey,* 21.
68. Judy Rummerman, *Aviation Security* (Washington, DC: U.S. Centennial of Flight Commission, n.d.), www.centennialofflight.gov/essay/Government_Role/security/POL18.htm.
69. Brian Michael Jenkins, "Safeguarding the Skies," *San Diego Union Tribune,* September 30, 2001.
70. Martha T. Moore, "Mayors Unite to Get Guns Off the Street," *USA Today,* October 25, 2006.
71. Another game the pro-gun partisans play on the enforcement issue could be called the "How many gun laws do we have?" game. Often the "just enforce

existing laws" argument will be presented this way: "We already have 20,000 gun laws. We don't need another gun law; we need to enforce the laws we have." If there really were 20,000 gun laws on the books restricting access to firearms, it would at least superficially seem to strengthen the argument that another law would make little difference. The "20,000 gun law" figure has achieved a mythic status in the pro-gun community similar to the "2.5 million defensive gun uses" figure. Yet how was it derived and what does it include? Johns Hopkins University researchers Jon Vernick and Lisa Hepburn investigated the history and accuracy of the figure. Jon S. Vernick and Lisa M. Hepburn, "State and Federal Gun Laws: Trends for 1970–99," in *Evaluating Gun Policy*, 345. They found that it originated in 1965 testimony by Rep. John Dingell (D-Michigan), the same John Dingell who first called ATF agents "a jack-booted group of fascists." Dingell gave no source or basis for the figure, nor apparently has anyone else. The Hopkins researchers actually did attempt a count of existing laws. They identified approximately 300 different state gun laws, and about 90 local laws in cities of at least 250,000 population, that apply to the manufacture, design, sale, purchase, and possession of guns, to add to the handful of federal gun laws. Of course, if you add laws relating to the use of guns—like the Texas law prohibiting the shooting of a gun across Lake Texarkana (I'm not kidding)—you would get a higher count. But it is fanciful to think the number would be anything close to 20,000. In any event, the number of gun laws on the books is utterly immaterial. The issue is whether the laws are sufficient to protect the public. As should be readily apparent from the discussion in this text, the answer is clearly no.

72. Wayne LaPierre, *America's 1st Freedom*, December 2002, 34.
73. Chris Cox, *Chris Cox's Political Report*, July 1, 2005, http://www.nraila.org/Issues/Articles/Read.aspx?ID=173.

CHAPTER 6: "IS BUDWEISER RESPONSIBLE FOR DRUNK DRIVERS?"

1. Ruby L. Bailey, "Showdown over Guns Drags on in Courts," *Detroit Free Press*, January 3, 2003.
2. "New Gun Control Efforts Draw Mixed Support from Americans," Gallup News Service, July 13, 1999.
3. *Cathey v. Bernard*, 467 So.2d 9, 11 (La. Ct. App. 1985).
4. *Perkins v. Wilkinson Sword, Inc.*, 700 N.E.2d 1247, 1250 (Ohio 1998).
5. Ibid., 1252.
6. Philip J. Cook and Jens Ludwig, *Guns in America: National Survey on Private Ownership and Use of Firearms*, Research in Brief (Washington, DC: Department of Justice, National Institute of Justice, May 1997), 7. See also Johnson and others, "Firearm Ownership and Storage Practices," 173, 175. (Reviewing studies estimating that between 29 percent and 37 percent of gun owners keep guns loaded, 49 percent to 53 percent store guns unlocked, and 21 percent to 22 percent keep guns loaded and unlocked in the home. Studies also show somewhat lower percentages for households with both firearms and children in the home: 14–30 percent keep guns loaded, 43 percent keep guns unlocked, and 6–14 percent keep guns both loaded and unlocked.)
7. Mark A. Schuster and others, "Firearm Storage Patterns in U.S. Homes with Children," *American Journal of Public Health* 90 (April 2000): 588, 590.
8. Garen J. Wintemute and others, "When Children Shoot Children: 88 Unintended Deaths in California," *JAMA* 257 (June 12, 1987): 3107, 3108.
9. *City of Cincinnati v. Beretta U.S.A. Corp. et al.*, 768 N.E.2d 1136, 1147 (Ohio 2002).
10. *Hurst v. Glock*, 684 A.2d 970 (NJ App. Div. 1996).

11. Ibid., 972.
12. Ibid., 973.
13. *Smith v. Bryco Arms,* 33 P.3d 638 (Ct. App. N.M. 2001).
14. Ibid., 645.
15. Ibid., 649.
16. Ibid., 645.
17. See, e.g., *Barker v. Lull Engineering Co.,* 573 P.2d 443, 453 (Cal. 1978).
18. *LeBouef v. Goodyear Tire & Rubber Company,* 623 F.2d 985, 989 (5th Cir. 1980).
19. The National Traffic and Motor Vehicle Safety Act expressly provides that compliance with a federal safety standard "does not exempt any person from any liability under common law." 15 U.S.C. §1397(k) (1988 ed.). Thus where federal safety standards create a minimum floor, common law liability can be based on the failure to exceed the minimum. Where such common law liability would conflict with federal law, the conflict can be the basis for federal preemption of civil tort liability. See *Geier v. American Honda Motor Co., Inc.,* 529 U.S. 861 (2000) (holding federal safety standards requiring air bags preempt tort lawsuits).
20. The Consumer Product Safety Act includes language providing that "compliance with consumer product safety rules or other rules or orders under this chapter shall not relieve any person from liability at common law or under State statutory law to any other person." 15 U.S.C.§2074(a). Some courts have held that certain product defect liability suits are barred if they conflict with federal consumer safety regulations. See, e.g., *BIC Pen Corp. v. Carter,* 51 Tex. Sup. Ct. 783 (2008) (liability suit for failure to make disposable lighter more child-resistant preempted as conflicting with federal safety standards). But see *Colon ex rel. Molina v. BIC USA, Inc.,* 136 F.Supp. 2d 196 (S.D.N.Y. 2000) (product liability suit involving disposable lighters held not preempted).
21. Tom Gresham, "Safety First," *Guns and Ammo,* June 2002, 22.
22. The gun industry's argument for special treatment should be distinguished from claims by other industries that they should be exempt from product liability suits because those suits conflict with existing federal safety standards. See, e.g., *Geier v. American Hondo Motor Company, Inc.,* 529 U.S. 861 (2000). The gun industry is arguing that it should be exempt from design defect product liability suits, even though federal safety standards on guns are nonexistent.
23. The factual discussion that follows is taken from the opinion of the California Court of Appeal in *Merrill v. Navegar, Inc.,* 89 Cal. Rptr. 2d 146(1999), a lawsuit in which I represented victims of the shootings at 101 California Street.
24. *Merrill v. Navegar, Inc.,* 89 Cal.Rptr.2d 146, 163 (1999), *rev'd on other grounds,* 28 P.3d 116 (2001).
25. Ibid.
26. *Palma v. U.S. Industrial Fasteners, Inc.,* 36 Cal. 3d 171 (1984).
27. *Merrill v. Navegar, Inc.,* 89 Cal. Rptr. at 169.
28. *Merrill v. Navegar, Inc.,* 28 P.3d 116 (2001).
29. *Merrill v. Navegar, Inc.,* 28 P.3d at 135 (J. Werdegar dissenting).
30. Expert Report of Joseph J. Vince Jr., *City of New York v. Beretta,* No. CV-3641 (E.D.N.Y. 2005).
31. Bureau of Alcohol, Tobacco and Firearms, *Commerce in Firearms in the United States* (Washington, DC, February 2000), 2.
32. Ibid., 23.
33. Department of Justice, Memorandum of Points and Authorities in Opposition to Motion for Preliminary Injunction filed in *Trader Sports v. Gonzales,* No. C 06-001136 VRW (N.D. Cal.), 1.

34. Bureau of Alcohol, Tobacco and Firearms, *Crime Gun Trace Reports (2000) Oakland* (Washington, DC, July 2002), 6.
35. Declaration of Sania Franken in Opposition to Motion for Preliminary Injunction filed in *Trader Sports, Inc. v. Gonzales*, No. C 06-001136 VRW (N.D. Cal.), Exhibit B.
36. Ibid.
37. Ibid.
38. Bureau of Alcohol, Tobacco and Firearms, *Report to the Secretary on Firearms Initiatives* (Washington, DC, November 2000), iii.
39. Garen Wintemute and others, "Risk Factors Among Handgun Retailers for Frequent and Disproportionate Sales of Guns Used in Crime," *Injury Prevention* 11 (2005): 357.
40. See Second Amended Complaint, *Chicago v. Beretta U.S.A. Corp.*, No. 98-CH-015596 (Cook County Circuit Court, November 12, 1998).
41. See Complaint, *McNamara v. Arms Technology*, No. 99-912662 NZ (Wayne County Circuit Court, April 26, 1999).
42. See Complaint, *City of New York v. A-1 Jewelry & Pawn, Inc., et al.*, No. CV 06-2233 (E.D.N.Y. May 15, 2006); *City of New York v. Bob Moates' Sport Shop, Inc., et al.*, No. CV-6504 (E.D.N.Y. December 7, 2006).
43. Amended Complaint, *Anderson v. Bryco Arms*, No. 00-L-7476 (Cook County Circuit Court, April 10, 2002), 151.
44. Ibid., 53–58.
45. Plaintiffs' Memorandum in Opposition to Defendant Old Prairie Trading Post's Motion to Dismiss, *Anderson v. Bryco Arms*, No. 00-L-7476 (Cook County Circuit Court, April 10, 2002), 5–7, 8–11.
46. Expert Report of Joseph J. Vince Jr., *Jefferson v. Rossi*, No. 02218 (Pa. Common Pleas, May 3, 2002), 23–24, 31.
47. Deposition of Perry Bruce, *Jefferson v. Rossi*, 32, 39.
48. Ibid., 35–37, 40.
49. Ibid., 25, 51.
50. Ibid., 38.
51. Complaint, *Jefferson v. Rossi*, No. 02218 (Pa. Common Pleas, May 3, 2002).
52. *Kitchen v. K-Mart Corporation*, 697 So.2d 1200 (1997).
53. Ibid., 1206. (quoting *Skinner v. Ochiltree*, 5 So.2d 605 (1941)).
54. See, e.g., *Phillips v. Roy*, 431 So.2d 849 (La. Ct. App. 1983).
55. See, e.g., *Pavlides v. Niles Gun Show, Inc.*, 679 N.E.2d 728 (Ohio Ct. App. 1996).
56. See, e.g., *Johnson v. Bull's Eye Shooter Supply*, WL 21639244 (June 27, 2003).
57. According to ATF, traced "crime guns" include "any firearm that is illegally possessed, used in a crime, or suspected by enforcement officials of being used in a crime." Bureau of Alcohol, Tobacco and Firearms, *The Illegal Youth Firearms Market in 17 Communities* (Washington, DC, 1997), 3.
58. Bureau of Alcohol, Tobacco and Firearms, "Treasury, ATF Release Firearms Report, Gun Trafficking Actions," news release, February 4, 2000, 2.
59. Documents produced by Plaintiffs in the *Judicial Council Coordination Proceeding No. 4095* (Cal. Super Ct.) (PLTF 101149-53).
60. Documents produced by Sturm, Ruger in the *Judicial Council Coordination Proceeding No. 4095* Cal. Super. Ct. (SR 21972).
61. National Alliance of Stocking Gun Dealers, *The Alliance Voice*, February 1994.
62. Ibid.
63. Ibid.
64. Declaration of Robert A. Ricker, *People v. Arcadia Machine & Tool, Inc. et al.* (January 31, 2003), 7–8.

65. Documents produced by plaintiffs in the *Judicial Council Coordination Proceeding No. 495* (Cal. Super. Ct.) (PLTF 100007-10).

66. Paul M. Barrett, "Loaded Words: A Dealer Breaks Rank; Blaming Gun Makers," *Wall Street Journal*, June 22, 1999, A1.

67. Documents produced by plaintiffs in the *Judicial Council Coordination Proceeding No. 4095* (Cal. Super. Ct.) (PLTF 101388-89).

68. Deposition of Robert Lockett on August 9, 2002, *Judicial Council Coordination Proceeding No. 4095*, 39:5–19.

69. Ibid., 41:21–42:12.

70. The quotations from Bob Ricker are taken from his Declaration in *People v. Arcadia Machine & Tool, Inc. et al.* (January 31, 2003).

71. Document produced by NSSF in the *Judicial Council Coordination Proceeding No. 4095* (Cal. Super. Ct.) (NSSF 13898-13900).

72. Document produced by Beretta in the *Judicial Council Coordination Proceeding No. 4095* (Cal. Super. Ct.) (BUSA 16843).

73. Ibid.

74. Deposition of Donald Campbell, *Judicial Council Coordination Proceeding No. 4095* (Cal. Super. Ct.), 89.

75. Ibid., 155.

76. Bureau of Alcohol, Tobacco and Firearms, *2000–2005 Strategic Plan* (Washington, DC, 2000), 11.

77. Department of Justice, *Gun Violence Reduction*.

78. Deposition of Chris Killoy, *Judicial Council Coordination Proceeding No. 4095* (Cal. Super. Ct.), 425–426.

79. Document produced by Smith & Wesson in *Judicial Council Coordination Proceeding No. 4095* (Cal. Super. Ct.) (SW17537).

80. Settlement Agreement between Department of the Treasury, Department of Housing and Urban Development and Smith & Wesson (March 17, 2000).

81. Craig Gordon, "Gun Giant Agrees to Regulations; Government Will Drop Lawsuits in Exchange," *Newsday*, March 18, 2000, A5.

82. David Ho, "Officials Praise Smith & Wesson," Associated Press, March 17, 2000.

83. Fox Butterfield and Raymond Hernandez, "Gun Maker's Accord on Curbs Brings Pressure from Industry," *New York Times*, March 30, 2000, A1.

84. Ibid.

85. Documents produced by Sturm, Ruger in *Judicial Council Coordination Proceeding No. 4095* (Cal. Super. Ct.) (SR 20910-69).

86. *Philadelphia v. Stephan Chemicals Co.*, 544 F.Supp. 1135 (E.D.Pa. 1982).

87. *Hunnings v. Texaco, Inc.*, 29 F.3d 1480 (11th Cir. 1994).

88. *Suchomajcz v. Hummel Chemical Co.*, 524 F.2d 19 (3d Cir. 1975).

89. *City of Cincinnati v. Beretta U.S.A. Corp.*, 768 N.E.2d 1136 (Ohio 2002).

90. *James v. Arms Technology, Inc.*, 820 A.2d 27 (N.J. Super. Ct. App. Div. 2003).

91. *City of Gary v. Smith & Wesson Corp.*, 801 N.E.2d 1222 (Ind. 2003).

92. *NAACP v. Acusport, Inc.*, 271 F.Supp.2d 435 (E.D.N.Y. 2003).

93. 151 Cong. Rec. S8910 (July 26, 2005) (emphasis added).

94. 151 Cong. Rec. S9088 (July 27, 2005).

95. 151 Cong. Rec. S9226 (July 28, 2005) (emphasis added).

96. 151 Cong. Rec. S9017 (July 26, 2005).

CHAPTER 7: "FROM MY COLD, DEAD HANDS . . ."

1. *United States v. Miller*, 307 U.S. 174, 178 (1939).

2. Ibid.

3. *District of Columbia v. Heller*, 128 S.Ct. 2783, 2833 (2008) (J. Stevens dissenting).
4. Some of the leading historical texts supporting the "militia purpose" view of the Second Amendment include Saul Cornell, *A Well Regulated Militia: The Founding Fathers and the Origins of Gun Control in America* (New York: Oxford University Press, 2006); H. Richard Uviller and William G. Merkel, *The Militia and the Right to Arms, or, How the Second Amendment Fell Silent* (Durham, NC: Duke University Press, 2002); and the collection of essays in Carl T. Bogus, ed., *The Second Amendment in Law and History* (New York: New Press, 2000).
5. Warren Burger, interview on *MacNeil/Lehrer Newshour*, Show #4226, December 16, 1991.
6. *Heller*, 128 S.Ct. 2792, n.7.
7. Ibid., 2793, n.8.
8. Antonin Scalia, *A Matter of Interpretation: Federal Courts and the Law* (Princeton: Princeton University Press, 1997), 37.
9. *Heller*, 128 S.Ct. 2789–2790.
10. It is hardly surprising that the Supreme Judicial Court of Massachusetts has held that this provision is directed at "service in a broadly based, organized militia, not "to guaranteeing individual ownership or possession of weapons." *Commonwealth v. Davis*, 343 N.E.2d 847 (1976). The *Heller* majority claims, *without even acknowledging the Davis case*, that the state's highest court has determined that the Massachusetts right is not confined to a state-organized militia. *Heller*, 128 S.Ct. 2803. While ignoring the controlling authority of *Davis*, the *Heller* opinion instead relies on an 1825 libel case, *Commonwealth v. Blanding*, in which the scope of the "right to keep and to bear arms" was not even before the Court and which suggests only that the right to be armed does not extend to those who use arms irresponsibly.
11. *Heller*, 128 S.Ct. 2803.
12. Ibid., 2790, n.3.
13. Scalia, *A Matter of Interpretation*, 134.
14. Ibid., 43.
15. *Wright v. United States*, 302 U.S. 583, 588 (1938).
16. *Myers v. United States*, 272 U.S. 52, 151–152 (1926).
17. *Wright*, 302 U.S. 588.
18. *Holmes v. Jennison*, 39 U.S. 540, 571 (1840).
19. Scalia, *A Matter of Interpretation*, 132.
20. *Heller*, 128 S.Ct. 2821.
21. It is notable that the *Heller* majority largely avoids invoking the "insurrectionist theory" of the Second Amendment long urged by the NRA and other gun partisans, emphasizing instead the right to have guns for personal self-defense in the home. The notion that the Constitution itself guarantees a right to be armed for potential insurrection against the government likely proved far too frightening a concept to command a majority of the Supreme Court. Nevertheless, Justice Scalia veers close to this theory when, in discussing why the militia might be regarded as "necessary to the security of a free state," he comments that "when the able-bodied men of a nation are training in arms and organized, they are better able to resist tyranny." *Heller*, 2801. This observation occurs in a self-contradictory paragraph in which he also observes that the militia "is useful in repelling invasions and suppressing insurrections." *Heller*, 2800. Assuming that insurrection is the means by which the able-bodied men would resist tyranny, Scalia appears to be asserting that the militia is a means both to foment insurrection and suppress it.

22. Ibid., 2835 (J. Stevens dissenting).
23. The history of the consideration of the Second Amendment by the First Congress is ably described in Uviller and Merkel, *The Militia and the Right to Arms*, 97–106.
24. Scalia, *A Matter of Interpretation*, 38.
25. *Heller*, 128 S.Ct. 2796.
26. Ibid., 2783 (J. Stevens dissenting) (emphasis added).
27. Ibid., 2836.
28. Ibid., 2796.
29. Ibid., 2836 (J. Stevens dissenting).
30. Ibid., 2834–2835 (J. Stevens dissenting).
31. Ibid., 2789–2790.
32. Ibid., 2790, n.4.
33. Ibid., 2799–2800.
34. Ibid., 2799.
35. Ibid., 2830 (J. Stevens dissenting).
36. Act of May 8, 1792, 1 Stat. 271–272.
37. *Heller*, 2817.
38. Ibid., 2830 (J. Stevens dissenting).
39. Ibid., 2831.
40. See Adam Liptak, "Ruling on Guns Elicits Rebuke from the Right," *New York Times*, October 21, 2008, A1.
41. Douglas W. Kmiec, "Guns and the Supreme Court: Dead Wrong," *The-Tidings. com*, July 11, 2008, http://www.the-tidings.com/2008/071108/kmiec.htm.
42. Richard A. Posner, "In Defense of Looseness: The Supreme Court and Gun Control," *New Republic*, August 27, 2008, 32.
43. J. Harvie Wilkinson III, "Of Guns, Abortions, and the Unraveling Rule of Law," forthcoming in the *Virginia Law Review*, http://ssrn.com/abstract=1265118.
44. Ibid.
45. Ibid., 4.
46. *Heller*, 128 S.Ct 2816.
47. Ibid., 2816–2817, 2820.
48. Ibid., 2817, n.26.
49. Ibid., 2820.
50. Ibid., 2815, n.24.
51. Ibid., 2851 (J. Breyer dissenting) (quoting *Abrams v. Johnson*, 521 U.S. 74, 82 (1997)).
52. Ibid. (J. Breyer, dissenting).
53. Ibid., 2821.
54. James Oliphant, "Gun-Rights Ruling Could Ricochet across Nation," *Chicago Tribune*, March 16, 2008.
55. Rick Montgomery, "D.C. Handgun-Ban Case Could Put Controls in the Crosshairs," *Kansas City Star*, April 6, 2008.
56. Wayne LaPierre, "An Individual Right Affirmed," *America's 1st Freedom*, August 2008, 8.
57. These challenges to local handgun ban laws raise the threshold issue of whether the new private right to possess handguns applies to states and the cities and counties that derive their existence from states. Because the District of Columbia is a federal district, with a hybrid of local and federal legislative authority, the *Heller* Court did not address whether the new right to be armed applies as a limit on state and other local gun laws. *Heller*, 128 S.Ct., 2813, n.23.

This raises the issue of "incorporation" of the Bill of Rights; that is, whether the Bill of Rights, though originally applicable only as a restraint on federal laws, has been incorporated against the states and their localities through the post–Civil War enactment of the due process clause of the Fourteenth Amendment. The incorporation issue is beyond the scope of our discussion here. But, as argued in the text, the *Heller* opinion suggests that, even if the Second Amendment is held incorporated against the states, most state and local gun laws short of a handgun ban likely will survive constitutional challenge.

58. Chris Cox, "The Court Speaks, and the Fight Goes On," *America's 1st Freedom*, September 2008, 51.
59. Spitzer, *The Politics of Gun Control*, 17.
60. *Washington Post* Poll, "Most Say Amendment Covers Individuals and Militias," March 16, 2008, http://www.washingtonpost.com/wp-dyn/content/graphic/2008/03/16/GR2008031600072.html?sid=ST2008031502430.
61. On the day of the *Heller* ruling, Obama released a statement saying, "I have always believed that the Second Amendment protects the rights of individuals to bear arms, but I also identify with the need for crime-ravaged communities to save their children from the violence that plagues our streets through common-sense, effective safety measures." In that same statement, he reiterated his support for "closing the gun show loophole and improving our background check system, so that guns do not fall into the hands of terrorists or criminals." Statement of Barack Obama on Supreme Court decision in *District of Columbia v. Heller*, June 26, 2008, http://my.barackobama.com.
62. Pew Research Center for the People and the Press, "Public Continues to Oppose Banning Handgun Sales," press release, May 14, 2008, 2.

EPILOGUE: FROM LETHAL LOGIC TO SENSIBLE SOLUTIONS

1. The account of the Virginia Tech shooting is taken from *Mass Shootings at Virginia Tech, the Report of the Virginia Tech Review Panel* (Richmond, VA, August 2007) (Hereafter referred to as Panel Report).
2. Ibid., 71.
3. Ibid., 73.
4. Department of Justice, Bureau of Justice Statistics, *Improving Criminal History Records for Background Checks, 2005* (Washington, DC, July 2006) (estimates that, as of 2006, 234,628 disqualifying mental health records were in the system); General Accounting Office, *Gun Control: Options for Improving the National Instant Criminal Background Check System* (Washington, DC, March 2000) (estimating that at least 2.6 million disqualifying mental health records should be in the system). See also Jim Kessler, *Missing Records: Holes in Background Check System Allow Illegal Buyers to Get Guns* (Washington, DC: Third Way, May 2007).
5. Owing in large part to the impassioned efforts of some of the Virginia Tech victims and their families, Congress enacted into law the NICS Improvement Amendments Act of 2007, Pub.L. 110–180. The act provides new financial incentives for states to submit records of prohibited purchasers to the Brady Act's National Instant Criminal Background Check system. This statute is yet another illustration that sometimes it is necessary to enact new laws in order to better enforce existing laws.
6. Panel Report, 82.
7. Ibid.
8. Ibid., 84.

SELECTED BIBLIOGRAPHY

Americans for Gun Safety Foundation. *The Enforcement Gap: Federal Strategy Neglects Sources of Crime Guns.* Washington, DC, October 2004.

———. *No Questions Asked: Background Checks, Gun Shows and Crime.* Washington, DC, April 2001.

Azrael, Deborah, and David Hemenway. "'In the Safety of Your Own Home': Results from a National Survey on Gun Use at Home." *Social Science & Medicine* 50 (2000): 285.

Bailey, James E., and others. "Risk Factors for Violent Death of Women in the Home." *Archives of International Medicine* 157 (April 14, 1997): 777.

Beck, Allen, and others. *Survey of Adult Inmates 1991,* NCJ-136949. Washington, DC: Department of Justice, Bureau of Justice Statistics, 1993.

Black, Dan A., and Daniel S. Nagin. "Do Right-to-Carry Laws Deter Violent Crimes?" *Journal of Legal Studies* 27 (January 1998): 209.

Bogus, Carl T. "The Hidden History of the Second Amendment." *UC Davis Law Review* 31 (1998): 309.

———, ed. *The Second Amendment in Law and History.* New York: New Press, 2000.

Boor, Myron, and Jeffrey H. Bair. "Suicide Rates, Handgun Control Laws, and Sociodemographic Variables." *Psychological Reports* 66 (1990): 923.

Brady Center to Prevent Gun Violence. *Assault Weapons: "Massed Produced Mayhem."* Washington, DC, 2008.

———. *Brady Background Checks: 15 Years of Saving Lives.* Washington, DC, 2008.

———. *Death Valley: Profile of a Rogue Gun Dealer: Valley Gun.* Washington, DC, June 2006.

———. *Forced Entry: The National Rifle Association's Campaign to Force Businesses to Accept Guns at Work.* Washington, DC, 2005.

———. *Guns and Terror: How Terrorists Exploit Our Weak Gun Laws.* Washington, DC, 2001.

———. *Guns and the 2008 Elections: Common Sense Gun Laws Won, the NRA Lost, & What it Means.* Washington, DC, 2008.

———. *Guns for Gangs: Profile of a Rogue Gun Dealer: D'Andrea's Gun Case.* Washington, DC, 2007.

———. *Lethal Lou's: Profile of a Rogue Gun Dealer: Lou's Loan.* Washington, DC, 2006.

———. *No Gun Left Behind: The Gun Lobby's Campaign to Push Guns into Colleges and Schools.* Washington, DC, 2007.

———. *The NRA: A Criminal's Best Friend—How the National Rifle Association Has Handcuffed Federal Gun Law Enforcement.* Washington, DC, 2006.

————. *On Target: The Impact of the 1994 Federal Assault Weapons Act.* Washington, DC, 2004.

————. *Shady Dealings: Illegal Gun Trafficking from Licensed Gun Dealers.* Washington, DC, 2007.

————. *Smoking Guns: Exposing the Gun Industry's Complicity in the Illegal Gun Market.* Washington, DC, 2003.

————. *Targeting Safety: How State Attorneys General Can Act Now to Save Lives.* Washington, DC, 2001.

————. *Trading in Death: Profile of a Rogue Gun Dealer: Trader Sports.* Washington, DC, 2006.

————. *"Trivial Violations"? The Myth of Overzealous Federal Enforcement Actions against Licensed Gun Dealers.* Washington, DC, 2006.

————. *Unintended Consequences: What the Supreme Court's Second Amendment Decision in* D.C. v. Heller *Means for the Future of Gun Laws.* Washington, DC, 2008.

————. *Without a Trace: How the Gun Lobby and the Government Suppress the Truth about Guns and Crime.* Washington, DC, 2006.

Brady, Sarah. *A Good Fight.* New York: Public Affairs, 2002.

Brent, David A., and others. "Firearms and Adolescent Suicide: A Community Case-Control Study." *American Journal of Diseases of Children* 147 (1993): 1066.

Bureau of Alcohol, Tobacco and Firearms. *Commerce in Firearms in the United States.* Washington, DC, February 2000.

————. *Following the Gun: Enforcing Federal Firearms Laws against Firearms Traffickers.* Washington, DC, June 2000.

————. *Gun Shows: Brady Checks and Crime Gun Traces.* Washington, DC, January 1999.

————. *The Illegal Youth Firearms Market in 17 Communities.* Washington, DC, 1997.

————. *Report to the Secretary on Firearms Initiatives.* Washington, DC, November 2000.

————. "Treasury, ATF Release Firearms Report, Gun Trafficking Actions." News release, February 4, 2000.

————. *2000–2005 Strategic Plan.* Washington, DC, 2000.

————, Youth Crime Gun Interdiction Initiative. *Crime Gun Trace Analysis Reports: The Illegal Youth Firearms Market in 27 Communities.* Washington, DC, October 1998.

Card, Josefina. "Lethality of Suicidal Methods and Suicide Risk: 2 Distinct Concepts." *Omega Journal of Death & Dying* 5 (1974): 37.

Carr, Brendan G., and others. "Outcomes Related to the Number of Anatomic Placement of Gunshot Wounds." *Journal of Trauma* 64 (2008): 197.

Carter, Gregg Lee. *The Gun Control Movement.* New York: Twayne Publishers, 1997.

————, ed. *Guns in American Society: An Encyclopedia of History, Politics, Culture, and the Law.* Santa Barbara, CA: ABC-CLIO, 2002.

Carville, James, and Paul Begala. *Take It Back: Our Party, Our Country, Our Future.* New York: Simon & Schuster, 2006.

Center to Prevent Handgun Violence. *Concealed Truth: Concealed Weapons Laws and Trends in Violent Crime in the United States.* Washington, DC, 1999.

Centers for Disease Control, NCHS Vital Statistics System. *United States, Firearms Deaths and Rates per 100,000.* Washington, DC, 2002.

City of Cincinnati v. Beretta U.S.A. Corp. et al., 768 N.E.2d 1136 (Ohio 2002).

City of Gary v. Smith & Wesson Corp., 801 N.E.2d 1222 (Ind. 2003).

Clinton, Bill. *My Life.* New York: Knopf, 2004.

Commonwealth v. Davis, 343 N.E.2d 847 (1976).

Cook, Philip J. *Guns in America: Results of a Comprehensive National Survey on Firearms Ownership and Use.* Washington, DC: Police Foundation, 1996.

———. "The Technology of Personal Violence." In *Crime and Justice, A Review of Research,* edited by Michael Tonry. Chicago: University of Chicago Press, 1991.

———, and Jens Ludwig. "The Effects of the Brady Act on Gun Violence." In *Guns, Crime, and Punishment in America,* edited by Bernard E. Harcourt. New York: New York University Press, 2003.

———, and Jens Ludwig. "Guns and Burglary." In *Evaluating Gun Policy: Effects on Crime and Violence,* edited by Jens Ludwig and Philip J. Cook. New York: Oxford University Press, 2003.

———, and Jens Ludwig. *Guns in America: National Survey on Private Ownership and Use of Firearms,* Research in Brief. Washington, DC: Department of Justice, National Institute of Justice, May 1997. http://www.ncjrs.gov/pdffiles/165476.pdf.

———, and Jens Ludwig. "The Social Costs of Gun Ownership." *Journal of Public Economics* 90 (2006): 379.

———, and others. "Criminal Records of Homicide Offenders." *JAMA* 294 (August 3, 2005): 598.

———, and others. "Regulating Gun Markets." *Journal of Criminal Law & Criminology* 86 (1995): 59.

Cornell, Saul. *A Well Regulated Militia: The Founding Fathers and the Origins of Gun Control in America.* New York: Oxford University Press, 2006.

———, ed. *Whose Right to Bear Arms Did the Second Amendment Protect?* Boston: Bedford/St. Martin's, 2000.

Cummings, Peter, and others. "The Association between the Purchase of a Handgun and Homicide or Suicide." *American Journal of Public Health* 87 (June 1997): 974.

Cunningham, Kevin M. "When Gun Control Meets the Constitution." *St. John's Journal of Legal Commentary* 10 (1994): 59.

Davidson, Osha Gray. *Under Fire: The NRA and the Battle for Gun Control.* New York: H. Holt, 1993.

Department of Justice. *Gun Violence Reduction: National Integrated Firearms Violence Reduction Strategy.* Washington, DC, April 5, 2001.

———. *National Instant Criminal Background Check Regulation,* 66 Fed. Reg. 6471 (January 22, 2001).

———. *National Instant Criminal Background Check System,* 66 Fed. Reg. 35,567 (July 6, 2001).

——— and Department of Treasury. *Gun Shows: Brady Checks and Crime Gun Traces.* Washington, DC, January 1999.

Department of Justice, Bureau of Justice Statistics. *Background Checks for Firearms Transfers, 2005.* Bureau of Justice Statistics Bulletin. Washington, DC, November 2006.

———. *Background Checks for Firearm Transfers, 2006.* Washington, DC, March 19, 2008. http://www.ojp.usdoj.gov/bjs/pub/html/bcft06st/table/bcft06st01.htm.

———. "Crimes Committed with Firearms, 1973–2006." In *Key Facts at a Glance.* Washington, DC, January 5, 2008. http://www.ojp.usdoj.gov/bjs/glance/tables/guncrimetab.htm.

———. *Criminal Victimization, 2004.* Washington, DC, September 2005.

———. *Guns Used in Crime.* Washington, DC, July 1995.

———. *Homicide Victimization, 1950–2005.* Washington, DC, July 11, 2007. http://www.ojp.usdoj.gov/bjs/homicide/tables/totalstab.htm.

———. *Improving Criminal History Records for Background Checks, 2005.* Washington, DC, July 2006.

Department of Justice, Federal Bureau of Investigation. *Uniform Crime Reports*, Expanded Homicide Data Table 7 (Murder Victims, by Weapon, 2003–2007). Washington, DC, September 2008. http://www.fbi.gov/ucr/cius2007/offenses/expanded_information/data/shrtable_07.html.
———. *Uniform Crime Reports*, Expanded Homicide Data Table 14 (Justifiable Homicide by Weapon, Private Citizen, 2003–2007). Washington, DC, September 2008. http://www.fbi.gov/ucr/cius2007/offenses/expanded_information/data/shrtable_14.html.
Department of Justice, Office of Inspector General. *Inspections of Firearms Dealers By the Bureau of Alcohol, Tobacco, Firearms and Explosives.* Washington, DC, July 2004.
———. *Review of the Bureau of Alcohol, Tobacco, Firearms and Explosives' Enforcement of Brady Act Violations Identified Through the National Instant Criminal Background Check System.* Washington, DC, July 2004.
District of Columbia v. Heller, 128 S.Ct. 2783 (2008).
Donahue, John J. "The Impact of Concealed-Carry Laws." In *Evaluating Gun Policy: Effects on Crime and Violence*, edited by Jens Ludwig and Philip J. Cook. New York: Oxford University Press, 2003.
Duggan, Mark. "Guns and Suicide." In *Evaluating Gun Policy: Effects on Crime and Violence*, edited by Jens Ludwig and Philip J. Cook. New York: Oxford University Press, 2003.
Duncan, Otis Dudley. "Gun Use Surveys: In Numbers We Trust?" *Criminologist* 25 (January/February 2000): 1.
Eagan, Margery. "Letting an 8-year-old Play with a Machine Gun; Are You Crazy?" *BostonHerald.com*, October 28, 2008. http://www.bostonherald.com/news/columnists/view.bg?articleid=1128272.
Ehrman, Keith, and Henigan, Dennis A. "The Second Amendment in the Twentieth Century: Have You Seen Your Militia Lately?" *U. Dayton L. Rev.* 15 (1989): 5.
Elnour, A. A., and J. Harrison. "The Lethality of Suicide Methods." *Injury Prevention* 14 (2008): 39.
General Accounting Office. *Firearms Purchased from Federal Firearms Licensees Using Bogus Identification.* Washington, DC, March 2001.
———. *Gun Control: Implementation of the National Instant Criminal Background Check System.* Washington, DC, February 2000.
———. *Gun Control: Options for Improving the National Instant Criminal Background Check System.* Washington, DC, March 2000.
———. *Potential Effects of Next-Day Destruction of NICS Background Check Records.* Washington, DC, July 2002.
Government Accountability Office. *Gun Control and Terrorism, FBI Could Better Manage Firearm-Related Background Checks Involving Terrorist Watch List Records.* Washington, DC, January 2005.
Greenberg Quinlan Rosner Research and the Tarrance Group. *Americans Support Common Sense Measures to Cut Down on Illegal Guns.* Washington, DC, April 2008.
Gresham, Tom. "Safety First." *Guns and Ammo*, June 2002.
Grossman, David C., and others. "Gun Storage Practices and Risk of Youth Suicide and Unintentional Firearm Injuries." *JAMA* 293 (February 9, 2005): 707.
Halbrook, Stephen. "Does the United States Need a National Database for Ballistic Fingerprints?" *Insight*, November 26, 2002.
Harcourt, Bernard E., ed. *Guns, Crime, and Punishment in America.* New York: New York University Press, 2003.
Hemenway, David. "Gun Accidents." In *Guns in American Society: An Encyclopedia of*

History, Politics, Culture, and the Law, edited by Gregg Lee Carter. Santa Barbara, CA: ABC-CLIO, 2002.

———. *Private Guns, Public Health*. Ann Arbor: University of Michigan Press, 2004.

———, and Deborah Azrael. "The Relative Frequency of Offensive and Defensive Gun Uses: Results from a National Survey." *Violence and Victims* 15 (2000): 257.

———, and Matthew Miller. "Firearm Availability and Homicide Rates Across 26 High-Income Countries." *Journal of Trauma* 49 (December 2000): 985.

———, and others. "Firearms and Community Feelings of Safety." *Journal of Criminal Law & Criminology* 86 (1995): 121.

———, and others. "Gun Use in the United States: Results from Two National Surveys." *Injury Prevention* 6 (2000): 263.

Henigan, Dennis A. "Arms, Anarchy and the Second Amendment." *Valparaiso University Law Review* 26 (1991): 107.

———. "Ashcroft's Bad Aim." *Legal Times*, July 29, 2002.

———. "Dances with Guns." *Legal Times*, January 28, 2008.

———. "Exploding the NRA's Constitutional Myth." *Legal Times*, April 22, 1991.

———. "Gun Control Through Tort Law." *Legal Times*, August 19, 1991.

———. "The *Heller* Paradox." *UCLA L. Rev.* 56 (2009).

———. "Militias Misinterpret Constitution." *National Law Journal*, June 12, 1995.

———. "The Mythic Second: Constitutional Fantasy at the D.C. Circuit Should Not Destroy Our Nation's Gun Policies." *Legal Times*, March 26, 2007.

———. "N.R.A. Should Not Rejoice: Brady Act Lives On." *National Law Journal*, July 28, 1997.

———. "The Right to Be Armed: A Constitutional Illusion." *San Francisco Barrister Law Journal*, December 1989.

———. "Self-Inflicted Wounds: the D.C. Circuit on the Second Amendment." *Geo. Mason U. Civ. Rts. L.J.* 18 (2008): 209.

———. "Shooting Blanks." *The Recorder*, August 3, 1992.

———. "Should Cities Be Allowed to Sue Firearms Manufacturers?" *Insight*, April 26, 1999.

———. "Victims' Litigation Targets Gun Violence." *Trial*, February 1995.

———, and Judith Bonderman. "Paying the Bill for Violence." *National Law Journal*, January 21, 1991.

———, E. Bruce Nicholson, and David Hemenway. *Guns and the Constitution: The Myth of Second Amendment Protection for Firearms in America*. Northampton, MA: Aletheia Press, 1995.

Higgins, Steven. Statement in U.S. House of Representatives, Subcommittee on Crime and Criminal Justice, *Federal Firearms Licensing: Hearing before the Subcommittee on Crime and Criminal Justice of the House Committee on the Judiciary*. 103rd Cong., 1st. sess., 1993.

Hurst v. Glock, 684 A.2d 970 (NJ App. Div. 1996).

James v. Arms Technology, Inc., 820 A.2d 27 (N.J. Super. Ct. App. Div. 2003).

"John R. Lott, Jr.'s Reply to Otis Duncan's Recent Article in The Criminologist." *Criminologist* 25 (September/October 2000): 1.

Johnson, Renee, and others. "Firearm Ownership and Storage Practices, U.S. Households, 1992–2002, A Systematic Review." *American Journal of Preventive Medicine* 27 (2004): 173.

Johnson v. Bull's Eye Shooter Supply, WL 21639244 (June 27, 2003).

Kalodimos v. Village of Morton Grove, 470 N.E.2d 266 (Ill. 1984).

Kates, Don. *Proposition H: Mythology Instead of Criminology*. Oakland, CA: Independent

Institute, November 23, 2005. http://www.independent.org/newsroom/article. asp?id=1621.

Kates, Don, Michael Krauss, Abigail Kohn, and Wendy Kaminer. "Straight Shooting on Gun Control: A Reason Debate." *ReasonOnline*, May 2005. http://www. reason.com/0505/fe.ak.straight.shtml.

Kellermann, Arthur L., and Donald T. Reay. "Protection or Peril? An Analysis of Firearm-Related Deaths in the Home." *New England Journal of Medicine* 314 (June 12, 1986): 1557,

Kellermann, Arthur L., and others. "Gun Ownership as a Risk Factor for Homicide in the Home." *New England Journal of Medicine* 329 (October 7, 1993): 1084.

Kellermann, Arthur L., and others. "Injuries and Deaths Due to Firearms in the Home." *Journal of Trauma* 45 (1998): 263.

Kellermann, Arthur L., and others. "Suicide in the Home in Relation to Gun Ownership." *New England Journal of Medicine* 327 (1992): 467.

Kellermann, Arthur L., and others. "Weapon Involvement in Home Invasion Crimes." *JAMA* 273 (June 14, 1995): 1759.

Kennedy, Donald. "Research Fraud and Public Policy." *Science* 300 (April 18, 2003): 393.

———. Response to John Lott. *Science* 300 (June 6, 2003): 1505.

Kessler, Jim. *Missing Records: Holes in Background Check System Allow Illegal Buyers to Get Guns.* Washington, DC: Third Way, May 2007.

Kitchen v. K-Mart Corporation, 697 So.2d 1200 (1997).

Kleck, Gary. "Struggling Against 'Common Sense,' The Pluses and Minuses of Gun Control." *The World & I*, February 1997, 287.

———. *Targeting Guns: Firearms and Their Control.* Edison, NJ: Aldine Transaction, 1997.

———, and Don B. Kates. *Armed: New Perspectives on Gun Control.* Amherst, NY: Prometheus Books, 2001.

———, and Marc Gertz. "Armed Resistance to Crime: The Prevalence and Nature of Self-defense with a Gun." *Journal of Criminal Law & Criminology* 86 (1995): 150.

Kmiec, Douglas W. "Guns and the Supreme Court: Dead Wrong." *The-Tidings.com*, July 11, 2008. http://www.the-tidings.com/2008/071108/kmiec.htm.

Kopel, David B. "Lawyers, Guns, and Burglars." *Arizona Law Review*, Summer 2001, 345.

Kovandzic, Tomislav V., and Thomas B. Marvell. "Right-to-Carry Concealed Handguns and Violent Crime: Crime Control through Gun Decontrol." *Criminology and Public Policy* 2 (2003): 363.

LaPierre, Wayne. *Guns, Crime, and Freedom.* Washington, DC: Regnery Publishing, Inc., 1994.

Lester, David, and Mary E. Murrell. "The Influence of Gun Control Laws on Suicidal Behavior." *American Journal of Psychiatry* 137 (January 1980): 121.

Levitt, Stephen D., and Stephen J. Dubner. *Freakonomics: A Rogue Economist Explores the Hidden Side of Everything.* New York: William Morrow, 2005.

Liptak, Adam. "Ruling on Guns Elicits Rebuke from the Right." *New York Times*, October 21, 2008.

Lode, Eric. "Slippery Slope Arguments and Legal Reasoning." *California Law Review* 87 (1999): 1469.

Loftin, Colin, and others. "Effects of Restrictive Licensing of Handguns on Homicide and Suicide in the District of Columbia." *New England Journal of Medicine* 325 (1991): 1615.

Lott, John R., Jr. "Childproof Gun Locks: Bound to Misfire." *Wall Street Journal*, July 16, 1997.

———. "Gun-Lock Proposal Bound to Misfire." *Chicago Tribune*, August 6, 1998.

———. Letter to editor. *Science* 300 (June 6, 2003): 1505.

———. "Letting Teachers Pack Guns Will Make America's Schools Safer." *Los Angeles Times*, July 17, 2003.

———. *More Guns, Less Crime: Understanding Crime and Gun-Control Laws.* Chicago: University of Chicago Press, 1998.

———. "The Real Lesson of the School Shootings." *Wall Street Journal*, March 27, 1998.

———, and David B. Mustard. "Crime, Deterrence, and Right-to-Carry Concealed Handguns." *Journal of Legal Studies* 26 (January 1997): 1.

Lowy, Jonathan E. "Litigating Against Gun Manufacturers." *Trial*, November 2000.

Ludwig, Jens. "Concealed-Gun-Carrying Laws and Violent Crime: Evidence from State Panel Data." *International Review of Law & Economics* 18 (1998): 239.

———, and Philip Cook. "Homicide and Suicide Rates Associated with Implementation of the Brady Handgun Violence Prevention Act." 284 *JAMA* (2000): 585.

———, and Philip Cook. "Impact of the Brady Act on Homicide and Suicide Rates (Letter)." *JAMA* 284 (2000): 2721.

Malkin, Michelle. "The Other Lott Controversy." *WorldNetDaily*, February 5, 2003. http://www.worldnetdaily.com/news/article.asp?ARTICLE_ID=30873.

Marttila Communications Group. *National Gun Control Survey.* Boston, July 11–14, 2003.

McClurg, Andrew Jay. "The Rhetoric of Gun Control." *American University Law Review* 42 (1992): 53.

McDowall, David. "John R. Lott, Jr.'s Defensive Gun Brandishing Estimates." *Public Opinion Quarterly* 69 (Summer 2005): 246.

———, and Brian Wiersema. "The Incidence of Defensive Firearm Use by US Crime Victims, 1987 through 1990." *American Journal of Public Health* 84 (December 1994): 1982.

———, and others. "Did Mandatory Firearm Ownership in Kennesaw Really Prevent Burglaries?" *Sociology and Sociological Research* 74 (October 1989): 48.

Merrill v. Navegar, Inc., 89 Cal.Rptr.2d 146 (1999), *rev'd on other grounds*, 28 P.3d 116 (2001).

Michael, Lou, and Dan Herbeck. *American Terrorist: Timothy McVeigh and the Oklahoma City Bombing.* New York: Harper, 2001.

Miller, Matthew, and others. "Household Firearm Ownership and Rates of Suicide Across the 50 United States." *Journal of Trauma* 62 (2007): 1029.

———, and others. "Rates of Household Firearm Ownership and Homicide Across US Regions and States, 1988–1997." *American Journal of Public Health* 92 (December 2002): 1988.

———, and others. "State-level Homicide Victimization Rates in the US in Relation to Survey Measures of Household Firearm Ownership, 2001–2003." *Social Science & Medicine* 64 (2006): 656.

Moncure, Thomas M., Jr. "The Second Amendment Ain't About Hunting." *Howard Law Journal* 34 (1991): 589.

NAACP v. Acusport, Inc., 271 F.Supp.2d 435 (E.D.N.Y. 2003).

National Alliance of Stocking Gun Dealers. *The Alliance Voice*, February 1994.

National Center for Injury Prevention and Control. "Rates of Homicide, Suicide, and Firearm-Related Death Among Children—26 Industrialized Countries. *Morbidity and Mortality Weekly Report* 46 (1997): 101.

National Center for Policy Analysis. *Will Banning Assault Weapons Reduce Crime?* Brief Analysis No. 102. Dallas, TX, February 7, 1994. http://www.ncpa.org/ba/ba102.html.

National Institute of Justice. *Felony Defendants in Large Urban Counties.* Washington, DC, 1998.

———. *Research in Brief.* Washington, DC, May 1997.

National Rifle Association v. Reno, 216 F.3d122 (D.C. Cir. 2000), *cert. denied,* 533 U.S. 928 (2001).

National Safety Council. *Odds of Death Due to Injury, United States, 2005.* Itasca, IL, n.d. http://www.nsc.org/research/odds.aspx.

Noah, Timothy. "The Bellesiles of the Right? Another Firearms Scholar Whose Dog Ate His Data." *Slate,* February 3, 2003. http://slate.msn.com/toolbar.aspx?action=print&id=2078084.

Olson, Joseph E., and David B. Kopel. "All the Way Down the Slippery Slope: Gun Prohibition in England and Some Lessons for Civil Liberties in America." *Hamline Law Review* 22 (1999): 399.

O'Matz, Megan, and Maines, John. "Investigation Reveals Criminal Pasts of Those Toting Guns." *South Florida Sun-Sentinal,* January 29, 2007.

Pavlides v. Niles Gun Show, Inc., 679 N.E.2d 728 (Ohio Ct. App. 1996).

Perkins, Craig. *Weapon Use and Violent Crime,* NCJ-194820. Washington, DC: Department of Justice, Bureau of Justice Statistics, September 2003.

Phillips v. Roy, 431 So.2d 849 (La. Ct. App. 1983).

Polsby, Daniel D., and Dennis Brennen. *Taking Aim at Gun Control.* Chicago: Heartland Institute, 1995.

Polston, Mark D. "Civil Liability for High Risk Gun Sales: An Approach to Combat Gun Trafficking." *Seton Hall Legislative Journal* 19 (1995): 821.

———. "Suing Firearm Dealers for Gunshot Injuries—Liability without Defect." *Product Liability Law Reporter,* July 1994.

———, and Douglas S. Weil. "Unsafe by Design: Using Tort Actions to Reduce Firearm-Related Injuries." *Stanford Law & Policy Review* 8 (1997): 13.

Posner, Richard A. "In Defense of Looseness: The Supreme Court and Gun Control." *New Republic,* August 27, 2008.

Powell, Elizabeth C., and others. "Incidence and Circumstances of Nonfatal Firearm-Related Injuries among Children and Adolescents." *Archives of Pediatrics and Adolescent Medicine* 55 (December 2001): 1364.

Printz v. United States, 521 U.S. 898 (1997).

Raphael, Steven, and Jens Ludwig. "Prison Sentence Enhancements: The Case of Project Exile." In *Evaluating Gun Policy: Effects on Crime and Violence,* edited by Jens Ludwig and Philip J. Cook. New York: Oxford University Press, 2003.

Reagan, Ronald. "Why I'm for the Brady Bill." *New York Times,* March 29, 1991.

Reuter, Peter, and Jenny Mouzos. "A Massive Buyback of Low-Risk Guns." In *Evaluating Gun Policy: Effects on Crime and Violence,* edited by Jens Ludwig and Philip J. Cook. New York: Oxford University Press, 2003.

Ridgeway, James, Daniel Schulman, and David Corn. "There's Something about Mary: Unmasking a Gun Lobby Mole." *Mother Jones,* July 30, 2008. http://www.motherjones.com/news/feature/2008/07/mary-mcfate-sapone-gun-lobby-nra-spy.html.

Rostron, Allen. "Gunning for Justice." *Trial,* November 2001.

———. "Lawyers, Guns & Money: The Rise and Fall of Tort Litigation Against the Firearms Industry." *Santa Clara Law Review* 46 (2006): 481.

Saltzman, Linda, and others. "Weapon Involvement and Injury Outcomes in Family and Intimate Assaults." *JAMA* 267 (June 10, 1992): 3043.

Sanchez, Julian. "The Mystery of Mary Rosh." *ReasonOnline*, May 2003. http://www.reason.com/0305/co.js.the.shtml.

Scalia, Antonin. *A Matter of Interpretation: Federal Courts and the Law*. Princeton: Princeton University Press, 1997.

Schauer, Frederick. "Slippery Slopes." *Harvard Law Review* 99 (1985): 361.

Schuster, Mark A., and others. "Firearm Storage Patterns in U.S. Homes with Children." *American Journal of Public Health* 90 (April 2000): 588.

Shenassa, E. D., S. N. Catlin, and S. L. Buka. "Lethality of Firearms Relative to Other Suicide Methods: A Population Based Study." *Journal of Epidemiology & Community Health* 57 (2003): 120.

Shields, Pete. *Guns Don't Die—People Do*. Westminster, MD: Arbor House Publishing, 1981.

Siebel, Brian J. "Blind Eye for Killers." *Legal Times*, October 2003.

———. "The Case Against Guns on Campus." *George Mason University Civil Rights Law Journal* 18 (2008): 319.

———. "The Case Against the Gun Industry." *Public Health Reports* 115 (2000): 410.

———. "City Lawsuits Against the Gun Industry: A Roadmap for Reforming Another Deadly Industry." *St. Louis University Public Law Review* 18 (1999): 247.

———. "Gun Industry Immunity: Why the Gun Industry's Dirty Little Secret Does Not Deserve Congressional Protection." *University of Missouri–Kansas City Law Review* 73 (2005): 911.

Smith, Tom W. *1998 National Gun Policy Survey of the National Opinion Research Center: Research Findings*. Chicago: National Opinion Research Center, 1999.

———. *1999 National Gun Policy Survey of the National Opinion Research Center: Research Findings*. Chicago: National Opinion Research Center, July 2000.

———. *2001 National Gun Policy Survey of the National Opinion Research Center: Research Finding*. Chicago: National Opinion Research Center, December 2001.

———. *Public Opinion on Gun Control*. Chicago: National Opinion Research Center, December 2003.

Smith v. Bryco Arms, 33 P.3d 638 (Ct. App. N.M. 2001).

Sorenson, Susan B. "Mental Health and Firearms in Community-Based Surveys." *Evaluation Review* 32 (June 2008): 239.

Spitzer, Robert J. *The Politics of Gun Control*. 3rd ed. Washington, DC: CQ Press, 2004.

Suchomajcz v. Hummel Chemical Co., 524 F.2d 19 (3d Cir. 1975).

Sugarmann, Josh. *Every Handgun Is Pointed at You: The Case for Banning Handguns*. New York: New Press, 2001.

———. *NRA: Money, Firepower, Fear*. Washington, DC: National Press Books, 1992.

Tushnet, Mark V. *Out of Range: Why the Constitution Can't End the Battle Over Guns*. Oxford: Oxford University Press, 2007.

United States v. Miller, 307 U.S. 174 (1939).

United States v. One Assortment of 89 Firearms, 465 U.S. 354 (1984).

U.S. Senate Committee on the Judiciary. *Whose Right to Keep and Bear Arms? The Second Amendment as a Source of Individual Rights: Hearing before the Subcommittee on the Constitution, Federalism and Property Rights of the Senate Committee on the Judiciary*. 105th Cong., 2nd sess., 1998.

Uviller, H. Richard, and William G. Merkel. *The Militia and the Right to Arms, or, How the Second Amendment Fell Silent*. Durham, NC: Duke University Press, 2002.

Vernick, Jon S., and Lisa M. Hepburn. "State and Federal Gun Laws: Trends for

1970–99." In *Evaluating Gun Policy: Effects on Crime and Violence*, edited by Jens Ludwig and Philip J. Cook. New York: Oxford University Press, 2003.

Vernick, Jon S., and others. "Unintentional and Undetermined Firearm Related Deaths: A Preventable Death Analysis for Three Safety Devices." *Injury Prevention* 9 (2003): 307.

Virginia Tech Review Panel. *Mass Shootings at Virginia Tech, the Report of the Virginia Tech Review Panel.* Richmond, VA, August 2007.

Vizzard, William J. *Shots in the Dark: The Policy, Politics, and Symbolism of Gun Control.* Lanham, MD: Rowman & Littlefield Publishers, Inc., 2000.

Volokh, Eugene. "The Mechanisms of the Slippery Slope." *Harvard Law Review* 116 (2003): 1026.

Walton, Douglas N. *Informal Logic: A Handbook for Critical Argumentation.* New York: Oxford University Press, 1989.

Webster, Daniel, and Marc Starnes. "Reexamining the Association Between Child Access Prevention Gun Laws and Unintentional Shootings Deaths of Children." *Pediatrics* 106 (December 2000): 1466.

Webster, Daniel, and others. "Association Between Youth-Focused Firearm Laws and Youth Suicides." *JAMA* 292 (August 4, 2004): 594.

Webster, Daniel, and others. "Flawed Gun Policy Research Could Endanger Public Safety." *American Journal of Public Health* 87 (June 1997): 918.

Webster, Daniel, and others. "Relationship between Licensing, Registration, and Other Gun Sales Laws and the Source State of Crime Guns." *Injury Prevention* 7 (2001): 186.

Weil, Douglas S. "Gun Control Laws Can Reduce Crime." *The World & I*, February 1997.

———. *Traffic Stop: How the Brady Act Disrupts Interstate Gun Trafficking.* Washington, DC: Center to Prevent Handgun Violence, 1997.

———, and David Hemenway. "I Am the NRA: An Analysis of a National Random Sample of Gun Owners." *Violence & Victims* 8 (1993): 353.

———, and Rebecca Knox. "Effects of Limiting Handgun Purchases on Interstate Transfer of Firearms." *JAMA* 275 (June 12, 1996): 1759.

Wells, William, and Julie Horney. "Weapon Effects and Individual Intent to Do Harm: Influences on the Escalation of Violence." *Criminology* 40 (2002): 265.

Wiebe, Douglas J. "Homicide and Suicide Risks Associated with Firearms in the Home: A National Case-Control Study." *Annals of Emergency Medicine* 41 (June 2003): 771.

Wiener, Jon. *Historians in Trouble: Plagiarism, Fraud, and Politics in the Ivory Tower.* New York: New Press, 2005.

Winkler, Adam. "The Reasonable Right to Bear Arms." *Stanford Law & Policy Review* 17 (2006): 599.

Wintemute, Garen J. "Gun Shows across a Multistate American Gun Market: Observational Evidence of the Effects of Regulatory Policies." *Injury Prevention* 13 (2007): 150.

———. "Guns and Gun Violence." In *The Crime Drop in America*, edited by A. Blumstein and J. Wallman. New York: Cambridge University Press, 2000.

———, and others. "Mortality among Recent Purchasers of Handguns." *New England Journal of Medicine* 341 (1999): 1583.

———, and others. "Prior Misdemeanor Convictions as a Risk Factor for Later Violent and Firearm-Related Criminal Activity among Authorized Purchasers of Handguns." *JAMA* 341 (1998): 2083.

————, and others. "Risk Factors Among Handgun Retailers for Frequent and Disproportionate Sales of Guns Used in Crime." *Injury Prevention* 11 (2005): 357.

————, and others. "When Children Shoot Children: 88 Unintended Deaths in California." *JAMA* 257 (June 12, 1987): 3107.

Wright, James D., and Peter H. Rossi. *Armed and Considered Dangerous: A Survey of Felons and Their Firearms.* Piscataway, NJ: Aldine Transaction, 1986.

Wright, M. A., and others. "Effectiveness of a Program to Deny Legal Handgun Purchase to Persons Believed to be at High Risk for Firearm Violence." *American Journal of Public Health* 89 (1999): 88.

Yang, Bijou, and David Lester. "The Effect of Gun Availability on Suicide Rates." *Atlantic Economic Review* 19 (1991): 74.

Zimring, Franklin E. "Is Gun Control Likely to Reduce Violent Killings?" *University of Chicago Law Review* 35 (1968): 721.

————, and Gordon Hawkins. *Crime Is Not the Problem: Lethal Violence in America.* New York: Oxford University Press, 1997.

INDEX

ABOUT THE AUTHOR

DENNIS A. HENIGAN is the vice president for law and policy at the Brady Center to Prevent Gun Violence and founder of its Legal Action Project. For twenty years, he has been a leading advocate for stronger gun laws, appearing dozens of times on national television and radio shows, including *60 Minutes, The Today Show, Nightline, Larry King Live*, and *Dateline NBC*. He also has written and spoken extensively on liability and constitutional issues relating to gun laws and gun violence, including testifying before several congressional committees. Under his direction, Brady Center lawyers have recovered millions of dollars in damages for gun violence victims, as well as winning precedent-setting decisions on the liability of gun sellers. In 2004 he was named one of the top ten "Lawyers of the Year" by *Lawyers' Weekly* magazine. His work as a public interest lawyer has been profiled in *The New Yorker.*

Henigan received his BA from Oberlin College in 1973 and his law degree in 1977 from the University of Virginia School of Law. Prior to joining the Brady Center in 1989, he was a partner in the law firm of Foley & Lardner.